Summary Justice

Open Linguistics Series

Series Editor
Robin Fawcett, University of Wales, Cardiff

This series is 'open' in two senses. First, it provides an open forum for works associated with any school of linguistics or with none. Most practising linguists have long since outgrown the unhealthy assumption that theorizing about language should be left to those working in the generativist-formalist paradigm. Today large and increasing numbers of scholars are seeking an understanding of the nature of language by exploring one or other of various cognitive models of language, or in terms of the communicative use of language in social contexts – or both. This series has played a valuable part in re-establishing the traditional 'openness' of the study of language and works have been published in and on the borders of Pike's Tagmemics, Lamb's Stratificational Grammar, Starosta's Lexicase Grammar and especially – because it has been the most widely used of the major functional approaches to language – Halliday's Systemic Functional Grammar. The general trend of the series has been to a functional view of language, but this simply reflects the works that have been offered and the series continues to be open to all approaches – including works in the generativist-formalist tradition.

The second way in which the series is 'open' is that it encourages works that open out 'core' linguistics in various ways: to encompass discourse and the description of natural texts, to explore the relationship between linguistics and its neighbouring disciplines such as psychology, sociology, philosophy, and cultural and literary studies, and to apply it in fields such as education, language pathology and law.

Relations between linguistics and artificial intelligence are covered in a sister series, *Communication in Artificial Intelligence*, and works that are primarily descriptive are published in a new sister series, *Functional Descriptions of Language*. Cassell also has a strong and widely used series of linguistics textbooks, again with a strong functional and discourse-centred orientation.

Recently published titles in the series:

Thematic Development in English Texts, ed. Mohsen Ghadessy
Ways of Saying: Ways of Meaning: Selected Papers of Ruqaiya Hasan, eds Carmel Cloran, David Butt and Geoffrey Williams
Language Policy in Britain and France: The Processes of Policy, Dennis Ager
Genre and Institutions: Social Processes in the Workplace and School, eds Frances Christie and J. R. Martin
Educating Eve: The 'Language Instinct' Debate, Geoffrey Sampson
Summary Justice: Judges Address Juries, Paul Robertshaw
Pedagogy and the Shaping of Consciousness: Linguistics and Social Processes, ed. Frances Christie

Summary Justice

Judges Address Juries

Paul Robertshaw

CASSELL
London and Washington

Cassell
Wellington House, 125 Strand, London WC2R 0BB, England
PO Box 605, Herndon, Virginia 20172-0605, USA

First published 1998

British Library Cataloguing in Publication Data
A catalogue for this book is available from the British Library.

ISBN 0-304-33701-3

Typeset by BookEns Ltd, Royston, Herts.
Printed and bound in Great Britain by Biddles Ltd, Guildford and King's Lynn

Contents

Preface

As with my previous books I have tried to break new ground, in terms of both method and topic. I have at the same time maintained a degree of continuity: *Jury and Judge* derived from 'inverted' legal need in my first book *Rethinking Legal Need*, and this book, *Summary Justice*, begins to humanize the statistics and main findings of *Jury and Judge*.

The final version of the book is shorter than I originally intended, but the contractual amputations were made without pain or rancour and have resulted in a more focused text: the history of the Summing-up is absent and so is a section on summing-up in civil trials concerning criminal process issues. I am grateful to Janet Joyce, my publisher, and Robin Fawcett, my Linguistics colleague and editor, for their tolerance in leaving these choices to my discretion.

Apart from that my thanks for encouragement and advice are also gladly given to Bernard Jackson at Liverpool – particularly for the *Biezanek* Summing-up despite its being largely edited out – and to Ottmar Ballweg and Katharina Sobota, then at Mainz. Between them they set me on the road to legal linguistics and legal rhetoric.

The transcripts on which this book is based are subject to Crown copyright and have been reproduced with the permission of the Controller of Her Majesty's Stationery Office.

Finally, a special mention of thanks is overdue to Val Simpson whose skill, patience and stamina in producing the typescript is something I can only aspire to.

Paul Robertshaw
Cardiff, April 1997

Abbreviations

a.b.h.	actual bodily harm
AC	Appeal Cases
ALJ	*Australian Law Journal*
All ER	*All England Law Reports*
Anglo-Am. L. Rev.	Anglo-American Law Review
BMLR	*Butterworth Medico-Legal Reports*
CA	Court of Appeal
Camb. L. Rev.	*Cambrian Law Review*
Chic. Linguistics Soc.	*Chicago Linguistics Society*
Cir	Circuit
CJ	Chief Justice
Cm	Command Paper
Col. L. Rev.	*Columbia Law Review*
Cr. App. R.	*Criminal Appeal Reports*
Crim. L. Rev.	*Criminal Law Review*
ER	*English Reports*
F	(US) *Federal Law Reports*
HL	House of Lords
HMSO	Her Majesty's Stationery Office
IJ Semiotics L.	*International Journal for the Semiotics of Law*
IJSL	*International Journal of the Sociology of Law*
JC	Justiciary Cases
KB	*Law Reports, King's Bench Division*
Law and Soc. Rev.	*Law and Society Review*
Liverpool L. Rev.	*Liverpool Law Review*
LJC	Lord Justice Clerk
LJG	Lord Justice General
Med. Law Internat.	*Medical Law International*
MLR	*Modern Law Review*
NLJ	*New Law Journal*
Ox. Lit. Rev.	*Oxford Literary Review*
PC	Privy Council
PD	Practice Direction
QB	*Law Reports, Queen's Bench Division*
QBD	Queen's Bench Divisional Court

s.	section (of an Act)
SCCR	*Scottish Criminal Case Reports*
SLT	*Scottish Law Times*
SN	*Scottish Law Notes*
Th.	The, this, that
TLR	*Times Law Reports*
UK	United Kingdom
US	*United States Law Reports*
USA	United States of America
WLR	*Weekly Law Reports*

1 Legal language and Summing-up to juries

Legal linguistics and structuralist rhetoric

An autobiographical introduction

It is difficult to extract from my memory how I became interested, then involved in legal linguistics. It certainly was not because of any flowery speeches I read by advocates nor judicial peroration when sentencing villains. I think it is most likely that it was a by-product of another jurisprudential interest which gripped me as a postgraduate in the late 1960s when totally out of fashion (not that it had ever been in fashion in insular Britain) and has influenced me ever since: American Legal Realism (Frank on fact-finding, Llewellyn on precedent and the Canadian, Willis, on statutory interpretation). In the heady intellectual climate of the time, this interest in American Legal Realism was coupled with a devotion to the structuralist movement in cultural anthropology (especially Levi-Strauss and Leach).

At first, those divergent interests were without focus, but as I began to publish they became employable, and when I used to teach on David Miers' Juristic Technique course at Cardiff, the realism became routine.

With hindsight one can see a long-term but interrupted move in a particular direction, towards what I now call Structuralist Rhetoric. This was a personal development, aware of but separate from allied developments such as legal semiotics (Jackson 1996; Goodrich 1987), applied linguistics (exemplified for me by the Cardiff Language Symposium), forensic linguistics, and the Mainz School of Rhetoric (Sobota 1990) as well as critical discourse analysis (Stygall 1994). It is therefore necessary to outline how I reached the perspective and method I am using here, by way of a selective academic autobiography.

One section of my Master's thesis (1970) concerned the issue of 'standing' for third parties aggrieved by others' development proposals. Before its reform in 1977 the Anglo-Welsh Common Law of judicial review remained a bastion of mediaeval formalism in the shape of the Prerogative orders (Certiorari, Mandamus, Prohibition; and in Chancery, the Declaration). Frankly the jurisprudence was a mess, at least it was in terms of judicial utterance. However, by taking a structuralist-realist approach to the caselaw in terms of 'action', outcomes in relation to 'territory' – internal (judicial) and external (government) review – and ignoring the particular formal device, a rational and largely defensible pattern emerged: *Public Law* (1971), 'American realism', a mere quarter of a century behind the Americans.

I then attempted something more social-psychological, a consideration of the relationship between the superior judiciary as an elite autonomous, 'invaded', work group and their reaction to novel doctrinal claims. Here it was necessary to focus on a variety of topics: locus standi again, the doctrine of intention in contract, and negligence. The organizing concept was homeostasis. I was able to publish this in Australia, 47 *ALJ* (1973). This produced a strong reaction from a High Court of Australia judge, Blackburn J, 48 *ALJ* (1974), to which I replied in 50 *ALJ* (1976). This was an essay in social-psychological realism.

I then took the notion of territory back to administrative law, combined with status, and produced for the first time an explicit structural analysis of the caselaw of relationships with land: *Public Law* (1975); also 8 *Camb. L. Rev.* (1977).

The next topic I examined demonstrated the constitutive function of law, but my vehicle was a structural analysis of agreements involving family members over several centuries in England, going beyond the limited group of cases on 'intention' in contract I had considered earlier. Again, a realist perspective on outcome for particular family relationships was revelatory. Here was the Common law constituting the nuclear and extended family: (Robertshaw and Curtin) 25 *Sociological Review* (1977) and (Robertshaw) 3 *Anglo-Am. L. Rev.* (1984).

At this stage some generalization, 'theorizing', seemed necessary and led to two further articles: 'Structuralism and Law' 2 *Liverpool L. Rev.* (1980) 31-43 and 'Judicial Politics within the State' 9 *IJSL* (1981) 201–24.

Despite this realist and structuralist activity none of this work had really entangled itself in the language of judgments. This began with another exploration of the law's constitutive function, and a fraught one at that: gender. Here my primary focus was on the cluster of tropes that ran through the judgments: 'Semantic and Linguistic Aspects of Sex Discrimination Judgments', in Carzo and Jackson (eds) (1985) and 'Contemporary Legal Constitution of Woman' 8 *Ox. Lit. Rev.* (1986).

This was followed by an exploration of another cluster of metaphors in a series of cases regulating power relations primarily between Trade Union officials and their members: 'Hierarchies, Metaphors and Judicial Decisions' *Semiotics* (1984).

I then produced another overview, a review article on the emergence of an exciting and long overdue interest in the variety of legal linguistics from a number of disciplines: 'Law, Language and Rhetoric' 50 *MLR* (1987); also a review of Walter's (1988) path-breaking 'The Jury Summation as Speech Genre' – a study of *advocates'* final speeches in American criminal trials: 3 *IJ Semiotics L.* (1992).

I was then largely diverted from those pursuits by my PhD thesis and its publication, *Rethinking Legal Need* (1991), and moving from its finding of 'inverted legal need' (chs 14 and 15) to a full-scale study of bench and courts' local and regional variation, a statistical re-encounter with legal realism: *Jury and Judge* (1995).

This book brought me full circle to legal language in that it did not consider the most blatant relationship between judge and jury in the Anglo-Welsh trial, the Summing-up by the trial judge after counsel's final speeches. Where the current study differs from earlier work is in that it considers entire judicial statements, but not the judgments I once had in mind for rhetorical analysis.

One of the great ironies of Western intellectual history is that Plato's victory over the rhetoricians was secured by his mastery of their discipline and topics. This has had two principal consequences. One is that rhetoric is still mainly perceived as an artifice of prettification of language, of cosmetic embellishment; or worse, of bad faith in dressing up poor arguments in false attire. The other is that rhetoric has been torn from its roots in criminal (and public) law, particularly in its more developed Roman form (Goodrich 1987). So it is necessary to provide a brief introduction to Rhetoric.

Rhetoric and law

Species of argument

Rhetoric's original focus was on the *effective* use of language: perlocution as persuasion. I would argue that the three types of Aristotelian argument (pistis) although analytically separable, are all apposite to the trial. Clearly *forensic* argument for the proof of facts is relevant. However, *deliberative* argument on policy is frequently relevant; and surely *epideictic* argument for praise or blame is inescapable in the criminal trial?

In my specific focus of study, the genre of trial judge's Summing-up to the jury, I argue, however, that the three classical types of pistis are insufficient; and have introduced my own types which I will discuss below.

Mode of argument

Ethos, Pathos and Logos may be the three musketeers of rhetoric, but they cannot win the war of words without a strategy, that is some structure or morphotactics.

Ethos, the character or status of the speaker, is essential and we can take it that save in the rarest of cases the judge's authority and presence at the very least engages the attention and consideration of juries (see Moscovici 1976: 110 *et seq.*).

It is *Pathos* which has carried the false image of rhetoric down the millennia, but it is only part of the equipment, the appeal to the emotions by means of tropes.

Logos in my view needs development because it is too abstract. Logos connotes the positive content or substance of argument including its logic and consistency; it will embody its strategy, that is the relationship between topoi and tropes, in its structure. It will also embody quasi-tropes such as analogy, exemplification and differentiation; also consequentialism. I will be arguing that the Summing-up, at least in its Anglo-Welsh version, entails three other divisions within Logos, of such prominence and regularity that they must be added by name to the map, or at least its map.

So far I have considered three types of rhetoric and found them all to be relevant to this study. I have also considered three types of pistis, and considered them all to be relevant but not necessarily sufficient. We now come to the four cognitive methods of rhetoric: heuresis, style, memorability, and performance.

Cognitive aspects

Heuresis is the most difficult aspect, not least because Aristotle treated it at a totally abstract level. Heuresis – invention, in Ciceronic terms – is the choice of appropriate paradigms, structure and concepts in formulating argument towards the objective desired: the topoi (Viehweg 1993). The *topoi* emerge from a consideration of one's starting position, one's location in a situation (topology) and from a consideration of consensual ideas, invocation of 'the natural order', 'common-sense' and mental dockets – such as archetypes, stereotypes, foundational myths – into which they can be loaded. (See Sobota 1990.) Also there will be a perspective, a way of looking at the issue from a particular point-of-view or standpoint which will need to mesh with the former aspects, so that a 'map' of argumentative movement can be drawn and traversed. With those one can make one's topos or topoi concrete, because one has built one's argumentative premises on firm foundations from which to sortie (Hollander 1996).

It would be unfair to criticize the topoi for ignoring structuration of argument: topology itself suggests structure. Nevertheless I believe that the structuring of public speeches intended to influence or persuade, needs highlighting. Contemporary rhetoric and allied disciplines emphasize such structural matters as sequencing (Bourcier and Bruxelles 1984: 126–46) and the 'framing' of subject in matter in opening or prefatory remarks (Munkman 1991). Structuration has in my opinion a special relationship with Pathos. Pathos is what engages the audience because it involves surface phenomena; the pathic elements' value to the rhetor is that they disenable the audience from engagement with structure, which operates more or less subliminally. Certainly structure is far easier to comprehend in a visual (and repeatable through rescanning) text, than in a single oral representation. This, of course, is what advocacy and the judge's final speech to the jury comprise for them, but not for an appeal court (Ong 1982).

One must note that within the legal genre of the Summing-up heuresis is to an extent reduced as a moment in its rhetoric because so much of it is foreclosed by binding legal requirements and the pre-existing arguments of the advocates that must be addressed: a narrative of narratives.

Stylistics have always been rather unimaginatively listed as high, mid or low level methods of appropriate language, linked to the overall objective of effectiveness. In this study we will certainly encounter 'low' stylistic modes such as colloquialisms; jokes are almost absent; but the resort to the first person plural is, I think, important.

Mneme – memory, or rather memorability – the effective mobilization of this mental resource – is the third aspect of rhetoric and must be relevant to all long or complex trials and their Summings-up. It is clearly linked to the mental 'pigeon-hole' aspect of topoi.

Finally there is performance (*parastasis*), a dramaturgical concept concerned with the actual on site delivery of speech by the rhetor. There will be some kind of linkage between this and the rhetor's ethos. It includes all the stereotypical pejorative aspects of rhetoric: volume, pitch, speed, silence, direction, body language and movement of all in court, not excluding jurors. These are of course all absent from my text-centred text and must be acknowledged as a gap in the study because the trial Summing-up is delivered as a live once-and-for-all speech (Ong 1982).

The audience

In my view the major deficiency of classical rhetoric was a matter ignored by its critics: the audience or rather audience selection. This may have been because of the considerable homogeneity of the Athenian jury or the Roman senate. Nevertheless, with hindsight one has to say that the abstraction of the topoi may reflect this lack of engagement, especially with problematic or multiple audiences. For example tropotactics or heuretic strategy and morphotactics hardly makes sense outwith such concern: when to denigrate; how to denigrate; will sarcasm rebound; will rhetorical questions offend; when does repetition bore rather than emphasize; does enumeration confuse; does one metaphorize or colloquialize; are proverbs or fables effective; should one jab the finger at the opposition?

Such concerns are in the UK – unlike the USA – of enormous difficulty to those who address juries because, today, all that one has is gender (normally), an indication of age (18–69), dress and body language and proxemics of the group. Given this opaqueness the resort to Lowest Common Denominator images, and consensual topoi is hardly surprising: Ham rather than Hamlet is the safest choice.

The linkage between rhetor and audience can take two forms, both problematic. Behaviourally one can observe a vote, a verdict, an outcome as a correlation between that and what one has interpreted as the objective of the rhetor's delivered speech to the audience/s. That correlation does not in itself prove that the audience were persuaded, not least because there will be further rhetorical turns – and in trials the law demands it – within the audience/jury. But leaving that aside (along with its multiplex aspects), one might be able to show that persuasion had occurred if one could lawfully observe the audience's deliberation. (In Brazil juries are not permitted to deliberate together. They vote immediately the trial ends by secret ballot.)

In Anglo-Welsh law, the judge's functions are ambiguous and within the limits of 'fairness' include persuasion of the jury. As we shall see the judge is free to opine in any direction on the narrative presented, so long as both sides' narratives are considered, and a 'Disclaimer' is issued to the jury. The official function is to clarify rather than to persuade; this of course assumes confusion and presumably explains why the more robust Americans do not permit judges to survey the evidence in 'instructing' juries; American juries tend to receive these legal instructions with incomprehension (see for example Charrow and Charrow *Col. L. Rev.* (1979); Stygall 1994: 182–90).

That said I have to state that in my reading most Summings-up to juries, in their survey of the evidence in the trial, have 'directionality' in that they point towards acquittal or conviction. For what it is worth I think the judges' estimates of which way to lean are usually right, but that does beg the basic question of whether this genre should include this species of rhetoric. So I conclude with three possibilities of proof of persuasion, if one could observe it:

(1) confirmatory: the attitudes and action of the audience are reinforced.
(2) adaptive: the action of the audience is not altered but its justification shifts in some way.
(3) radical: there is a change of opinion and therefore of action.

The current study: genre-specific rhetorical categories

The path into this study was oblique in other respects. By happy chance I came upon a copy of the transcript of Caulfield J's extraordinary Summing-up to the jury in the world-famous libel case of *Archer* v. *Express Newspapers* in 1987 (Raphael 1993: chs 1–5). It immediately became clear to me that there was far more to it than the 'fragrant' references to the plaintiff's wife. I made a number of analyses of aspects of the transcript (112 pages) and gave some papers from them. I considered writing a book on this Summing-up alone. I acquired a small number of other Summings-up in libel trials, some also of considerable interest, and considered writing a book on Summing-up in libel trials. In working on *Archer* I had to develop a method to enable me to cope with its bulk.

I started with a laborious sentence-by-sentence and paragraph-by-paragraph analysis. This demonstrated what every literary critic knows, but is not so evident for verbally delivered texts: that sequencing and location can be significant regardless of themes or tropes. For example in 'The Archers, an Everyday Story of County Folk' I was able to demonstrate how by factual narrative interspersed between other participants' narratives and histories, Jeffrey Archer's life trajectory echoed the 'Tombstone' heralding and framing page one of the Summing-up, with a series of –/+ (down/up) episodes in which the final episode, the trial itself (– down), is left to be completed by the jury, in concordance with the preordained Archer destiny (+ up). There was also: 'Monica Coghlan – the Public Construction of a Born Loser'; but I will not consider that further nor 'Aziz Kurtha – a Study in Denigration' (apart from aspects of their naming, *infra*).

Sentence and paragraph analysis enabled me to construct thematic analyses. At that stage I did not see the need for any more abstract, truly structural categories for analysis.

However, *Archer* yielded another topic, which permeated the entire Summing-up and led to an analysis which now permeates this study: terms of address – nomenclature – and their relationship with credibility by a hierarchy of relative status. This I will reproduce below.

It was not until I chanced upon the much shorter but equally interesting Summing-up by Stable J in '*The Philanderer*' published in full: *R* v. *Secker and Warburg* [1954] 2 All ER 683, that I was prompted to develop the necessary structural categories appropriate to this specific genre.

Without the contact and encouragement of the colleagues in rhetoric, both classical and modernist, in the Law Faculty at the Johannes Gutenberg University, Mainz, this might not have happened. Nevertheless it must be stated that just as Sobota has developed a Statistical Rhetoric, so have I developed a Structuralist Rhetoric.

What is constant with tradition is the focus on particularity rather than general laws and on perlocution, persuasion as speech intended, usually strategically, to produce a particular effect relevant to the speech situation. These categories of rhetorical structure are designed for use with the Summing-up genre, though they could be adapted to judgments. Thematic analysis is not ousted as such, but can be made within the more abstract patterns constructed by the structural analysis. Again, within that any amount of analysis of tropes and other forms can take place.

The categories now follow:

Mythos

Narrative or story: typically in a criminal trial's Summing-up this will cover any reference by any person – defendant or witness, or counsel – to the contested events. It does not matter at all that these narratives are confused, contradictory or selective. A variant, still within the term Mythos, would be references to events leading to or in the course of the trial itself: Trial-Mythos. Jackson pithily distinguishes these variants as 'The Story in the Trial' and 'The Story of the Trial' (Jackson 1996: 445–52).

Next, there are two types of Nomos:

Nomo-dogma
Here the judge is instructing, ruling on law by stating what it is and how it must be interpreted or applied. Examples would include the elements of murder, the elements of manslaughter and the differences between them; the elements of rape; the Direction on the Burden of proof; a *Turnbull* Direction on identification, and so on.

Nomo-doxa
Here the judge is not instructing or directing on law but advising or opining on it, usually to assist the jury.

Krito-doxa
This category refers to the expression of judicial opinion on matters other than the law or facts in issue in the trial itself: opinionation. Krito-doxa is clearly closed related to Ethos, the speaker's role, status and charisma.

Intermediate categories are possible, for example *Mytho-doxa* where the judge comments on a version of events in a narrative. *Nomo-doxa* would occur if the judge gave an opinion on the value or utility of a law.

These terms appear to cover all the possibilities, and allow for thematic analysis within that frame and for tropic and other micro-level analysis within both. One classical category, Logos, does occur in particular forms in the Summing-up genre – exemplification, analogy, consequentialism, parameter and probability – but is not in my view independent of the rhetorical categories.

Pathos
Pathos, a category in classical Rhetoric, is not a structural but a surface category. It covers all those emotive features – stereotyped pejoratively as being the all-and-nothing of Rhetoric – which parade under the general label of trope, along with a number of miscellanea such as quotation and question-and-answer (Erotesis–Apocrisis).

Here are some examples of the above categories, excepting Pathos:

Mythos
The example I provide here is from a case considered only in relation to the successful appeal on 'unfairness' in the Summing-up of *R* v. *Spencer (John) The Times* 13 July 1994. My point is solely to show that the term Mythos is neutral between all accounts and narratives of action and motive constructed before the court. In this case the narratives can be considered as layers relating to the perspective of particular actors in the story in the trial (Wagenaar, Van Koppen and Crombag 1993).

I A man, not a resident of the locality (the defendant) may have inveigled a young girl across a street, where she lived, as a prelude to abduction in his car parked nearby.

II The young girl may have said that he invited her to cross the street as an excuse for breaking her mother's injunction against crossing the road to play with friends.

III The man who apprehended the defendant and reported him to the police had previous convictions including blackmail, and may have attempted unsuccessfully to blackmail the defendant before reporting him.

IV The defendant had a previous conviction for kerb-crawling for adult prostitutes. He had not declared that previous conviction to his employer, the Royal Air Force, as required, and may therefore have been unwilling to admit that that was his purpose for visiting the district.

From the structuralist perspective two comments can be added.

First, the *ordering* combinations of the layers might be important e.g. II, I, IV, III against I, II, III, IV or I, III, IV, II.

Second, the *omission* of one or more Mythos layers can alter the overall Mythos significantly, such as the omission of II. Equally *additional* layers could appear (typically on appeal or review), for example (V or IVA) that the defendant's visits to prostitutes may have begun because although his relationship with his wife was good, she felt unable to continue sexual intercourse during and after her menopause.

The layering of Mythos is not simply a matter of what is included or excluded, played down or highlighted at trial. Much of plea-bargaining's ethical risk is that layers of the Guilty plea narrative may be consensually excluded from the sentencing judge (Baldwin and McConville 1978). In addition the newer practice of 'down-charging' by police or prosecutors without negotiation to meet administrative objectives or financial constraints, has the same impact. Here is an example known to me in which the 'Story of the Trial' itself was radically shifted from Crown Court to the Magistrates.

Three men broke into a car repair garage at 3 a.m. They were inside it loading equipment into the two cars inside the garage for more than an hour. In this task they were sophisticated in that they did not load any of the pre-metrication tools that were present. They were about to drive the cars out of the garage when the police were called, because at that stage they had switched the lights on and had been quite noisy. They were arrested without incident, and searched. The police discovered small quantities of amphetamines on the men. The men said that the burglary had been a spontaneous event caused by the drugs they had taken.

The men were charged with possession of the drugs to which they pleaded Guilty. No reference of any kind was made to the burglary, nor the attendant criminal damage which cost the garage owners £1000 to repair (without insurance because of previous burglaries) – 'The Story of the Victims'.

Neither the Crown Prosecution Service nor the Magistrates received any indication of the burglary layer in the Mythos.

Mytho-doxa

Here a judicial comment on a narrative or narrative segment is inserted. An example might be: '... a likely tale you may think, given the witness's infatuation with the defendant, but it is of course, a matter for you ...'

Nomo-dogma

As examples of basic legal instruction I am going to cite from the two Canadian trials I have regretfully largely omitted from this study.

First from the beginning of the 'Charge to the Jury' in *R* v. *Horne* (Superior Criminal Court of the Province of Alberta at Edmonton 1995 per Ritter J):

> Your duty to your community is to ascertain if crimes have been committed and whether the accused committed those crimes. You have a responsibility to the accused to ensure that he is not improperly convicted. (Transcript 1080)

From the beginning of the Charge in *R* v. *Starr* (Supreme Court of British Columbia at Vancouver 1995 per Smith J):

> The first thing I want to say to you is that you will decide the case on the evidence adduced in the courtroom, and nothing else. You will try it without prejudice against or sympathy for any person involved in the proceedings. Consider the evidence rationally, and do not let your emotions affect your judgment. (Transcript 208)

Nomo-doxa

An example is the categorization of the case in *Bourne* [1939] 1 KB 687 as serious: 'The case is a grave case, and no doubt raises matters of grave concern both to the medical profession and to the public.' (Per MacNaghten J at 695. See also Stable J in *R* v. *Secker and Warburg* [1954] 2 All ER 683, 684D. Both these cases are analysed in later chapters.)

Krito-doxa

An example, one of a number, is from Stable J in '*The Philanderer*' *R* v. *Secker and Warburg* at 685 DE, on sex: 'I, at all events, approach that great mystery with profound interest and at the same time a very deep sense of reverence. We cannot get away from it. It is not our fault that but for the love of men and women and the act of sex the human race would have ceased to exist thousands of years ago ...'

Situational and pragmatic features of the Summing-up: 'The jury in the trial'

The location of the Summing-up in the trial

The trial judge's Summing-up occurs at the end of the trial process immediately before the jury withdraw to their sequestered deliberation towards verdict. At that culminating point the judge is free within the obligation to instruct the jury on all relevant law, to survey – in England and Wales – any aspect of the evidence adduced by either side at any stage. As we shall see the legal controls on the survey of evidence are not strong. No particular order is prescribed; more time may be spent on one matter than another might wish to, and less on another; comments of all kinds can be made, provided that the requirement of 'fairness' is not breached, and, that at least one 'disclaimer' be given asserting the jury's control of the verdict on the facts and that the judge's opinion is no more than that, which they are free to accept or reject. This speech is what the jury 'take out' with them. In many trials it is the only significant input from the judge that they observe.

Types of story

What the jury get to hear in the courtroom is a product of a complex set of choices in a sequence of procedures and tactical moments, usually over months: 'The Story of the Case', a story they may be ignorant of. There is also 'The Story of the Jury', how they came to be selected and empanelled together (see Robertshaw, Cox and Van Hoen 20 IJSL (1992)). Then follows what Jackson calls 'The Story of the Trial', much of which is observed directly by the jurors – assuming they are attentive and comprehending (Jackson 1996: chs 11–12; Bennett and Feldman 1981). What they have to evaluate is 'The Story in the Trial'.

Decision-making on the facts

The Summing-up to the jury by the trial judge epitomizes the out-of-normal situation in which jurors find themselves. The jurors' role as 'decision-makers on the facts' is misleading and serious academic discussion occurs from time to time as to what exactly their verdict connotes, even the dichotomous Anglo-Welsh choice between conviction or acquittal ('Guilty' or 'Not Guilty'). Does 'Not Guilty' equate with moral innocence, or is it merely an indication that the jury were not sufficiently convinced by what they heard and saw to make a statement of 'guilt', combining legal closure, moral culpability and factual probability to a very high degree? It is not impossible that the jury's deliberation and verdict were on altogether different grounds. Some instances of their situation can be gleaned from the language itself: the verdicts allowed lie around the stem 'guilt': Guilty or Not Guilty. Guilt is both a legal and a lay term whereby the legal and the moral are fused. The alternative to guilt is imposed in negative terms rather than as a positive assertion of innocence, a moral term not mirrored in legal language. Equally the jury can be said to convict or acquit; these are purely legal terms, though 'convict' has acquired a lay gloss relating to the consequences of conviction. In addition both verdicts are probabilistic, 'beyond reasonable doubt' (coupled with the possibility of a majority verdict since 1967). Excellent accounts of this problem are to be found in Jackson (1996: 26–31) and Dershowitz (1996 ch. 4).

My position on this is more socio-linguistic. First, the jury verdict is a striking example of social closure, a means whereby a contentious matter may be resolved authoritatively, in which that finality lies in the legitimacy accorded to the jury's deliberation and verdict as the appropriate truth-certifying procedure (Bankowski, ch. 1 in Findlay and Duff 1988) or 'veridication' (Jacquemet 1996).

In addition this linguistic ambiguity in the verdict requirement gives *legal* scope for moral elements to enter the jury's deliberation (Dershowitz 1996: ch. 4; Abramson 1994: ch. 2).

Passivity and activity

As decision-makers the publicly visible role of the jury is characterized by extreme passivity, of inert consumption of the spectacle provided to them, over which they have no control whatsoever for as long as the trial lasts, whether days or months.

It is true that notes may be passed or questions asked through the judge, but this is rare, discouraged and restricted to points of clarification.

The attribute of silence

This passivity is signalled by the jury as collective mutes. Public discussion in trial, even whispering, is rare and frowned upon.

Further they are always instructed at the beginning of the trial not to discuss the trial or any aspect of it, not only with their friends and relatives, but also with each other even in the jury room, until formal deliberation commences. So mediating effects, from all sources, are excluded.

In turn the deliberation is in secret conclave and will be delivered by the foreman without elucidation or reasoning (*R* v. *Jameson* (1896) 12 TLR 551, 594 CJ). Further, any post-trial discussion of the deliberation is currently prohibited by s.8 Contempt of Court Act 1981: *Attorney-General* v. *Associated Newspapers Ltd* [1993] 2 All ER 535 QBD.

Enforced strangers-together

Despite the residential tie to the trial court required throughout the history of jury service, jurors rarely serve more than once in a lifetime, and unless research were to provide evidence to the contrary, are usually strangers to each other (as well as the defendant). During waiting times before empanelment jurors-in-waiting are free to talk to each other and this may even continue throughout their service without actually hearing a trial, or, more likely, hearing a trial but not necessarily in the company of those with whom time has been passed in so waiting. Such shared conversation and experience gives no control at all as to its continuance into the trial experience. Interesting conversation may be suddenly disrupted by call to empanelment or end of service by any or all concerned. The one topic which cannot be discussed is previous jury experience, if any, and by definition, hypothetical trials to come. In other words there is a degree of enforced superficiality in pre-trial jurors' in-court experiences.

From beck-and-call to power

The juror's experience is more – or rather less – than passivity. It involves induction into mobility without obvious purpose, at the behest of jury bailiffs, low-level court staff. The most common instances of such shunting are:

(i) 'Cracked' trials (Robertshaw *Crim. L. Rev.* (1992)), that is very late changes of plea to guilty by defendants.
(ii) Pre-empanelment discharge, 'ordered' acquittals by the trial judge, usually in consultation with counsel or because the prosecution decide for good reason to discontinue (Robertshaw 1995: ch. 6; Block, Corbett and Peay 1993).
(iii) During the trial jury exclusion can occur because of legal discussion over procedure and issues over the admissibility of evidence. (See J. Jackson in Davies, Lloyd-Bostock, McMurray and Wilson 1995.)
(iv) When breaks occur they are usually decided with the jury in mind, but they are at the behest of the judge, who also controls their duration. This is particularly important in the context of the Summing-up because it allows for the strategic introduction of openings, framings and finales.
(v) Jury trial can be abruptly ended by a Directed acquittal by the judge to the jury, usually because of failure of witnesses or the facts disclosed not amounting to relevant illegality (Robertshaw 1995: ch. 5).

This heteronomous experience is an imperfect preparation for the exercise of responsibility for the defendant's reputation and future liberty or incarceration. Since 1996, a Lord Chancellor's Department–Interlink Videotape has been available for jurors (in English and Welsh), but this is the first attempt at formal jury induction.

Individual atomism to group collectivism

Whatever the degree of camaraderie and superficial conversational interchange achieved during the waiting period, as far as a trial is concerned the juror remains an individual atom isolated from others with the same experience right up until the moment deliberation commences. Whilst one can appreciate the risks in formally allowing or encouraging running commentary and interchange within a jury during trial, equally one can assert that this is not the best training for deliberation, which has in effect to commence from a 'cold' start. It is hardly surprising that juries frequently resort to preliminary straw-polls which are rightly frowned upon as foreclosing full discussion of the evidence and creating factions unnecessarily (Hastie, Penrod and Pennington 1983: 163–7).

The shock of responsibility

Not all trials in the Crown Court are of national or local scandals, and not all are of extremely serious offences, but the vast majority are. The consequences for those defendants convicted are highly stigmatic on first conviction, and usually involve loss of liberty in a deteriorating prison system. Jurors are well aware of this, though it is only in exceptional cases that they have any knowledge of the defendant's previous convictions. This imposes a special burden on the jury because although entirely responsible for the verdict they have no responsibility at all for its consequences. It must be difficult to bracket this out, although often so directed by the trial judge in the Summing-up. Since jury qualification was democratized in 1974 with the basic qualification being registration as an elector, those available for jury service have undoubtedly been drawn from a far wider social spectrum than in the past. There is hearsay evidence that the 'excusing process' reduces the number of those with professional and middle-class occupations (and not disqualified by law) who serve. This may have an impact on intra-jury relations – selection of foreman and 'silent free-riders' for example – which I will not go into here. What must be stated is that this in itself is an extraordinary moment in the life history of most jurors, whose lives will not normally have involved making decisions on difficult, non-consensual evidence about strangers with drastic potential impacts on their lives and those of their dependants. In extreme cases one can hypothesize the identification of the juror as failed excusee with the defendant as failed representative of the dark figure of crime.

This is more basic than shocking forensic evidence and disturbing evidence about motivation which may occur in a minority of trials, which simply compound this background stress. It is also distinct from the disruption of routine normality that any jury trial induces (Lindley 1993: 5, 155–6).

Power disequilibrium: judge and jury

The outcome in a jury trial combines two sources of authority, in law of equal standing, yet this is negated by the structure of the trial event and the judge–jury relations. Perhaps it could not be otherwise, but it remains a tension or contradiction. The judge is the epitome of Galanter's 'Repeat Player' (9 *Law and Soc. Rev.* 1974) and the jury as 'One-Shot-Players' (by definition they would be disqualified, if they had been convicted and sentenced for certain terms). In that, the judge may be similar to counsel, solicitors, and ironically, even defendants. But the authoritative location of the judge in the courtroom architecture is more than symbolic, combined with the superior status indicators of wig and robes. The judge faces the defendant directly, whereas the jury do so obliquely. All procedural moves and sequences pass through the judge, to whom, deferential behaviour and speech forms are routine. The judge's silence may compete over time with that of the jury, but there is no restraint on his or her initiative to puncture it. Both judge and jury are observers and listeners, but the judge is listening 'for the jury' whereas jurors listen solely for themselves. The role-expectation for the jury throughout the trial is one of dependence on the judge.

Switching from margin to centre

The focus on the defendant, and witnesses, throughout the trial has a consequence on the jury who will be on-stage marginals for that period, and then transmute into central actors as soon as off-stage for deliberation.

Alienation effects

A number of the points already made suggest that the jury experience can be an alienating one, separating the jury from each other and from that which they are convened to achieve. There are aspects of the trial which may exacerbate these tendencies: the courtroom architecture; the language of counsel; the ritual of procedure; the extreme control of narrative sustained by the examination and cross-examination mode; the sloth of progress and degree of repetition; in some instances the subject-matter of the offence event and defendant's biography. In such instances the ability of jurors to evaluate evidence or narrative by reference to their own experiences of life may be reduced or entirely absent: 'The Story of the Juror' has no reference to the 'Story in the Trial'.

Disruption of linguistic normality

Alienation features in the jury's position as spectator-audience of the trial in terms of the specific linguistic performance witnessed. I am not referring here to trial matters such as legal terminology, which actually is not a major feature of most criminal trials; nor to legal ponderosity, such as confusing double negatives; nor to the risks of enumeration when unsystematic (Charrow and Charrow 1979).

One prominent example which is structured into trial process affects all concerned. It is the breach of the conversational norm of Question: Answer-to-Questioner. This affects defendants and witnesses most, but there is no reason to think that jurors are not also affected by being the recipients of answers actually intended for others.

Related to this is another well-known feature of much of the trial process, what I call here the anti-narrativity mode of trial narration. Witnesses do not 'tell their story' in the courtroom. It is extracted from them via the Question-Answer-to-Jury mode by affirmative or negative responses to selections (not necessarily sequences) from competing narratives, usually with considerable overlapping and therefore considerable repetition. The only preparation jurors have for this unique narrative mode is (unless they have visited trials) from novels and the media. The generalized effect is that these lay decision-makers are deprived of all control over the information sources and quantity of information from which they will construct their decision.

The site of the Summing-up

The Summing-up itself has a salience regardless of content. It is the finale of the entire pre-deliberation trial process in which there is a survey in retro-prospective as preparation for the dénouement of all those competing narratives presented through the medium of the trial process. In addition it is the only input of any length from the judge, witnessed by the jury. It is the trial's culmination. This special effect is best brought out by comparison with the USA. There the trial judge does have the final say but it is short and confined to arid legal instruction. It is not a culminating but a coda moment. (See Walter 1988.)

Conclusion

I have considered here the jury's situation pre-Summing-up and pre-deliberation and verdict. It appears that jurors are put through a process of disorientation, in which they cannot – at least legally – turn to each other for assistance and support by discussing the trial events and issues. This I suggest creates the conditions for dependency and for the reception of authoritative resolution of difficulties and tensions by the trial judge. That moment is the Summing-up in which not only definitive legal rulings are given but the entire trial event and its advocates' narratives mediated by a selective survey of the evidence adduced by both sides. The form of the Summing-up and the issue of its directionality towards or against either side is the focus of this book. The relevance of structural Rhetoric is that it considers the ways in which this monologue, punctured by judicially controlled breaks, can attempt to persuade a passive, silent, subdued audience. The verbal monologue form should be emphasized here; jury interruptions are very rare. The monologue form means that any sequencing strategy is masked. It is only by after-the-event *textual* analysis that it is reasonably possible to elicit structural patterns, and also the spacing of surface forms such as extended families of metaphor. Rhetoric it must be remembered was, in origin at least, the study of persuasion in speech, not written, mode.

In addition a set of caveats must be entered. Because I have had to analyse texts, many important, even crucial features, are omitted: tone, silences, speed and face, hand and upper body language, all in relation to speech delivery.

All the points made here concern the jury situation prior to deliberation. That presents its own problems, but these are beyond the scope of this book, not least because of s.8 Contempt of Court Act 1981.

2 The law of Summing-up

England and Wales

Overall structure

The Judicial Studies Board produces specimen Directions in what are known as Judicial Benchbooks. These are not publicly available, but the Board gave me the Contents list for the December 1994 and May 1996 editions. The Board was unwilling to provide me with examples of any of the specific Directions, and this was for a sound policy reason: they are not in general intended to be tablets of stone. This is put clearly by the then Lord Chief Justice Taylor in his foreword (December 1994):

> I would have welcomed this useful aid to summing up when I sat regularly at first instance. These Directions are not, however, intended as a substitute for thorough preparation and will of course require careful adoption where the circumstances of the case so dictate. In particular specimen Directions drafted for one purpose should not be used for a different purpose (*R* v. *Taylor (Anthony) The Times* 15 June 1993 CA).

This statement fits into a broader philosophy of purpose of the Summing-up expressed by Lord Chancellor Hailsham:

> It has been said before but obviously requires to be said again. The purpose of a direction to a jury is not best achieved by a disquisition on jurisprudence or philosophy or a universally applicable circular tour round the area of law affected by the case. The search for universally applicable definitions is often productive of more obscurity than light. A direction is seldom improved and may be considerably damaged by copious recitations from the total content of a judge's notebook. A direction to a jury should be custom-built to make the jury understand their task in relation to a particular case. Of course it must include references to the burden of proof and the respective roles of jury and judge. But it should also include a succinct but accurate summary of the issues of fact as to which a decision is required, a correct but concise summary of the evidence and arguments on both sides and a correct statement of the inferences which the jury are entitled to draw from their particular conclusions about the primary facts. (*R* v. *Lawrence* [1982] AC, 510, 519 HL. See also *Arthurs* v. *A-G for Northern Ireland* 55 *Cr. App. R.* (1970) 161, 170 per Lord Morris of Borth-y-Gest)

Another obvious risk of slavish imitation would be failure to adapt a specimen direction to a particular issue of law that might arise in a particular trial (*R* v. *Jackson* [1992] *Crim. L. Rev.* 214 CA).

As it happens the Benchbooks have recently been the subject of some controversy. Roderic Munday recently criticized the Court of Appeal for its tendency to criticize or overturn convictions because aspects of particular Directions did not conform to the Benchbook model, in other words that the Directions had changed status: *Crim. L. Rev.* (1996) 296–305. This led to correspondence from Kennedy LJ (*ibid.*: 529–30); with Munday's reply (*ibid.*: 530–2). The Judicial Studies Board then decided that it will publish the specimen Directions, but has made it clear that there will be no change in their general status (*ibid.*: 533 Ed.).

That said I can report on the overall contents of the specimen Directions. The headings are 'General', 'Intention and Recklessness', 'Evidence', 'Defendant's failures' (introduced in 1996); 'Defences'; 'Jury Management/Verdicts'. The 1996 edition no longer covers under 'General': aiding and abetting, and counselling and procuring; and under 'Evidence' the former detail under 'corroboration' is omitted: 'what constitutes; lies as; accomplice; sexual offences'.

It would be tedious for the reader to read all the sub-headings under each main heading in the 1996 edition. There are eleven under 'General' including the functions of judge and jury; the Burden and Standard of proof and the separate treatment of each defendant. There are seven sub-headings under 'Intention and Recklessness' focusing on six types of offence. Under 'Evidence' there are 18 sub-headings covering such matters as circumstantial evidence, the defendant's character – good and bad – and the defendant's confession or lies, and expert evidence. New topics are 'system evidence', dishonesty, hearsay, and drugs-allegation of supply. There are eight sub-headings under 'Defendant's failures' of which five are new, covering the defendant's total or partial silence at trial: failure to mention facts when charged; failure to account or refusal to account for presence at a particular place. My study does not cover or attend to those recent changes in the legal situation. Under 'Defences' are nine sub-headings ranging alphabetically from alibi to sexual offences-consent, 'domestic circumstances'. Finally there are three sub-headings under 'Jury Management/Verdicts': unanimous verdict; majority verdict, and the '*Watson*' direction (on oppressively obtained confessions).

My objective here is not to enter into a detailed examination of the caselaw relating to the Summing-up today, but to give the reader the necessary background within which trial judges prepare and deliver these final speeches to jurors.

For example, it is not widely known that there is an active duty on prosecuting counsel to draw attention to any omission or failure in the directions to the jury and that all the basic requirements are met (*R* v. *McVey* [1988] *Crim. L. Rev.* 129 CA; *R* v. *Donoghue* 86 *Cr. App. R.* (1988) 267 CA; *R* v. *Lang-Hall The Times* 24 March 1989 CA; *R* v. *Roberts*

[1992] *Crim. L. Rev.* 375 CA). Clearly this can be seen as necessary and reasonable appeal-proofing. The law is less clear on the obligation of the defence counsel – with their primary obligation to their client (*R* v. *Cocks* 63 *Cr. App. R.* (1976) 79, 82 CA) – but there is also an obligation to the court, particularly on basic errors and omissions such as the Standard of proof (*R* v. *Edwards (N.W.)* 77 *Cr. App. R.* (1983) 5 CA) or the law of provocation (*R* v. *Southgate* 47 *Cr. App. R.* (1963) 252 CA). Should an error in direction come to the judge's attention by whatever means after the jury have started their deliberation, s/he must have the jury brought back into court so that the error can be explained and a correct Direction given; the jury should then be asked to retire again to consider their verdict in the light of the correct version (*R* v. *Plimmer* 61 *Cr. App. R.* (1975) 264 CA).

Burden of proof

As far as the Burden (and Standard) of proof is concerned there is no escape from the duty to direct upon every element in each charge. The Burden of proof lies on the prosecution and remains there throughout the trial (*Woolmington* v. *DPP* [1935] AC 462, 482; *R* v. *Hunt* [1987] AC 352 HL). There is authority that these directions should be given once at the beginning of the Summing-up (*R* v. *Ching* 63 *Cr. App. R.* (1976) 7 CA; *R* v. *Milligan The Times* 11 March 1989 CA). Repetition is not normally considered necessary, but circumstances such as jury confusion and request for assistance may necessitate it (*R* v. *Gibson* 77 *Cr. App. R.* (1983) 151 CA). Should a misdirection on the Burden occur, the mistake must be corrected in the clearest possible terms (*R* v. *Moon* [1969] 1 WLR 1705 CA; *R* v *Johnson* [1972] *Crim. L. Rev.* 180 CA).

An example of the application of this overriding principle is where the judge considers that self-defence can be left to the jury. Here the judge must reassert that it is for the prosecution to disprove self-defence, and not for the defence to prove that the defendant was so acting (*R* v. *Abraham* 57 *Cr. App. R.* (1973) 799, 803 CA).

Standard of proof

As far as the Standard of proof is concerned the prosecution must satisfy the jury on the whole of the evidence called by all the parties that the defendant is guilty beyond all reasonable doubt (*Woolmington* v. *DPP supra*; *Ferguson* v. *R* [1979] 1 WLR 94, 99 PC; *R* v. *Sang* [1980] AC 402 HL; *R* v. *Lawrence supra* HL). The degree of satisfaction does not have to amount to certainty (*Miller* v. *Minister of Pensions* [1947] 2 All ER 372, per Denning J at 373–4). Goddard CJ's formulation 'satisfied so that you are sure' in *R* v. *Kritz* 33 *Cr. App. R.* (1948) 169, 177 and *R* v. *Summers* 36 *Cr. App. R.* (1951) 14, 15 is much used and was approved by the Privy Council in *Walters* v. *R* [1969] 2 AC 26, 30. Weaker variants have been disapproved by the Court of Appeal, such as 'pretty certain' or 'pretty sure' (*R* v. *Law* [1961] *Crim. L. Rev.* 52; *R* v. *Head* 45 *Cr. App. R.* (1961) 225; *R* v. *Woods* [1961] *Crim. L. Rev.* 324). Should the jury request a further explanation, the correct practice is to state that a reasonable doubt is the sort of doubt that might affect the mind of a person in dealing with matters of importance in their own affairs (*Walters* v. *R supra*; *R* v. *Gray* 58 *Cr. App. R.* (1974) 177, 183). Again weaker variants have been disapproved such as a reference to 'everyday affairs' without 'matters of importance' (*R* v. *Stafford* 53 *Cr. App. R.* (1969) 1 CA; *R* v. *Gray supra*).

In addition to the Burden and Standard of proof the judge must direct on the law applicable in the particular case (*R* v. *O'Meara The Times* 15 December 1989 CA) and must direct on the different functions of judge and jury (*Broadhurst* v. *R* [1964] AC 457, 459 per Lord Devlin). The jury must also be instructed to give separate consideration to each count (*R* v. *Fisher* 49 *Cr. App. R.* (1965) 116; *R* v. *Lovesey* 53 *Cr. App. R.* (1969) 461) and separate consideration to each defendant (*R* v. *Smith* 25 *Cr. App. R.* (1936) 119; *R* v. *S/C* [1996] *Crim. L. Rev.* 346).

As far as the evidence is concerned it is, in England and Wales, standard practice to go through the evidence and comment on it. There seems to be a proportionality convention in that in complex trials the judge is expected to assist the jury by considering the most important features, whereas in a short, simple trial that may not be necessary. (*R* v. *Attfield* 45 *Cr. App. R.* (1961) 309.) In particularly complicated cases the judge may sum-up in sections, and even take the verdict for each charge at the conclusion of each section: *R* v. *Newland* 37 *Cr. App. R.* (1954) 159; *R* v. *Simmonds* 51 *Cr. App. R.* (1969) 316; *R* v. *Houssein* 70 *Cr. App. R.* (1980) 267 CA. In summing-up the evidence for the defence must be considered (*R* v. *Dinnick* 3 *Cr. App. R.* (1903) 77; *R* v. *Weiner The Times* 3 November 1989 CA). However, where the defendant makes no attempt at a defence the judge is not under a duty to provide one in the Summing-up (*R* v. *Briley* [1991] *Crim. L. Rev.* 444 CA; *R* v. *Hillier* 97 *Cr. App. R.* (1993) 349 CA). Although there is no duty on the judge to take up every point made by the defence, nor to stick to the structure presented (*R* v. *Goodway* 98 *Cr. App. R.* (1994) 11, 14 CA; *R* v. *Richardson* 98 *Cr. App. R.* (1994) 174, 178 CA), yet the survey and comment must be balanced and fair (*R* v. *Mills* 25 *Cr. App. R.* (1936) 138; *R* v. *Waters* [1954] *Crim. L. Rev.* 147; *R* v. *Olliffe* [1955] *Crim. L. Rev.* 570; *R* v. *Badjan* 50 *Cr. App. R.* (1966) 141; *R* v. *Hamilton* [1972] *Crim. L. Rev.* 266). This extends to stating a defence that arises from the evidence adduced, even if it has not been relied on by the defence counsel (*Kops* v. *R* [1894] AC 650 PC; *R* v. *Courtnell* [1990] *Crim L. Rev.* 115 CA; *R* v. *Williams* (*Winston Anthony*) *The Times* 11 November 1993 per Neill LJ). So long as comment is based on evidence adduced in the trial, the judge is not restricted to the argument put forward by either side (*R* v. *Evans* (*David John*) 91 *Cr. App. R.* (1992) 173 CA); however, where this happens notice should be given to counsel and an opportunity to discuss its appropriateness given, which will be in the absence of the jury (*R* v. *Cristini* [1987] *Crim. L. Rev.* 505 CA; *R* v. *Feeny* 94 *Cr. App. R.* (1992) 1 CA). If the trial judge goes his or her own way and sums up on a different basis from that canvassed at trial this flouts the adversarial principle and may result in a successful appeal. In *R* v. *Redman The Times* 25 April 1994 counsel had drawn the trial judge's attention to the lack of correspondence between the Summing-up and advocate's arguments, to no avail.

The judge may direct that the suggestions, theories or opinions of counsel made either in cross-examination or closing speeches are not evidence (*R* v. *Hill* 96 *Cr. App. R.* (1993) 456, 463 CA).

In appropriate cases the judge should give a Warning that the jury should not be swayed in any direction by the emotions that might be released by the case (*R* v. *Bowditch* [1991] *Crim. L. Rev.* 831 CA).

The demarcation in roles between judge and jury must be explained at the outset, that it is for the jury to decide on the facts (*R* v. *West* 4 *Cr. App. R.* (1910) 179; *R* v. *Frampton* 12 *Cr. App. R.* (1917) 202). However, in the Anglo-Welsh tradition the judge is entitled to comment and even to do so strongly where appropriate, provided always that the jury is aware that the decision remains with them (*R* v. *Cohen* 2 *Cr. App. R.* (1909) 197). In addition the point already made remains relevant: the defendant's case must be fairly presented, so the usual Warnings to the jury will not transcend any unfairness; *Mears* v. *R* 97 *Cr. App. R.* (1993) 239 PC; *R* v. *Berrada* 91 *Cr. App. R.* (1992) 131 CA. The comment must not be tantamount to a Direction to convict: *R* v. *Gent* 89 *Cr. App. R.* (1990) 247 CA.

There are a number of special Directions on particular matters which are not common to all trials, but some of which arise frequently and certainly feature in this study. They include:

- *The defendant's failure to testify*
  Here there is a strong Direction, in effect buttressing the Burden of proof, and reminding the jury not to take this 'failure' as any evidence of guilt (*R* v *Jackson* 37 *Cr. App. R.* (1953) 43; *R* v. *Bathurst* 52 *Cr. App. R.* (1968) 251 CA; *R* v. *Hubbard* [1991] *Crim. L. Rev.* 449 CA). This is now subject to s.35 of the Criminal Justice and Public Order Act 1994: *R* v. *Cowan/Gayle/Ricciardi* [1995] 4 All ER 939 provides authoritative assistance to trial judges on how to instruct juries in the context of s.35, including the lack of change in the Burden and Standard of proof.
- *The defendant's lies*
  Lies go to the defendant's credibility and judges should comment on the possible causes for lying, but they should not go beyond this unless the context gives no logical room but for an inference of guilt – and here a full direction to that effect must be given (*R* v. *Lucas (R)* 73 *Cr. App. R.* (1981) 159 CA; *R* v. *Goodway supra*).

- *The consequences of conviction*
  This is not normally considered desirable, but if given will not automatically flaw the Summing-up (*R* v. *Peart The Times* 12 November 1992 CA).
- *Circumstantial evidence*
  There is no obligation to give a special Direction: *McGreevy* v. *DPP* 57 *Cr. App. R.* (1973) 424 HL, but if given it should be in the appropriate form: see Judicial Studies Board specimen/terms: *R* v. *S/C* [1996] *supra*.
- *Corroboration*
  My sample has been overtaken by s.32(1) of the Criminal Justice and Public Order Act 1994, which abolishes the former rules requiring judges to give corroboration warnings, typically in rape cases. The approach trial judges should take to the discretion they now have has been laid down by the Court of Appeal in *R* v. *Makanjuola/Easton* NLJ 20 June 1995. However, it should be noted that in Scotland corroboration is generally required in all prosecutions.
- *The defendant's character*
  Good character
  When a defendant has given evidence a Direction on the relevance of good character to credibility should be given: *R* v. *Vye/Wise/Stephenson* 97 *Cr. App. R.* (1993) 134 CA. Where the facts support it the Direction need not be given, that is where there is clear or agreed evidence of dishonesty without previous convictions: *R* v. *Buzalek* [1991] *Crim. L. Rev.* 116 CA; *R* v. *Zoppola-Barraza The Times* 6 May 1994 CA. The judge has a discretion as to the amount of significance that is attached to the relevance and weight of previous convictions: *R* v. *H* [1994] *Crim. L. Rev.* 205 CA.
  Bad character
  Again, where the defendant has given evidence the jury should be told that this goes solely to credibility and is not evidence as to whether the particular offence tried has been committed; also that the jury has a choice whether to take such evidence into account regarding credibility: *R* v. *Prince* [1990] *Crim. L. Rev.* 49 CA.
- *Identification*
  There is now a standard Direction on identification (*R* v. *Turnbull* 63 *Cr. App. R.* (1977) 132 CA); failure to follow it in detail may result in a conviction being quashed: *R* v. *Hinjan* 68 *Cr. App. R.* (1978) 99 CA; *R* v. *Pattinson* (1996) 1 *Cr. App. R.* 51 CA.

Finally, there are Directions which almost invariably occur at the end of the Summing-up and relate to the jury's deliberation and verdict.

There will be one on the need to appoint a 'foreman' to chair the deliberations and report the verdict. There is also one on unanimity – rather than majority: PD 51 *Cr. App. R.* (1967) 454; *R* v. *Georgiou* 53 *Cr. App. R.* (1969) 428; this stress on unanimity includes a lack of indication as to the amount of time that may pass before a majority verdict would become acceptable: *R* v. *Thomas (IJ) The Times* 4 August 1983 CA; *R* v. *Guthrie The Times* 23 February 1994 CA held that mention of the minimum time did not in itself amount to an irregularity. The requirement of unanimity applies to all the elements essential to the commission of an offence: *R* v. *Brown (K)* 79 *Cr. App. R.* (1984) 115 CA, though jurors are free to reach these conclusions by differing evidential routes.

Scotland

Because I shall be proposing serious consideration of the Scottish judge's Charge to the Jury as an alternative model to that in England and Wales, I add here a brief résumé of the relevant Scots law.

The leading case remains *Hamilton* v. *HM Advocate* (1938) JC 134 per Lord Normand LJG:

> ... the primary duty of the presiding judge is to direct the jury upon the law applicable to the case. In doing so it is usually necessary for him to refer to the facts on which questions of law depend. He may also have to refer to evidence in order to correct any mistakes that may have occurred in the addresses to the jury, and he may have occasion to refer to the evidence where controversy has arisen as to its bearing on question of fact which the jury has to decide. But it is a matter very much in his discretion whether he can help the jury by resuming the evidence on any particular aspect of the case, I am confident that the anxious willingness of judges to give every help that they can to the jury may be relied on to guide them aright on the extent to which they ought to review the evidence in the case, and I am little disposed to attend with patience to the criticism that more should have been said about the evidence by way of exposition or explanation than the judge thought proper at the time. A Court of appeal is not in a position to review this discretion of the presiding judge on matters which concern the best way of conducting the case before him.

In consequence judges and sheriffs in Scotland very rarely review the whole evidence. Attempts to mount appeals on the basis of factual errors in the Charge are unlikely to succeed. What matters is that the legal issues have been clearly identified in the trial itself by advocates for the Crown and defence. So the emphasis is on the legal issues prosecuted in the Charge. The judge must not exceed the demarcation between judge and jury by trespassing on their verdict: *Ogg* v. *HM Advocate* (1938) JC 152; *Sinclair* v. *HM Advocate* (1990) SCCR 412. In particular 'Disclaimers' of the type universally found in the Anglo-Welsh Summing-up will not cancel out any excessive opinion on the facts: *McPhelim* v. *HM Advocate* (1960) JC 17, LJC at 21. In fact comment on the evidence as opposed to showing how it fits into the legal issues is strongly discouraged: *Simpson* v. *HM Advocate* (1952) JC 1; *McArthur* v. *HM Advocate* (1989) SCCR 646; *Sutherland* v. *HM Advocate* (1994)

SCCR 80, indeed there is no obligation in law to deal with the evidence: *Vetters* v. *HM Advocate* (1994) SCCR 305, 308B. Nor will such a Disclaimer override inaccurate or confusing reference to evidence: *Larkin* v. *HM Advocate* (1977) SCCR 30; if that cannot be achieved it should not be attempted: *Scott (A.T.)* v. *HM Advocate* (1946) JC 90; *Tonge* v. *HM Advocate* (1982) JC 130.

This is not to suggest that evidence is prohibited from the Charge, the position is subtler than that. The basic function of the presiding judge is to explain the legal framework, the relevant legal elements of each charge on the indictment: *M'Kenzie* v. *HM Advocate* (1959) SC 32, and any special defences that are relevant: *Owens* v. *HM Advocate* (1946) JC 119; *Elliott* v. *HM Advocate* (1987) SCCR 278. Focused legal relevance is the primary consideration: *McTavish* v. *HM Advocate* (1975) SLT (Notes) 27; *McIntyre* v. *HM Advocate* (1981) SCCR 117; *McGougan* v. *HM Advocate* (1991) SCCR 49. Within that – again on the principle of relevant necessity – evidence may be referred to within each such context, so as to enable the jury to be clear on the issue or issues they have to decide: *Rubin* v. *HM Advocate* (1984) SCCR 96, 112 per Lord Grieve; *MacNicol* v. *HM Advocate* (1986) SCCR 288. It follows therefore that the Charge is not a Summing-up or survey of all the evidence, but is limited by relevance, by even-handedness: *Gilmour* v. *HM Advocate* (1982) SCCR 590; *Meek* v. *HM Advocate* (1982) SCCR 613; *King* v. *HM Advocate* (1985) SCCR 322, 328 per LJC Wheatley; and by concentration on the conflicts of the evidence between Crown and defence: *Mills* v. *HM Advocate* (1935) JC 77; *Tonge* v. *HM Advocate supra*.

Comment by the judge on this evidence is risky because usurpation of the jury's role as master of the facts is a fundamental misdirection: *Simpson supra*, *Tallis* v. *HM Advocate* (1982) SCCR 91. If comment is considered essential it should be restrained: *Brown* v. *MacPherson* (1918) JC 3; *Costello* v. *MacPherson* (1922) JC 9, and neither emphasized nor repeated: *Scott (A.T.) supra*, *Stewart* v. *HM Advocate* (1980) SLT 245.

There is no special order or procedure laid down; what matters is relevance to the legal issues and clarification: *McAvoy* v. *HM Advocate* (1991) SCCR 123. If a charge is appealed the tendency of appeal courts is to consider it as a whole against what occurred in the trial itself rather than to focus on detail or details in isolation: *Reynolds* v. *HM Advocate* (1928) SN 103; *Muir* v. *HM Advocate* (1933) JC 46; *McPhelim supra* at 21.

Examples of matters on which Directions should be given are:

- Burden of proof is on the Crown:
  Slater v. *HM Advocate* (1928) JC 94; *M'Kenzie supra*; *Black* v. *HM Advocate* (1974) JC 43; *Earnshaw* v. *HM Advocate* (1981) SCCR 279.
- The Standard of proof beyond reasonable doubt:
  M'Kenzie supra; *Shewan* v. *HM Advocate* (1989) SCCR 364.
- Corroboration of facts relevant to the Crown's case:

Dorrens v. *HM Advocate* (1982) SCCR 407; *Kyle* v. *HM Advocate* (1987) SCCR 116.

- No requirement of corroboration for the defence case:
  Hillan v. *HM Advocate* (1937) JC 53.
- The Three Verdicts:
  MacDermid v. *HM Advocate* (1948) JC 12,
  but not the difference between Not Proven and Not Guilty:
  McDonald v. *HM Advocate* (1989) SCCR 29; *McNicol* v. *HM Advocate* (1964) JC 23.
- The majority required to convict:
  McPhelim v. *HM Advocate supra*.
- Separate verdict on each charge:
  Bergson v. *HM Advocate* (1972) SLT 242.
- 'Concert' where two or more charged:
  Martin v. *HM Advocate* (1992) SCCR 356.
- Alternative conviction verdicts available where relevant:
  Muir v. *HM Advocate supra*.
- Identification Warning:
  McAvoy supra.
- Status of admitted prejudicial or hearsay evidence:
  Paterson v. *HM Advocate* (1974) JC 35; *Jones* v. *HM Advocate* (1981) SCCR 192; *Higgins* v. *HM Advocate* (1974) SCCR 542.

No Directions are required for:

- Unanimity or time for deliberation:
  Crowe v. *HM Advocate* (1989) SCCR 681.
- Request to Jury for further Directions:
  Alexander Thompson v. *HM Advocate* (1988) SCCR 534.

'Unfairness'

My purpose in analysing Summings-up will not be to demonstrate that they were 'right' or 'wrong' in their legal or moral direction, but to demonstrate the nature of any direction, and that 'directionality' is the norm where there is a survey of the evidence. I will also suggest that the use of the 'Disclaimer' is ineffective, a rhetorical gesture that obscures directionality, when considered in the context of the morphotactics and tropotactics of most such addresses to juries.

Nevertheless the Court of Appeal can and does occasionally allow appeals because the trial judge's Summing-up was unfair. By unfair I do not mean there was some specific defect of law, for example the recent test case on the appropriate Direction when defendants exercise their Common Law right to silence (to keep their previous convictions away from the jury) in the context of s.35 of the Criminal Justice and Public Order Act 1994 (*R* v. *Cowan/Gayle/Ricciardi* (*supra*) CA 7).

Alleged 'unfairness' may be an important problem for those convicted. Apparently in 1963 the then National Council for Civil Liberties received 321 applications for legal advice, of which 10 per cent, 32, were concerned with judges' Summings-up (Dyson 1994: 42).

A recent example of a successful appeal based on a perverse or unfair Summing-up is *R* v. *Gibbons and Winterburn* 22 June 1993 CA. I quote here illustratively, at some length from the Court of Appeal transcript per Lord Taylor CJ:

> By his second ground, Mr De Silva complains of substantial passages in the Summing-up which he argues were prejudicial to a fair trial. The learned judge properly directed the jury, at page 3 of the transcript, that they were the sole judges of the facts and that they should disregard anything he said about the facts unless they agreed with it. The prosecution had a formidable case. It is right to acknowledge that the learned judge put the defence case to the jury and indeed it is not contended to the contrary.
>
> However, the complaint is that some of the judge's observations went far beyond legitimate comments. The first passage relied upon is at page 20 of the transcript where he said:
>
> > Do not draw any inference adverse to Mr Lawrence Gibbons from the fact that the police were given information about him, and information which resulted in a Deputy Commissioner authorising the use of an undercover officer. The Crown cannot call the informant for obvious reasons, and what the informant told the police is not evidence that the police are allowed to give in evidence, and their evidence would be second-hand, and would infringe against what lawyers call 'the rules against hearsay evidence'.
> >
> > But what we do know is that the central drug squad obtained authority from the Deputy Commissioner of the Metropolitan Police, who is a very senior officer, to use the services of a specially trained undercover officer, and later used a second undercover officer, in the shape of Maggie.
>
> There had been evidence that a Deputy Commissioner would be at the head of this type of investigation, but there was no evidence as to whether the police could have called an informant or whether his evidence, even if it had been admissible, would have implicated Mr Gibbons in the offence charged. Although beginning with a Warning not to draw an adverse inference, the effect of the passage was to maximise the gravity of the case and the importance of the undercover operation being authorised. It also implied that there existed an informant who could tell them a lot more if the technical rules did not prevent it. This was compounded in a later passage at page 25, where the learned judge said that:
>
> > Members of the jury, Mr Ferguson is a police officer. As you know he works only on the authority of the Deputy Commissioner at New Scotland Yard and whilst on assignment has to report regularly to a senior supervising officer.
> >
> > He was employed in this case to try and obtain information which could be given in court that Mr Lawrence was a drugs' dealer. Perfectly obviously, police had been given that information from a source that could not be put

> into the witness box. Therefore, they had to use an undercover agent to see if it was true or not. His employment on this job as an undercover man was, as I say, authorised at a very high level.

Again that passage conveyed that there was an informant who could have given cogent evidence that Mr Gibbons was a drugs' dealer, that the jury were prevented from hearing him by rules of procedure and that the police had had to resort on the personal authority of the Deputy Commissioner to the use of an undercover officer to see if the informant was right or not.

At page 21, straight after the passage building up the importance of the case as evidenced by two undercover officers being employed, the learned judge went on as follows:

> Members of the jury, undercover officers are extremely brave people. They put their lives at risk on almost all the operations they embark on. The fact that a man is enormously courageous does not necessarily mean of itself that he must necessarily be telling the truth, but that Mr Ferguson is a really brave man cannot be gainsaid.
>
> I am bound to say that the picture Mr Higginson tried to paint, of the shallow deceptive charmer, who was the best placed officer in the whole police force to obtain drugs for planting on innocent men, in my view, was very wide of the mark. Mr Higginson knows as well as I do the enormous precautions that are taken by the police to ensure drugs held by the police in pending cases do not get misused, and he knows as well as I do the precautions that are taken over the destruction of drugs that are no longer needed in pending cases, to ensure that they do not fall into the wrong hands.

Mr De Silva makes a number of criticisms of that passage. The bravery and courage of undercover officers had nothing to do with the case. The learned judge said that he was 'bound to say' that counsel's submissions were in his, the judge's view 'very wide of the mark'. The position is that the learned judge was not bound to say that. Indeed by saying it, he was in effect expressing a strong view on the very question the jury had to decide. Worse than that, his phrase that counsel 'knows as well as I do', implied that counsel was improperly advancing the case that the drugs had been planted. The truth is that counsel had a duty to put his client's case that the drugs had been planted. The truth is that counsel had a duty to put his client's case, whatever his own view of the matter, or that of the judge. At page 26, the learned judge said:

> Most people in England who are approached by someone who holds himself out as acting for the IRA, if they think that that person may really be a representative of the IRA, would, you may think, go straight to the British police and report the matter, and that, you may think goes not only for people of good character, but for the old lags trying to go straight and trying to run an honest car business, which is how Mr Lawrence Gibbons would like you to view him.

It is unnecessary to spell out the objection to those remarks.

We have no doubt that the criticisms made of the passages quoted above are amply justified. The learned judge's observations were in some instances highly emotive, in others inaccurate and in regard to counsel, unfair.

> Mr Worsley QC, on behalf of the Crown has conceded that the remarks went too far and that the learned judge used stronger language and said more than he should.
>
> However, Mr Worsley argued that the misdirection by the learned judge did not render the convictions unsafe or unsatisfactory because the jury would inevitably have come to the same conclusions. Suffice it to say that we are not convinced that the verdict in the appellant Gibbons' case was inevitable. The learned judge's remarks, which we have quoted, had scarcely any foundation in relevant evidence but they may have had an important and prejudicial effect on the jury's approach to the case. This court has said before (e.g. in *Marr* 90 CR App R 154) that however strong the case for the Crown, or however tenuous the answer to it, a defendant has the right to have a fair trial.
>
> In our judgment, the passages we have cited prejudiced that right, not only in the case of Gibbons but also in the case of Winterburn against whom the evidence was much weaker. Other grounds were raised on behalf of Winterburn which it is not necessary to consider. For the reasons which we have now given, we decided to allow these appeals.

From the legal perspective these remarks of Lord Taylor CJ for the Court of Appeal provide a good example of a 'holistic' legal approach to 'fairness' in a Summing-up. From the perspective of this study the trial judge's remarks on the bravery of undercover police officers and on individual reactions to IRA approaches, are examples of Krito-doxa: judicial opinionation.

A recent Court of Appeal (Criminal Division) decision, *R* v. *Whybrow/Saunders* (*The Times* 14 February 1994), is particularly interesting in this context. First, because it specifically approved the unlegislated Royal Commission on Criminal Justice (Cm 2263 (1993) p. 19) support for greater judicial intervention in trials – to prevent them becoming protracted.

However, the Court of Appeal stated that such intervention: 'to curb prolixity and repetition and to exclude irrelevance, discursiveness and oppression of witnesses', most definitely had its limits (in a trial of conspiracy to murder). Lord Taylor CJ referred to the unreported serial metaphors of Cumming-Bruce LJ in *R* v. *Gunning* (7 July 1980) CA): 'The judge is not an *advocate*. Under the English and Welsh system of criminal trials he is much more like the *umpire at a cricket match*. He is certainly not *the bowler whose business is to get the batsman out* ...'

This judgment of Lord Taylor CJ was referred to by the Court of Appeal in *Thompson and Thomas* (22 March 1995 per Otton LJ with Hutchison and Forbes JJ). This was a Serious Fraud Office prosecution and with hindsight can be seen as a 'test case' because of the sophisticated technological assistance provided for the trial, including a 'minuscript' device for daily transcripts and computer terminals allowing for documents to be displayed on VDUs for all, including the jury. It was estimated that these cut the time of trial by 25%:

> Each appellant lodged a notice of appeal setting out a number of grounds. However, they made common cause in their criticism of the judge's

> Summing-up for its inadequacy and brevity. They submitted that he failed to summarise the issues, that he failed adequately to remind the jury of most of the evidence pertinent to them and in particular that he failed to remind the jury adequately of the defence and of the evidence in respect of each of them. (Transcript 17DE)
>
> ... The statements served by the Crown ran to some nine volumes, the exhibits were contained in 200 volumes. The indictment contained seven counts but four were severed so that there was a trial on three counts only against the four defendants. The events which these three alleged conspiracies entailed covered a period of some two years. (Transcript 17GH)
>
> ... The trial began on 7th March 1994 and verdicts were returned on 8th June. Thus it lasted, with a break for Easter and other short breaks, some three months. The Crown opening, evidence and closing speeches by five leading counsel took 49 days. In particular it should be noted that the appellant Thomas started his evidence on 12th May (day 37). His evidence in chief lasted one and a half days. His evidence in all lasted nearly four days and he left the witness box in the late afternoon of 17th May (day 40).
>
> Thompson was then called. His evidence in chief lasted even longer and he left the witness box at the end of 23rd May (day 44) after five days.
>
> At the end of speeches there was then a discussion between Bench and Bar on the form certain directions were to take. On 6th June (day 50) at 2 pm the learned Judge started to sum-up. He did so for about one and three quarter hours, during which time he dealt with all the preliminary directions including a definition and explanation of each count of conspiracy. The transcript of this part of his Summing-up occupied some 43 pages. Next day the court sat at 10 am. The first 15 pages of transcript contain further discussions between Bench and Bar as to the previous day's directions. The record does not show when the jury was finally summoned. The remainder of the Summing-up occupied some seven pages of transcript and the jury retired to consider their verdict at 10.43 am. We were told that the Summing-up was less than two hours in length overall and occupied a total transcript length of 50 pages. (Transcript 18C–19B)

The Summing-up was considered to be properly stated on the legal requirements: functions of judge and jury; Burden and Standard of proof, taking each count and defendant separately; types of evidence; co-defendants had given no evidence; 'good character'; the offence of conspiracy; also the meaning and centrality of dishonesty in this offence. At page 18 he said:

> Turning to evidence I will deal with what the Crown says are the *points of evidence* [our emphasis] on which you can rely to infer guilt on the part of each defendant and then I will deal with what each defendant says about those particular suggestions.

He then started with the Orion account. This part of the Summing-up occupied some eight pages. It would be more accurate to describe this passage not as 'points of evidence' but as a summary of the Crown case and that for the defence of each of the four defendants. There is a passing reference to each of the key documents by reference to its identification code but not its substance. There is no direct reference to any part of the evidence from either the minuscript transcript or the Judge's own notes of what any of the defendants had said in examination in chief or in cross-examination during the eight or more days they had been giving evidence. It is to be remembered that it was some three weeks since Thomas had given evidence in chief in which he had explained his part in the transactions.

At page 26 the judge performed a similar exercise in respect of count 2 (BAFIN). He stated the Crown case. He did not refer to any of the key documents or their terms and effect. He merely identified by code number some of the appropriate documents including chart 17. (Transcript 20F–21D.)

He then carried out a similar exercise in respect of Andrew and Eastaway. His Direction on this count lasted for some five pages in all.

He then dealt with count 1 (Crédit du Nord). This lasted five pages in all. It followed the same pattern, with an outline of the prosecution case, referring in general terms to some of the principal documents, and summarizing the six particular transactions from which the Crown suggested dishonesty. (Transcript 21H–22B.)

Then in 22 lines he dealt with the whole of Mr Thompson's case on count 3. He then dealt similarly with the defence of Andrew and Eastaway.

This brought him to the end of the afternoon session which he concluded in the following terms: 'Tomorrow, members of the jury, I shall summarise in a few sentences, what the Crown says against each defendant and what each defendant says in reply.' Thus it might have been anticipated that he was to remind the jury of the salient points of the defence evidence.

In the event, the first part of the morning was spent on a discussion in the absence of the jury. When they returned certain matters were clarified from the previous day, and at page 17 he said: 'What I said yesterday was that I would summarise briefly the main points for and against each defendant and I will do that now.'

In view of the penetrating criticism to which this part of the Summing-up has been subjected it is necessary to set out the relevant passages in full. He continued:

> The Crown's case against Mr Thomas is simply that he was the boss, as Mr Farrer described him, and he was not the sort of boss who allowed things to happen in his company without his knowing about it and the Crown says that he had access to as much information as anyone in the company and in short he knew exactly what was going on. It is up to you to say whether or not that is a fair assessment, but the Crown say that his activities in obtaining and thereafter retaining funding was dishonest and he knew that it was.
>
> His defence is that he employed a battery of accountants and other people, including Mr Eastaway, on whom he had considerable reliance. What he did in

> conducting the business of Blackspur was largely what he had learned at Atlantic, and which he not only believed was honest, but of which Orion at any rate was aware. If you think that is right, or that it might be right, then he is entitled to be acquitted. It is only if you are satisfied that he knew that what he was doing was dishonest that you will convict him.
>
> In the case of Mr Thompson, the Crown say that he has tried to disclaim knowledge of many documents saying that they were dealt with by subordinates, or at any rate other people in the company. The Crown say that there is no evidence that anyone tried to hide anything from him, and they say that you might take the view that when giving evidence to you in the witness box he was evasive and you should regard that as evidence of his dishonesty. It is a matter for you whether you take that view. The knowledge of what was right and who was wrong in the context of leasing ...

There then followed short directions on the need for a unanimous verdict and the appointment of a foreman. (Transcript 21G–23B.)

I will not retell here the strong attack mounted on this Summing-up on behalf of the appellants, nor the beguiling defence of it put forward on behalf of the Crown.

The Court of Appeal took into consideration *R* v. *Gregory* 14 January 1993, per Auld J:

> In our judgment, this cursory treatment of the evidence at the point of his Summing-up when he left his directory function on the law and moved to his reminding function on the evidence was unsatisfactory. His earlier references to the evidence in the course of his directions on the law, although useful to put those directions in context, were no adequate substitute for an orderly and suitably comprehensive reminder of the evidence on both sides at the point where, in the light of his opening remarks, the jury would have understood he was entering their territory.
>
> As to the adequacy of his references to the evidence, wherever they appeared in the Summing-up, the issue of intention may have been simple but the facts, particularly the appellant's employment status and the chronology of events, involved a considerable amount of important detail going to that issue. However difficult it may have been to understand the appellant's explanation for his conduct, he was entitled to have the jury reminded of all the important evidence going to it and to have it properly analysed.

Otton LJ then concluded:

> We can understand the temptation of the Judge to assume that because of the use of technology the jury had understood the terms and effect of the prosecution's documents, the implication of the documents and that the jury had a comprehensive recall of the evidence both for the Crown and for the defence.
>
> It was in accord with the desire of this Court (spearheaded by the Lord Chief Justice himself) to encourage judges to be concise. The outcome of this particular appeal must not be taken as in any way detracting from or undermining that initiative.

> Unfortunately we are obliged to conclude that the Judge was too ambitious in attempting to deal with the issues so economically. We feel that his Summing-up was too compact and too concise for the circumstances of this case, the number and complexity of the issues of fact the jury had to determine and the volume and density of the evidence, both documentary and oral, relating to them. We have come to the conclusion that he adopted a too broadbrush approach and thereby fell into error. (Transcript 27E–28E)
>
> ... Despite the strong case against the appellants they had a right to have it explained to the jury in sufficient detail to make it comprehensible and to be reminded of the evidence in support of it.
>
> In the view of this Court the learned Judge, without descending into prolixity, could and should have structured his Summing-up in a way that was less compact, which addressed the issues and spent more time on the salient parts of the evidence, particularly that of the defence.
>
> In our judgment the deficiencies in the Summing-up constituted a material irregularity which renders the convictions on each count unsafe and unsatisfactory. We can see no reason to distinguish any of the counts. (29A–C)

One can see some evidence of a quantitative 'proportionality' approach to the evaluation of fairness in this Summing-up.

From the perspective of the Serious Fraud Office the successful appeal was a loss to their politically sensitive 'batting-average' over which they had absolutely no control.

My one reservation about the Court of Appeal's decision is that a fuller consideration of the impact of high technology in the courtroom, its impact on the jury and the requirements of the survey of evidence would have been helpful.

I have referred previously to *R* v. *Spencer (John)* (*The Times* 13 July 1994) as a trial with a particularly interesting, layered Mythos. Here I consider solely the judgment of the Court of Appeal on its Summing-up per Henry LJ (Swinton Thomas, Turner JJ):

> There are then two linked complaints as to the overall fairness of the Summing-up. First it is alleged that the judge presented an unbalanced view of the defence by concentrating on points that were peripheral to the main defence, setting them up as Aunt Sallies, and then knocking them down in a way that was unfair to the defence case. (7BC)
>
> ... As the appellant was in no position to give any evidence in relation to either of those questions, those questions of him were not an attempt to elicit facts from him, but simply an invitation to argument. (8A)
>
> ... the judge then fastened on those answers to ask rhetorical questions so phrased as to reflect the unlikelihood of the girl lying (because she had been consistent in her story from the first) or Buckley having coached her to invent a false history. The judge introduced those matters in this way:
>
> > If, during my summary, as I intend to do, I raise various questions which may be put, I can say no more than that because it is your province and not mine. I hope that those questions may be useful, important, relevant and indicative for you to ask yourselves about the evidence.

He then went on to give the Direction that the jury not only were entitled to disregard any view they might detect in those questions, but were obliged to. (8C–E)
... In fact the judge asked those rhetorical questions no fewer than 7 times in his Summing-up. (9A)
... The 5 other occasions when those rhetorical questions were asked, they were asked in a less florid way. But in each case the context only permitted one reply: that it was unlikely that Chantelle had made the whole thing up, or that Mr Buckley had put her up to concocting this false story ... (10C)

With the defence having been put in that way, and the real issue being as we have described it, we think to ask essentially the same rhetorical question seven times was excessive, unhelpful to the jury, and unfairly damaging to the defence.

The linked complaint as to unfairness relates to comments the judge made as to the evidence he was summarising and the almost exclusively one-way nature of those comments – hostile to the defence. We deal first with his summary of Mr Buckley's evidence. This covers approximately fifteen pages in the transcripts. It includes the two examples of rhetorical questions quoted above, both of which are relied on in relation to the complaint on comment also. Of the fifteen Summing-up pages dealing with this evidence, roughly four pages can be said to be comment. The quoted rhetorical questions give an indication of the overall slant of the comment, but in our judgment the real complaint is as to the cumulative effects of them rather than any individual instance. (10G–11C)
... Next, the judge's account of the appellant's evidence. This occupies approximately ten pages of transcript. It includes two of the rhetorical questions. Slightly under half of the space occupied consists of comment ... (11GH)
... That passage gives the flavour of the comment introduced into the rehearsal of the defendant's evidence. As will be seen, the comment was argumentative, it was uniformly unfavourable to the defendant, and it was distracting, in that the story could not be coherently told with the judge descending into the arena to make points which were more suitable for and had very likely already been made by counsel for the prosecution. (12G–13A)
... Juries are more robust than people often give them credit for, and comment one way or the other is often necessary to keep a fair balance in adversarial proceedings, particularly where one side or the other (more usually but not invariably the defence) has in counsel's address apparently made headway with a point which in the view of the court is unmeritorious. Judges must not feel that they have to be Trappist in austerely eschewing comment, provided that the standard Direction is given ['the Disclaimer']. But the giving of that standard Direction will not excuse excessive and largely one-sided comment. And, quite apart from questions of fairness, excessive comment makes the jury's task more difficult because it interrupts the rehearsal of the evidence. In our judgment the rhetorical questions and the comment here were excessive, were unduly partisan, unbalanced the trial process, and made the jury's task more difficult. (13D–14A)

What is fascinating about this judgment is that although it does show some concern with quantitative proportionality, it is – as far as I know –

unique in its concentration on the rhetorical turn of the trial judge. Although it is limited to one trope – the rhetorical question – that is enough to carry the appeal.

From the perspective of this book I note that the nomenclature system covering defendant and complainant is also telling:

'The defendant/man' 100 (ex 113 references)
'Chantelle/the little girl' 118 (ex 88 references)

In *Thompson and Thomas* I also draw attention to the 49 questions left with the jury and the use of the 'dishonest-' stem 40 times against the 'honest-' stem 16 times.

3 An aspect of Pathos

Naming and credibility

When considering the use or deployment of names in a speech (recorded as text) one may, as I have done, devise a system of stratification from most formal to most informal. However, such a method may miss one possibility, that a particular name category or combination might not appear in that recorded text. This could be damaging in relation to the other aspect of a naming system: its relative social weighting. I am therefore commencing this chapter with an attempt at a complete nomenclature system from British names, and an (oversimplified) set of hypothetical value sets for them.

I commence at the most formal level. This is not as simple as one might suppose. Consider the example of medical practitioners: an eminent surgeon might be Mr Smith whereas his general practitioner brother would be Dr Smith. Similarly well-known Members of Parliament or Queen's Counsel may equally be Mrs Smith or Miss Smith. It seems therefore that the most formal type of naming requires something further to Mr/Dr, or even perhaps Lord/Lady or Sir/Dame. Against that one can posit that all non-M. addresses constitute a separate category (Dr/Lord/Lady/Sir/Dame). The most formal category would, regardless of the refinements just mentioned, contain some additional label; some that occur to me are 'The Right Honourable', 'The Honourable', 'The Reverend', 'The Worshipful', 'M. Justice'.

Thus so far we have considered:

1.	The XY M.	FnameSname
2.	L./S./Dr/	FnameSname
3.	M.	FnameSname

Even with these three possible categories further subdivision may occur, in particular with regard to forenames:

Mr Quentin	Allbery
Mrs	Allbery, or even
Miss Quince	(Allbery)

These possibilities may not be transformable in all instances. Thus, for Titles:

Lord Peter/Lord Peter Wimsey/Lord Wimsey,
but *not*: Sir Wimsey (except in American-English)

To keep it simple I will use category 3 as the foundation for the next part of the series:

3.	M. Forename	Surname
4.	M.	Surname
5.	M. Forename	(Surname)

and finally we can omit the M. prefix:

6.	Forename	Surname
7.		Surname
8.	Forename	(Surname)

That is not the end of the matter because, at least in British culture, there are two important final category sets. First are the nickname, abbreviations, diminutives:

9. 'Doxer'/'Jones the Ringpull'/Shá(ron – Cardiff dialect)/Freddie/Marge

Finally there are impersonal address forms; these can be:

10. 'Sir'/'Madam'/'Miss'/'Lady'/'Boy'/'Man'/'Woman'/'Flower' (S. Wales, to female) 'Hen' (Glasgow, to female) 'My Love' (West of England, to male) 'Darlin' (Cockney) 'Wack' (Liverpool) 'Marra' (Tyneside)

I move now to an hypothesized ranking system, bearing in mind that traditionally it was rank that name signified. As I wrote above, the system put forward here is a reduction. I am employing it solely to show an awareness of the inseparable nature of naming and evaluation of social status:

A. Class: upper–lower
B. Gender: male–female
C. Race: white–'black'

This is oversimplified. It does not cover Age: old–young, for example. It is not refined enough to prove a good fit for any intermediate categories. One might consider some of these relevant to the subsequent analysis. There are also specific legal categories which one should at least be aware, and they are not dyadic:

D. Plaintiff – Defendant – Witness etc.

That said, my working hypothesis is that in the context of courtroom persuasion the pragmatics of naming may deviate from expected norms. For example we might expect an upper class white male plaintiff to be named in ways which are nearer categories 1–4 than 6–10, but for situational or rhetorical reasons that might not occur; further there might be differentials between those of apparently similar social rank.

Non-pronoun naming system for humans in English

A 1 Extended Formal e.g. The Hon. Mr Justice X
2 Embellished Formal e.g. Lord X; Dr Y
B.3 Full Formal e.g. Mrs Anna Bibi
4 Standard Formal e.g. Mr Bibi
5 Reduced Formal e.g. Mrs Anna
C.6 Full Informal e.g. Joe Bloggs
7 Impersonal-Informal e.g. Bloggs
8 Personal-Informal e.g. Julia
D.9 Informal-Personal e.g. Dicky, Shá(ron)
10 Informal-Impersonal e.g. Sir, Miss, Madam, Love

Honorifics are no longer part of routine English linguistic culture; the prime example would be 'Your Honour' as opposed to 'Thou', the equivalent of vous–tu in French or Sie–du in German or lei–tu in Italian (see Jacquemet 1996: ch. 8).

There is little systematic or theoretical discussion of naming. On vocative Address naming there is a detailed taxonomy by Zwickey in his 'Hey, What's your Name!' (10 *Chic. Linguistics Soc.* (1974)). Zwickey comments (*ibid.*: 296): 'What is unexpected is that vocative Noun Phrases in English are almost never neutral, they express attitude ... status, intimacy, or a role relationship ...' He quotes their reduced effect amongst Finns (*ibid.*: 297). The most apposite work is from that discipline which bridges linguistics and anthropology: pragmatics. In *Politeness – Some Universals in Language Usage*, Brown and Levinson (1987) provide some valuable background to the analysis made here.

First, intimate forms (first names) are unusual in on-the-record discourse (*ibid.*: 18). Further, formal naming, such as Honorifics, are *motivated* not arbitrary forms, forming part of 'politeness strategies', which are linked to 'political' control of a situation (*ibid.*: 23–5). Intimate and non-intimate forms are associated in English usage with rank, anchored to the social properties of participants in the event (*ibid.*: 46–9), or as I would put it, with ranking by those who select such usage.

In this analysis I have made a number of methodological assumptions that others might not accept, so I have put them in the foreground. The reason for this was to achieve sufficient numbers in the category to enable a Chi-squared test for statistical significance to be made. These are taken from *Archer* v. *Express Newspapers*:

(1) Queen's Counsel representing both sides should be treated as one: 'QCs'.
(2) the various journalists should be amalgamated and treated as one: 'The Hacks'.
(3) Similarly Jeffrey Archer's restaurant cronies at The Caprice should be amalgamated and treated as one: 'The Caprice Set'.
(4) The remaining categories are individual solo performers: Mary Archer; Jeffrey Archer MP; Aziz Kurtha; and Monica (Debbie) Coghlan.

Method: Quantitative

First I counted the number of the four usages for each of the four categories and seven persons and groups set out above.

I then converted those into percentages of each usage of the total for each group or person. These are set out in the table.

It can be seen from it that there is a graph relating:

The QCs:	Mr Surname:	97.8%		1
Mary Archer:	Mrs Archer:	34.8%		
	Mary Archer:	43.5%	78.3%	2
'The Hacks':	Mr Surname:	30.4%		
	First Name:	60.4%	90.8%	3
Jeffrey Archer:	Archer	78.4%		
'Caprice' Set:	Surnames	92.5%		
Aziz Kurtha:	Kurtha	82.6%		4
Monica Coghlan:	Monica/Debbie:	69.6%		5

Here is the full table:

N:863	80 QCs	23 MA	207 Hacks	305 JA	40 Caprice	92 AK	116 MC
M. S'name	97.8	34.8	3.4	6.9	7.5	3.1	8.0
1st NS'name	0	43.5	30.4	9.5	0	6.5	12.8
Surname	0	0	60.4	78.4	92.5	82.6	7.2
1st name	0	21.8	0	4.9	0	6.5	69.6
Chi^2			<0.001		463		

From the general analysis it appeared that credibility was construed more from Mary Archer than from her husband in relation to Monica/ Debbie Coghlan. So I tested their figures independently for statistical significance as well as the general table.

'Madonna–Magdalena'	<0.001	26.8

It can be seen that both the general table and the Mary Archer–Monica Coghlan subset are statistically significant at 1%.

I then decided to take this method further to establish ranking between the cast(e) by unifying the appellations through the attribution of value to each level.

This is simple and crude:

	Rank
First Name	1 unit (Intimate)
Surname	2 units
1st Name + Surname	3 units
M. + Surname	4 units (Distant)

The ranking produced is as follows:

		Indicators		Scale	Rank
Ranges	MC		154.4:	1	7
	AK	203.6 –	154.4:	50	6
	Caprice	215.0 –	154.4:	62	4 =
	JA	217.9 –	154.4:	64	4 =
	Hacks	225.6 –	154.4:	92	3
	MA	291.5 –	154.4:	138	2
	QCs	390.0 –	154.4:	237	1

Here it is sufficient to note the extreme relativities of the credibility ranking for Mary Archer and Monica Coghlan (Madonna/Magdalena).

It is not fanciful to metaphorize Monica Coghlan as Magdalena: prostitution was her occupation. That in itself does not entitle one to link Mary Archer to her as Madonna; this polarization of rank may point that way, but it is the discourse itself relating to Mary Archer that enables one to metaphorize her thus (not developed here).

My proposition is that credibility in this Summing-up was constructed relatively, along a continuum such as has been demonstrated here. It illustrates well the relationship between subliminal rhetorical devices such as naming over a two-day period and the presenting of overt surface messages in the judicial discourse that have not been presented here for either credibility carrier.

In other words, Nomenclature is a valid category for analysis, independent of other co-relative rhetorical devices.

Monica Coghlan and the diminutive form

The analysis put forward here has in one respect been oversimplified. For example nothing has been made of typing as an alternative to naming. Thus Aziz Kurtha is sometimes referred to as 'the Arab'.

Typing also occurs for Monica Coghlan who is referred to as 'the prostitute' or even as 'the street-trader'.

I will not pursue typing further here.

However, there is a feature of the naming of Monica Coghlan which I have not yet addressed.

In her unique case there is a *choice* of First Name usage, and this is directly connected to the 'Madonna/Magdalena' dichotomy constructed between Mary Archer and Monica Coghlan. This is the use of her 'Trade Name', which is in diminutive – and hence more intimate – form: not Monica, not Deborah but Debbie.

This usage occurred in 65.5% (two-thirds) of the references to her by First Name.

In order to rank this usage a unit of less than 1 must be assigned, so I have arbitrarily assigned 0.5. This reduces her total indicator by 23.4 units to 121.0 and has a consequential effect on the relative inferiority of her ranking. In particular it magnifies the gulf between her and Mary Archer, which increased from 138 to 161.

If, as I have suggested the Summing-up constructs credibility around this dichotomy, that increase in social distance is significant.

Adjacencies and juxtapositions

(1) This analysis can be taken further. For example reference to 'Monica' is usually isolated, not as part of a *series* of references to Monica. Such solo instances occur twelve times; double the number for Debbie.

By contrast serial references above two, only occur three times for Monica (3, 4, 9) whereas they are the norm for Debbie: 5, 11, 3, 4, 4, 3, 3, 3, 7. The usage of Debbie therefore has a degree of *emphasis* by repetition generally lacking for Monica. It is the lower-ranking trade name that is stressed.

(2) Apart from such adjacencies, there are instances of juxtaposition of one name with another or others.

An interesting example occurs in the 'Heralding and Framing' remarks at the commencement of the Summing-up:

'Monica <u>Mary</u> Coghlan . . . and Aziz Kurtha . . . satisfied customer of Monica'.

There are two strategic aspects of such naming:

(a) Aziz Kurtha is situated as 'punter' though we learn later on that he has many other attributes.
(b) The first reference to Monica Coghlan is extremely formal and does not occur for any other members of the cast. It does in fact occur on two later occasions, one of which is as Monica Debbie Coghlan. The strategic value of such an opening is that it mirrors the language of *criminal* charging. It is precisely *her* credibility that is put in issue.

Most of these juxtapositions concern Jeffrey Archer in a variety of combinations. There are five involving Monica Coghlan, mainly also with Aziz Kurtha.

Here are three further examples:

The Judge	'... the past attributes of <u>Jeffrey Archer</u>, to consider whether his taste is such that he can take his place in virtually a queue ... for the services that <u>Debbie</u> has to offer.'
Aziz Kurtha	'That was <u>Archer</u>. I told <u>Miss Coghlan</u> on the spot.'
The Judge	'<u>Mr Archer</u> was the first to raise the visit of <u>Kurtha</u> to <u>Debbie</u> and the facts ... cover <u>Kurtha</u>, cover <u>Debbie</u> and they cover <u>John Lisner</u>.'

By their cars shall ye know them

In this section I take Naming a stage further. One of the issues relating to identification in this trial involved the registration number, colour and type of car allegedly driven by Jeffrey Archer. This facilitated some further juggling with the symbolism of car type, symbiotic rank with its owner, and (I am suggesting) the owner's resulting social credit with the jury audience. For aficionados of this species of male display the difference between a Jaguar and a Daimler at night lies solely in the scalloped radiator cover and boot-lift of the Daimler. Daimlers have higher price and status. The judge:

1. 'If Jeffrey Archer was in need of physical adventure ... he had the briefest of encounters with Debbie ... and seen the departure of the prostitute he had chosen in a blue Mercedes with the man Kurtha. His sexual urge driving him, as well as being driven in his powerful Daimler no doubt, he follows the prostitute, who is now accompanied by Kurtha.'
2. 'The Arab walked away and got into his customised Mercedes and watched Debbie lead Archer into the hotel.'

(AK) 3. 'The first time I saw her I was about to go to a casino in my Mercedes 380 SEL.'

(AK) 4. 'As I went towards my car I looked at the number plate of the car that was parked, the Jaguar-shaped car. I am little fond of cars of that type so am not sure whether it was a Daimler or a Jaguar but it was definitely that shape. I simply noted whether it was a Jaguar or a Daimler, that is all I noticed.'

5. 'Obviously members of the jury, you will conclude that the existence of the Daimler car and its colour are very material.' 'You might not like to have a drive with him in his Mercedes at quarter to one in the morning, going round Hyde Park Corner and down Park Lane.'

(AK) 6. 'The morally upright Mr Archer was spotted waiting in his green Jaguar car in Gillingham Street, Victoria SW1.'

(MC) 7. 'I stood there are waited for him and in a few minutes a dark Mercedes stopped on my left.'

(AK) 8. 'When I looked to my right on the opposite side of the road there was a dark Jaguar car and it was flashing its head lamps.'

The quotations involve some fencing between the judge and Aziz Kurtha over the proper appellation of Jeffrey Archer's vehicle:

The Judge:	'his powerful DAIMLER no doubt'
AK:	'the Jaguar-*shaped* car ... I simply noted whether it was a Jaguar or a Daimler ...'
The Judge:	'the existence of the DAIMLER car and its colour are very material.'
AK:	'in his green Jaguar car ...'
AK:	'there was a dark Jaguar car ...'

Although the judge is backing the Daimler with its higher status (and credibility ascription) and Aziz Kurtha is backing the Jaguar perception (lower status : lower credibility) one should not make too much of this, since the cars only have bit parts in the general drama, but it is interesting to note the tussle occurring despite the relative degree of equality of value between Daimler and 'customised' Mercedes. In these circumstances to have a Jaguar ascribed to a participant would be for that person to be put down.

As Brown and Levinson would put it, this was an FTS, 'face-threatening situation'.

Given this relative equality between the two male protagonists, and given Jeffrey Archer's self-inflicted damage in his reaction to the innuendoes and smears published, it should not be surprising that the relative ranking of his wife and of Monica Coghlan should have become so salient.

Naming a doctor defendant and her daughter

In the section of this book that considers Summings-up where doctors were on trial I have omitted *Biezanek*, because important aspects of it are protected by an order of court. The doctor was charged with possessing cannabis. Her defence was necessity, to preserve the life of her daughter who had a history of psychiatric treatment with powerful psychotropic drugs, which she said caused her great pain and distress.

The defendant doctor's full name was Ann Campbell Biezanek. This only occurred once, in conjunction with the words 'the defendant'. This is the formal necessity required by custom and tradition for the naming of a defendant on trial before a jury on indictment.

The defendant was named in four different ways, two predominantly:

	N	%
Dr Biezanek	69	43.9
The defendant	57	36.3
The mother	25	15.9
Woman/Lady	6	3.8
	157	(99.9)

From these simple statistics one may conclude that the use of *non*-defendant nomenclature predominated:

100	63.6

The Summing-up allowed for a further test of status. There were seven other doctors mentioned. On 24 occasions they were mentioned in conjunction with the defendant. This provides an opportunity to test for equivalence of rank:

Superior equal status:	Doctor
Inferior unequal status:	Defendant

The ratio was much higher than that for the full Summing-up.

		N	%
Doctor:	Doctor	15	62.6
Doctor:	Defendant	9	37.5

Thus, where one might have excepted some differentiation to occur between other doctors as witnesses and expert witnesses, and the defendant, the differentiation remained static at that level:

36.3 : 37.5%

but rose significantly on the equality indicator:

43.9 < 62.5%

The nomenclature system in this Summing-up was sympathetic to the defendant.

This Summing-up allows for a further test, an unusual one. The motivation and defence of the alleged crime was the defendant's daughter's situation. Naming of a daughter is in itself referential to the defendant.

There were in fact seven variations in naming her. One predominated, at 72%, which was a single first name reference: 'Lucy'. Here I make an overt, active interpretation. I argue that unlike 'Monica/Debbie' in *Archer* such intimate, personal naming does not have a reductive inferior value. In *Archer* v. *Express Newspapers* the function of the libel trial was the *defence* of reputation (of Jeffrey Archer, the plaintiff). By contrast in the Biezanek prosecution the function was the *assertion* of innocence.

The interpretation offered is that the rather massive reference to the defendant's daughter as Lucy (72%), a personal and intimate reference, is a sign of sympathy rather than an indicator of low credibility – since she was not a witness:

Name	N	Relationship	%
Lucy	201	Intimate	72.1
Daughter	72	Status	25.9
Gabrielle Waters	2	Alias I	0.8
Lucy Biezanek	1	Formal	0.4
Edwin Waters	1	Alias II	0.4
The patient	1	Role	0.4
	278		(100)

One can regroup these in various ways. I doubt that any such regrouping would affect the tendency created by the judge:

Aliases (the 'other' in court)	0.8
Formal (defendant linked)	26.2
Personal	72.0

The implicit coupling in this nomenclature is primarily 'Ann' (Dr Ann Biezanek) from 'Lucy'. It is a friendship marker. The secondary coupling is 'mother', from 'daughter'. From these one can then construct a mediating term combining both intimacy and status: 'Mum'.

Nomenclature and race

In this section I shall proceed by considering the nomenclature of four defendants, in the first place with almost no reference to the events causing the trial, nor to the verdict. After considering the operation of the naming system in the Summing-up I shall briefly describe the offences, verdict and consequences.

In considering the judge's reference system, it is important to bear in mind that two of the defendants were brothers and that the judge specifically stated at the beginning of his Summing-up (3, 21–2) that 'hereafter I am going to refer to them by their first names'.

Naming the defendants

There are ten references to 'the Ogunbusola brothers' which I am not considering here, since my focus is on – as was the case – individual charges.

I will show first the variety of namings of individuals, which demonstrates differences between individuals and between the black defendants and the white defendant.

1. Mr Olayinka Ogunbusola	/	1. Mr Olukayode Okefamkinde /		: 2
1. Mr Ogunbusola	/	/	37. Mr Birch	: 38
20. Mr Olayinka	6. Mr Olayini	/	/	: 26
30. Olayinka	19. Olayini	10. Olukayode	3. Shaun /	: 62
1. Dada, my brother	/	/		: 1
/	/	/	9. Birch	: 9
—	—	—	—	—
53	25	11	49	138

One can see that there is only one indicator in this seven-type naming system which is shared by all the defendants: single First name alone. This demonstrates well the differentials between the naming of individuals:

	%	Rank	
Olukayode	90.9	4	: Low
Olayini	76.0	3	
Olayinka	56.6	2	
Av.	41.6		
Shaun	5.0	1	: High

Since single first names are rated as having the lowest status and credibility in this context one can observe that all the black defendants have significantly above average referencing in this mode, notably the absconder (90.9%). The white defendant's referencing in this mode is marginal (5.0%).

Beyond that there are, because of the variety of referencing, difficulties of interpretation, which I shall confront now.

First there are the three types of 'Mr' naming of the first defendant. Second, only the white defendant is referred to by first name with surname, and by surname alone.

For the purpose of further analysis I shall amalgamate all varieties of 'Mr' naming as indicating an equivalent degree of impersonal respect. To them I shall add 'Shaun Birch', on the basis that it lies between 'Mr Birch' and 'Shaun' or 'Birch'.

Mr Birch
Shaun Birch
Shaun/
Birch

Thus:

				%	Rank
22.	Mr Olayinka/Ogunbusola	ex	53	41.5	2
6.	Mr Olayini	ex	25	24.0	3
1.	Mr Olukayode Okefamkinde		11	9.1	4
48.	Mr/Shaun Birch	ex	60	80.0	1
77			149	51.7	

Taking both indicators together as structurally related, one can observe the very wide differentials between the white defendant and the two black defendants: 90.1; 127.0 and the absconder: 156.8.

						Public indicator
1.	Mr/Shaun/Birch	80%>	5.0	Shaun	+ 75.0	White
Av.		51.7>	41.6		+ 10.1	
2.	Mr Olayinka/ Ogunbusola	41.5	<56.6	Olayinka	−15.1	Black
3.	Mr Olayini	24.0	<76.0	Olayini	−52.0	Black
4.	Mr Olukayode Okefamkinde	9.1	<90.9	Olukayode	−81.8	Black Absconder

There are three controls available on this finding, though limited by small numbers.

First there are references to the two women witnesses of the attack on the two black defendants.

1.	Mrs Normansell		/	1.	4.5%
6.	Vicky Normansell	7.	Tina Nicholson	13.	58.5%
4.	Vicky	4.	Tina	8.	36.0%
11		11		22	

First name alone for both occurred at the rate of 35%, slightly below the average (41.6%) for the four accused. Consequentially the other more formal references occurred at combined rates of 63.0% – above the average for the accused (51.70%). These figures have the effect

of reinforcing the separation between the white and black defendants.
There are also 19 references to the (white) doorman at the disco:

7.	Mr Amos	36.8%
1.	Neil Amos	5.3%
3.	Neil	15.8%
8.	Amos	42.1%

Here the two varieties of formal naming are very similar to that of the first black defendant (42.1%; 41.5%), but the single first name reference is much closer to that of the white defendant (Av. 41.6%: Neil 15.8%; Shaun 5.0%).

Finally there are the 26 combined references to the Counsel and the Police: 8 individuals. Without exception the address was formal:

2.	Mr Jackson	10.	PC Gannon
1.	Miss Amataye	5.	Sgt White
		3.	PC Stone
		2.	DC Widden
		2.	Inspector Dudley
		1.	PC Mayo
3 (100%)		23 (100%)	

The offences and verdicts

R v. *Shaun Birch, Olayini Ogunbusola and Olayinka Ogunbusola* was tried in Chelmsford Crown Court and the verdicts given on 1 November 1993.

In July that year the two Ogunbusola brothers and their friend Mr Olukayode Okefamkinde (who had absconded from bail and so was not present for trial) visited a night club and disco in the centre of Chelmsford.

During the evening Mr Olayinka Ogunbusola danced with one of the two women witnesses in the trial, Mrs Vicky Normansell and Miss Tina Nicholson. After that Mr Shaun Birch, who was with a group of friends comprising 'Darren Smith, known as Billy', 'Phil Windsor', and 'Glen', asked her to dance, which she did not agree to. Somebody then 'glassed' Mr Olayinka Ogunbusola with a bottle on the forehead. Eventually Mr Shaun Birch was charged with Wounding with Intent or Unlawful Wounding.

An immediate consequence of this 'out-of-the-blue' attack was that the three (black) defendants chased after Mr Shaun Birch, who had been apprehended by the doorman Mr Neil Amos but had escaped and got away in a taxi. These defendants picked up sticks and a wheel brace and chased after the taxi. They returned to the disco and behaved abusively. They were charged with Violent Disorder or Affray., also with having an Offensive Weapon.

Mr Shaun Birch was convicted of Wounding with Intent; the

Ogunbusola brothers were convicted of Violent Disorder and of Having an Unlawful Weapon. Mr Shaun Birch was sentenced to 30 months imprisonment; the Ogunbusola brothers to 18 months each.

On appeal by the Ogunbusola brothers the Court of Appeal overturned their convictions. This decision has not been reported but the Summing-up was considered unsafe in five respects concerning these defendants: the Burden of proof; good character and credibility; the racial element; Caution and the right to silence; and the Direction and invitation to draw inferences.

This was not an appeal where overall 'unfairness' was ruled to have occurred, but it is not unreasonable to draw the conclusion from the Court of Appeal that there was a multiplicity of legal problems with the Summing-up. What I have done here is to show how an apparently inconsequential matter – how the Judge names persons involved in the trial – may be a guide to the general drift, as much as the legal specifics, of a Summing-up, and in the same direction.

'Non-naming': referring by 'he' or 'she'

In *Archer* the term 'plaintiff' hardly figures as a description for Jeffrey Archer. One might be forgiven for expecting that that objective, neutral term would have been more prominent. Similarly the defendant newspapers are rarely referred to as such.

There is, however, an alternative to technical or proper naming, that is 'non-naming' through the use of the third person pronouns, 'he' or 'she'.

What hypotheses can one have about such usage? One might be stylistic: that their use is purely a matter for a given speaker, and that any patterns will be consistent for the speaker alone. Another might be negative, that such usage is entirely random. A further one might be that such usage correlates in some way with the general naming patterns.

In *Archer* 'non-naming' fits this last hypothesis, in this way: the greater the resort to non-naming the lower status of the referred-to person, *and* vice versa. Thus

			S/He %
Mr	Robert Alexander QC:	(for the plaintiff)	6.4
	Michael Hill QC:	(for the defendant)	14.3
	Jeffrey Archer (plaintiff)		38.6
	Mary Archer		43.9
	Aziz Kurtha		56.5
	Monica Coghlan		61.4

One can see immediately that the fit with proper naming is not perfect. In particular Jeffrey Archer gains status relative to Mary Archer; similarly Aziz Kurtha loses status relative to Monica Coghlan.

Nevertheless it can be read as a correlation with the pattern for proper naming, because, for example, the advocates have far lower rates than the other actors. Also, a small differential between them is reflected in Robert Alexander QC's particularly low rate (6.4%), since it was he, and he alone, who of all the actors was named twice at the beginning of the Summing-up as *Mr* Robert Alexander QC.

The plaintiff and his (character witness) wife fit in a middle band of 6%: 38.6%–43.9%.

Finally, although Aziz Kurtha has been 'demoted' (56.5%), Monica Coghlan remains definitely at the bottom of the pile (61.4%).

Perhaps more significant are the gaps based on gender and race. First, the Madonna–Magdalena gap. It is not small:

Mary Archer	43.9%
Monica Coghlan	61.4
	17.5
then plaintiff and punter:	
Jeffrey Archer	38.6%
Aziz Kurtha	56.5
	17.9

But does this relatively strong correlation follow through to other Summings-up?

In *Biezanek*, much depends on what one counts as 'proper-naming'. If one omits the terms 'defendant', 'mother', 'daughter' one constructs slightly different results. That is what I have done, to maintain consistency with the Archer Summing-up.

Dr Marks (Expert Witness)	30.6%
(Dr Pertwee – small sample	50.0)
Lucy Biezanek	40.3
Dr Biezanek (defendant)	77.2
[" " and full naming	59.8]

What is noteworthy is that Dr Biezanek's ranking does *not* echo her relatively strong position for proper-naming. A further hypothesis then might be that the differential between non-naming and proper-naming indicates the degree of judicial sympathy or support, for a given person, in this case 'sympathy'.

Finally we can consider the 'racial' element case of Birch and the Ogunbusola brothers. The 'non-naming' of the two women at the centre of the incident involves two very small samples. I have therefore excised them; for the same reason I have excised the absconder Olukayode:

Olayini O.	28.6%
Olayinka O.	32.1%
Shaun B.	52.8%

These figures contradict those for proper-naming.

However, it is worth noting that in the final twelve pages of the Summing-up all (20) 'he' references are to Shaun Birch. Moreover, after 96 minutes deliberation the jury were called back into court because they had sent a note to the judge asking for a definition of intent under count 1 of the indictment. This count was against Shaun Birch, and the note was immediately dealt with by the judge. This additional, final page of the Summing-up produced 12 of the 20 references – there were 67 in all. If these contingencies had not occurred the non-naming rate for Shaun Birch would have reduced to 43.9%, still higher than for the Ogunbusola brothers, but the rather dramatic differential would have been eradicated. After a further 75 minutes of deliberation the jury returned with their unanimous verdicts of guilty against all three defendants.

These differentials, between proper-naming and non-naming, might appear to support sympathy for the Ogunbusola brothers, the originating victims in the case, the one a social worker and the other a law student. But the alternative hypothesis remains; that non-naming simply does not carry the cultural weight of proper-naming.

Jury address

The issue of naming occurs equally for the jury. Basically there are two formal and two 'non-naming' possibilities:

Formal-polite:	Ladies and Gentlemen
Formal-distant:	Members of the jury
Informal-distant:	You
Informal-intimate:	We

In this study I am particularly interested in the first person plural 'We' form. It subtly breaks the judge/jury legal demarcation. It also signals an incorporating, even ingratiating mode, of which I imagine the judges are not conscious.

Conclusion

Naming and referral modes are basic aspects of human interaction. They should never be ignored. They are not inert, neutral labels but carry significance particularly as to actual or perceived social status.

I have not here developed the modes of jury reference employed by trial judges in Summings-up. That too is important, but will be considered in relation to particular trials.

4 The data

Selecting cases for study: a note on method

A cul-de-sac and a pragmatic solution

It is rare for a Summing-up to be reported in full in the Law Reports. Usually only a passage or passages appear when subject to appeal. For example in [1994] 2 All ER a small number of criminal appeals were reported in which the trial judges' direction/s to the jury were in issue. In none of these appeals was the full Summing-up reported – it is not suggested that they should have been. They were:

1. *R* v. *Chan-Fook* [1994] 2 All ER 562
   The issue was the appropriate Direction to the jury on psychiatric injury amounting to actual bodily harm.
   There were quotations (six paragraphs) from the trial judge; also one paragraph from a Direction by Willes J in *R* v *Ashman* (1858) 175 ER 638.
2. *R* v. *Rossiter* [1994] 2 All ER 752
   The quotations comprised about two pages. The issue was whether the trial judge had failed to leave the issue of provocation to the jury as required by s.3 of the Homicide Act 1957.
3. *R* v. *Cambridge* [1994] 2 All ER 760
   Here the issue was whether there was sufficient evidence to allow the judge to decide that provocation could be said to occur at all. There was one quotation from the trial judge's Summing-up.
4. *R* v. *Ryder* [1994] 2 All ER 859
   This appeal concerned (*inter alia*) the lack of any Direction to the jury on the absence of corroborative evidence as to lack of consent in rapes of five women. The trial judge's Direction was quoted (13 paragraphs).
5. *R* v. *H* [1994] 2 All ER 881
   This appeal concerned a Direction that the evidence of one girl against her stepfather could be used to corroborate the evidence of another girl in a trial of a number of counts of indecent assault. The trial judge's Direction was quoted (seven paragraphs).

These reports are typical. They concern Directions on points of law, and the quotations are, understandably, limited to relevant portions of the entire Summing-up. So the search for and acquisition of full Summing-up texts was essential.

Ideally I would have continued to work forward from data collected for my book *Jury and Judge* (1995) for five Circuits 1986–91 (and then added to for all England and Wales for 1992). These data allow one to look at the correlations between judicial action and jury verdict, positively and negatively. The kind of hypothesis one could test by referring to Summings-up would be: do high acquittal ('doubting') juries correlate with high acquittal (and low custodial sentence rate) judges, and vice versa?

For bailed defendants 1987–91 the correlations for judicial and jury acquittals were:

> Low × Low (QI × QI)
> [16.0%–24.7%; 19.2%–29.8%] four courts:
> Aylesbury, Reading, Worcester-Hereford, Dorchester
> High × High (QIV × QIV)
> [36.9%–46.2%; 35.7%–44.1%] seven courts:
> York, Sheffield, Nottingham, Lincoln, Plymouth, Exeter, Merthyr Tydfil
> Low × High (QI × QIV) three courts:
> Warrington, Liverpool, Northampton
> High × Low (QIV × QI) one court:
> Newport

[Custodial QI 36.8%–44.1%; QIV 53.1%–64.6%]

For remanded defendants the position was as follows:

> Low × Low (QI × QI)
> [6.8%–16.9%; 8.5%–10.1%] three courts:
> Reading, Aylesbury, Stafford
> High × High (QIV × QIV)
> [22.5%–30.1%; 21.0%–29.1%] two courts:
> Preston, Oxford
> Low × High (QI × QIV): no courts
> High × Low (QIV × QI): no courts

[Custodial QI 65.3%–74.8%; QIV 85.6%–95%]

Reading and Aylesbury are consistent between bailed and remanded defendants.

The 1992 figures which included the South-Eastern Circuit made almost no difference to those prosecuted:

Bailed:	High × High:	Snaresbrook
Remanded:	Low × Low:	Kingston
	Low × Low:	Inner London Sessions House

(Aylesbury and Reading had already been included to complete their Crown Prosecution Service Areas.)

From these correlations one might select the following courts for study (on the weak assumption of homogeneity between judges on the same bench).

I Consistently 'severe' judges and juries:
Aylesbury, Reading, Worcester-Hereford, Dorchester, Stafford
II Consistently 'lenient' judges and juries:
Sheffield
'Lenient' judges and juries:
York, Lincoln, Plymouth, Exeter, Merthyr Tydfil
III Contradicting judges and juries:
Liverpool, Warrington
Newport

One would then be left with the practical problem of acquiring a good sample of Summings-up from a cross-section of judges trying cases regularly in these courts.

It rapidly became clear that this was not a practical proposition. My funds only extended to the cost of photocopying in reasonable quantities. Very few Summings-up are transcribed from tape as the cost is formidable; almost always this occurs where an appeal is being seriously considered.

It follows that where acquittals occur a transcription is an unusual event. I clearly required Summings-up where both conviction and acquittal had ensued, so this line of research was stymied.

The hunt for transcriptions of these latter ('acquittal') Summings-up has produced a small sample, but I make no pretence as to their representativeness: three of them comprise the sum total of Summings-up reported in full, or edited, in the Law Reports and two of those were of unusual defendants, hospital doctors; another unreported transcript concerned another acquitted general practitioner. I acquired one for another unusual defendant, a police constable acquitted in one of the 'lenient' courts selected above – this had been transcribed for police training purposes. A further three 'acquittal' Summings-up had also been transcribed for training purposes: acquittals of charges for rape. I also acquired from the Serious Fraud Office the Summing-up in a trial where an acquittal followed, as well as an extremely long one where conviction followed. I was unsuccessful in my search for 'acquittal' Summings-up in Canada and Scotland.

By contrast it has been easier to acquire Summings-up where conviction followed, but perforce their representativeness has been deliberately skewed so as to enable reasonable comparison with those where acquittals occurred, such as rapes and a convicted police constable.

A scientific rather than a pragmatic approach to my research issue would have produced documentation on a very different basis. For example, it might have comprised convictions and acquittals solely of charges for burglary from a number of carefully selected court venues. So, my documentation has been founded on availability of Summings-up where acquittal followed. The 'sample' acquired is patently skewed, but at least a surprising degree of balance between acquittals and convictions has been achieved.

5 The Cases

'The Philanderer' – acquittal of obscenity

Introduction

The first Summing-up to be analysed was reported in full as *R* v. *Martin Secker and Warburg Ltd* [1954] 2 All ER 683. Its interest lies in its occurrence before the passage of the Obscene Publications Act 1959 with its safeguards for literary merit.

The book in question, by Stanley Kauffman, was originally published in the USA as *The Tightrope* in 1952, then in Britain as *The Philanderer* in 1953. In that year Boots' Library was successfully prosecuted for obscenity and fined by my native jurisdiction, the Isle of Man. The publishers, Martin Secker and Warburg Ltd, did not withdraw it from publication and eventually after police questioning and a preliminary hearing at Clerkenwell Police Court, the defendants reserved their defence and elected for trial by judge and jury. This was held at 'The Old Bailey' before Mr Justice Stable and a jury of nine men and three women (under the former property qualification).

Apart from the Summing-up at the end of the argument Stable J gave a Direction to the jury at the end of the first day's proceedings (29 June 1954) in adjourning the court until 2 July:

> Will you take this book home, and would you mind reading it, as I said, from cover to cover.
>
> Read it as a book. Do you follow? Not picking out bits that you think have, shall we say, a tendency here or there, or picking out bits that you think have a sort of immoral tendency, but read it as a book. Do not discuss it with your friends and relations, because they may not, possibly, appreciate the legal tests that you ultimately have to apply when you come to give your verdict.

Under the law as it then stood the jury's verdict had to be unanimous, and this was delivered as an acquittal.

The Summing-up

In this instance the reader can have the combined luxury and necessity of reading the entirety of a Summing-up in the Law Reports.

In '*The Philanderer*' the structural elements include Nomos and Mythos elements. Nomos elements are those of a legal, technical nature. They subdivide into Nomo-dogma and Nomo-doxa. Nomo-dogma consists of enunciation of law and legal rules, whereas Nomo-doxa consists of opinion on the meaning and application of such rules. These two categories cover what one may broadly call 'directing' or 'instructing' a jury, as opposed to 'reviewing' the evidence.

Nomo-doxa must be distinguished from Krito-doxa. With Krito-doxa the judge, the figure of authority, is *not* expounding or explaining the law but is passing on his or her personal opinions, in short: opinionating.

By Mythos is meant some narrative feature. In '*The Philanderer*' for example it consists entirely of description of that book, the subject of the prosecution.

These four categories comprise the four structural elements of analysis. In any given Summing-up other elements may well arise with prominence, but nevertheless they occur as sub-elements. They include for example the Antitheton, comprised of contrasting pairs or blocks of statement; also Quotation; another example is Erotesis-Apocrisis couplings: question-and-answer. All variants of such sub-elements will be played down in the analysis of structure.

Also absent from *structural* analysis will be the term Pathos. Pathos encompasses the huge variety of surface elements driving the emotional content of the text. My starting-point is that much of their emotional load is lost once they are divorced from their location in structure, which must be analysed prior to concern with tropes and figurative elements.

Structure of the Summing-up

684[1] para. and lines:

D1–4	*Nomo-dogma* I 'The charge against ... the verdict you will give.'
D4EF	*Nomo-doxa* I The burden of consequences on the jury: 'a matter of the utmost consequence. It is a matter of very real importance ... It is a matter of importance ... In addition to that it is of great importance ... Your verdict will have a great bearing on where the line is drawn ... The important duty of deciding rests fairly and squarely on your shoulders.'
G1–5	*Disclaimer* (Antitheton) 'It is not what I think about this book, it is the conclusion that you reach. You represent ... You and you alone ... I express my opinion about the matter, you are entitled to ignore it.'
G5–H3	*Krito-doxa* I: Criticism of Prosecution

	'During the closing speech for the prosecution . . . May I venture to suggest that your task is nothing of the kind.'
H3–H6	*Nomo-doxa* II: Aesthetics and Crime (Antitheton) 'We are not sitting here as judges of taste. We are not . . . We are not . . . You are here trying a criminal charge.'
H7–H9	*Nomo-dogma* II: Standard of Proof
685[2]C–H10	Burden of Proof
H11–15	Test for Obscenity (*Hicklin*)
A1–C	*Nomo-doxa* III: The Historical Factor 'Because that is a test laid down in 1868 . . . dressed up in a frock-coat or an equivalent feminine garment.' (Includes Rhetorical Question and Sarcasm)
D1–3	*Mythos* I 'This book . . . is a book which obviously and admittedly is absorbed with sex . . . of the human species.'
D3–686[3]C	*Krito-doxa* II: Role of Sex in Society. 'I, at all events, approach that great mystery . . . somewhere between those two poles the average, decent, well-meaning man or woman takes his or her stand.' (Includes historical allusion, and developed Antitheton)
D1,2	*Mythos* II 'Turning for a moment to the book . . . it is . . . in the form of a novel.'
D2–F2	*Nomo-doxa* IV: Literary Standards 'Remember that the charge is a charge that . . . but that does not mean that a publisher is guilty of a criminal offence for making those works available to the general public.' (Including Projected Erotesis–Apocrisis Quotation and interrogative serial Erotesis with a single emphasized Apocrisis)
F2–687[4]H12	*Krito-doxa* III 'I venture to suggest that you give a thought to what is the function of the novel . . . it may even be the only guide.'
686H12–687A1	*Mythos* III 'This is an American novel . . . life in New York.'
A1–D2	*Krito-doxa* IV: Literary Influence 'If we are going to read novels about how things go on in New York . . . directed to the ultimate fulfilment of a balanced individual life.' (Including Sarcasm)
D3–E1	*Disclaimer* II 'I am going to say a few words about the book itself . . . and your disagreement is paramount.'

E1–F4	*Krito-doxa* V: Pornography 'You may agree that it is a good book ... the literary output of Port Said and felt rather ashamed of themselves afterwards.'
F4–G3	*Mythos* IV 'The book purports to be a picture of contemporary ...' 'When the kissing had to stop' (Including Poetic Quotation – Rhetorical Question)
G4	*Krito-doxa* VI. Interjection 'I suppose men and women of all ages have wondered that.'
G5–H8	*Mythos* V 'The theme of the book is the story of ... the realities of human love and of human intercourse. There is no getting away from that.' (Includes Krito-doxic elements)
H8–688[5]	*Nomo-doxa* V: The Crown's Case 'and the Crown say: "Well that is sheer filth"'
H9–12	*Krito-doxa* VII 'Is it? ... but is it sheer filth?' (Projected Question) (serial interrogative Questions)
H12–13	*Nomo-dogma* III 'That is a matter which you have to consider and ultimately to decide.'
H14–16	*Nomo-doxa* VI 'There is another aspect of the book ... I have told you the test and I will not repeat it.'
H16–C1	*Mythos* VI 'There is another aspect of the book ... the example of a well-ordered, decent, home, stumbles.' (Includes Krito-doxa)
C3–C2	*Nomo-dogma* IV: Camouflaged Pornography 'You will have to consider whether ... to pass the critical standard of the Director of Public Prosecutions.'
D1–6	*Krito-doxa* VIII: Literary Standards 'The literature of the world ... is suitable for the fourteen-year-old schoolgirl to read?'
D5–E2	*Nomo-dogma* V: Pornography 'You must consider that aspect of the matter. And there is another aspect of the matter which I should like you to consider before you come to your conclusion.'
E2–F5	*Krito-doxa* IX: Consensus *Versus* Pornography 'I do not suppose there is a decent man or woman ... we can exclude and keep out.' (Includes Repetition and Hypothetical Consequentialism)

F5–G6 *Nomo-dogma* VI
'Remember what I said . . . "Not Guilty".'

The structure – abstract version

Para.					*Lines*
1	Nomo-dogma I	–			4
2		Nomo-doxa I			15
3	[Disclaimer I]	....			5
4			Krito-doxa I		5
5		Nomo-doxa II			6
6	Nomo-dogma II	–			9
7		Nomo-doxa III			14
8				Mythos I	3
9			Krito-doxa II		55
10				Mythos II	2
11		Nomo-doxa IV			13
12			Krito-doxa III		20
13				Mythos III	4
14			Krito-doxa IV		20
15	[Disclaimer II]	....			4
16			Krito-doxa V		8
17				Mythos IV	4
18			Krito-doxa VI		1
19				Mythos V	8
20		Nomo-doxa V			2
21			Krito-doxa VII		4
22	Nomo-dogma III	–			1
23		Nomo-doxa VI		—	3
24				Mythos VI	9
25	Nomo-dogma IV				4
26			Krito-doxa VIII		6
27	Nomo-dogma V				3
28			Krito-doxa IX		9
29	Nomo-dogma VI				7
					248

			Cover	*Range*		*%*
Nomo-dogma	28+	Disclaimer 9:	37	1–29	(29)	15
Nomo-doxa			53	2–23	(22)	21:36
Krito-doxa			128	4–28	(24)	52
Mythos			30	8–24	(16)	12
			248			100

Comment on structure

There are 29 blocks of these elements covering the 248 lines of Report. The number of blocks for each element does not vary much: from six for Nomo-doxa and Mythos to nine for Krito-doxa. However, the quantum for each element does vary considerably, ranging from 30 lines for Mythos and 37 lines for Nomo-dogma (including the two disclaimers) through 53 lines for Nomo-doxa to 128 lines for Krito-doxa. Thus Krito-doxa dominates this Summing-up in terms of both blocks and quantum. Spatially Krito-doxa is less concentrated than Nomo-dogma – comprising 24 blocks (9 to 28); whereas the latter covers the entire Summing-up (blocks 1 to 29). The most compact and central element is Mythos which comprises 16 blocks (8 to 24).

One can also consider the relations between elements. Thus the two Disclaimers both precede blocks of Krito-doxa. The first three blocks of Nomo-dogma are followed by Nomo-doxa, whereas the next two are followed by Krito-doxa. Five of the six blocks of Mythos form sandwiches with Krito-doxa.

Rhetorical analysis

So far my purpose has been to demonstrate the method of analysis of the structure of an *available* Summing-up. In later analyses there will not normally be such general availability from which readers can evaluate the method for themselves. First, I will draw attention to some of the questions which arise from this structural analysis.

The Mythos
What does it tell us about '*The Philanderer*'? How does it tell it? What is the role of Quotation in this Mythos? Is the Mythos a Mitigation?

Pathos
Here we are concerned with emotive surface elements. For example: how is this Summing-up 'framed', what is stated to be 'important'? What is the role and location of Antitheta? Is sarcasm a stylistic feature personal to Stable J or is it strategic: pathotactical? What is the role, if any, of metaphor? Does repetition and its location have a pathotactical content?

Krito-doxa
What impact would the Summing-up have if the nine segments discussed below were excluded?

Krito-doxa in 'The Philanderer'

1. 684 G5–H3. *Criticism of the Prosecution*
   Even if this segment is considered to be a type of nomo-doxa, it is

extremely rare for the trial judge to openly criticize the presentation of either side in front of the jury. To do so of, in this case the prosecution, may be doxatactical or as I call it 'directional'. It goes beyond the routine 'Disclaimer' wherein the judge warns the jury that he may pass opinions, or betray opinions on the evidence, but that the jury are absolutely free to ignore him and form their own opinions.

2. 685D3–686C. *The Role of Sex in Society*
   Some keywords:
   absorbed – great mystery – interest – reverence.
   'We cannot get away from it.'
   'It is not our fault that' × 2
   'Great motive forces ... essential condition ... the only possible foundation ...'
   'people thought and behaved' × 3
   Greece, Rome × 4: Venus ... Aphrodite ... Middle Ages
   Antitheton: 'you get two schools of thought:
   sex is sin ... dirty ... mistake × 2 ... wholly distasteful;
   frankness, plain speaking ...'
3. 686F2–687H12. *The Function of the Contemporary Novel*
   'holds up a mirror to the society of his own day ... record a picture not merely to entertain contemporaries'
   'understanding how life is lived ...' other countries.
4. 687A1–D2. *The Influence of Literature*
   'a very crude work'
   'You will consider whether or not
   it does seek to present a fair picture ...
   whether or not it is desirable ... we should close our eyes to a fact because we do not find it altogether palatable ...
   putting ideas into young heads ... is it books that put ideas into young heads (× 3) or is it nature? ...'
   'It is the business of parents and teachers and the environment of society ... to see that those ideas are wisely and naturally directed ...'
5. 687E1–F4. *Defining Pornography*
   '... the filthy bawdy muck that is just filth for filth's sake. Probably you ladies ... some of the men ... literary output of Port Said and felt rather ashamed of themselves afterwards.'
6. 687G4. *Interjection on Browning Quotation*
   'I suppose men and women of all ages have wondered that.'
7. 687H9–12. *Interrogating the Prosecution on Pornography*
   'Is it?
   Is the act of sexual passion sheer filth?
   It may be an error of taste to write about it.
   It may be a ... but is it sheer filth?'
8. 688D1–6. *The Yardstick for Literary Standards*
   '... Are we going to say in England that our contemporary literature is

to be measured by what is suitable for a 14-year-old schoolgirl to read ...'

9. 688E2–F5. *The Risk of Over-extending the Criminal Law* (Consequentialism)
'pornography, filthy books ... stamped out and suppressed.
... just filth ... ought to be stamped out; but in our desire for a healthy society;
if we drive the criminal law too far ... is not there a risk that there will be a revolt ... so that the pendulum will swing too far the other way and allow things to creep in ...'

Conclusion on structure

With '*The Philanderer*' I have made a pragmatic and tactical virtue of the accessibility of Stable J's Summing-up. This All England Law Report must be available in Law Society libraries up and down England and Wales; and almost always today in the libraries of solicitors. It is, of course, available in all University law libraries. It is only five pages long, so hardly a daunting read, even ignoring Stable J's captivating use of the English language.

Readers can therefore check my method and analysis without much difficulty. This degree of transparency will not be possible for most of the following analyses – at least in terms of structure.

So far I have not pursued a further set of analyses of the various rhetorical categories I developed in relation to structure. This follows and attempts to demonstrate 'directionality'. That is, that the Pathic elements taken together in relation to each other and in relation to the components of structure, point the reader – or rather the juror – in one, and only one, direction: in this case towards the acquittal given by the jury verdict.

'The Philanderer' linguistic aspects

Forms of address

The jury

Members of the Jury	0	
'We' etc.	45	
	45	(5 pages: 9:1)

This is an extreme example both in terms of intensity of address at nine times per page, but also in the incorporation-cooperative first person plural usage. It is unique in having no alternative forms.

The defendants

There are only six references to the accused companies and five to individuals. These references stress the reification of company over the personification of 'individual' or 'director', which suggests a degree of distancing with the visible in-court directors in whom responsibility can reside abstracted from the companies who are the formal defendants.

Exemplification

This is a frequently used mode of pedagogy in the Summing-up. In '*The Philanderer*' it includes sarcasm, euphemism and antitheton.

> At one extreme you get the conception ... illustrated in some of the teachings of the mediaeval church; that sex is sin; that ...; that ...; [parenthetic sarcasm] ... In speaking of the birth of a baby let us refer to '*the happy event on Monday*' instead of ... [parenthesis]. I suppose the high tide was reached in the Victorian era [parenthesis] ... in some houses legs of tables were actually draped and rather stricter females never referred to gentlemen's legs as such but called them their '*understandings*'. (686A–B) ... the extreme expression of that view is to be found in the nudist colonies where people ... walk about ... without any clothes on at all ... (*ibid.* C)

Metaphor

In this Summing-up contrastive differentiation by antitheton is salient. There are also a number of metaphors that fit into its structure. Stable J expresses a utilitarian approach to the problem of liberty of expression and offensive obscenity: 'millions of homes throughout this island ...' He then adds: 'This, after all, is the only possible *foundation* on which to *build* a vigorous, strong and useful nation' (686B). Then, talking of historically puritan attitudes to sex in Britain he states: 'I suppose the *high tide* was reached in the Victorian era ...' (686A). Later he remarks:

> When a boy or girl reaches that stage in life's *journey* when he or she is *passing* from the state of blissful ignorance *through that perilous part of the journey* which we call 'adolescence' and finds himself or herself *traversing an unknown country without a map, without a compass and sometimes*, I am afraid, from a bad home, *without a guide* ... (687C)

This metaphor of danger is amplified later in a sophisticated manner which links with the sexual imagery of 'filth' developed elsewhere in the Summing-up:

> It goes on to describe *the pitfalls of slime and filth* into which the unhappy adolescent, without knowledge or experience, *without the map or compass and without the guiding* hand of a wise parent ..., *stumbles*.

These metaphors can be reconstructed as an exemplar of commonsensical familial ideology:

> Homes are the only possible foundation on which to build a vigorous ... nation. In homes parents can guide children through adolescence, which can

be perilous. Without their guidance adolescents can stumble into pitfalls of . . . filth (which is equated with pornography).

In addition there is a metaphor, strictly a simile, of the anti-hero of the novel: 'He is like the drunkard who cannot keep away from drink although he knows where it will land him?' (687C). This is amplified by a quotation about the anti-hero's upbringing resulting in this judicial metaphor: 'left a sort of permanent *bruise* on his personality' (688B). Finally, there is another unrelated (mixed) metaphor related to the *mens rea* issue, the intention of the author and publishers:

> . . . or whether this was just a bit of *camouflage* to render the crudity, the sex of the book sufficiently *wrapped up* to pass the critical standard of the Director of Public Prosecutions. (688C)

Negatives

The first example is the primary item in a detailed antitheton; it is a double negative: 'Considering the curious change of approach from age to another, it is *not un*-interesting to observe that . . . (685B) . . . It is interesting that . . .' (685G). Within this antithetical space occurs a sarcastic negative implicature: '. . . you know that babies of either sex are not born into this world dressed up in a frock-coat or an equivalent feminine garment.'

As soon as the detailed antitheton occurs a serial negation follows, followed by another double negative with the same roots as that cited previously:

> Where should we be today if the literature of Greece, Rome and other past civilisations portrayed *not* how people really thought and behaved, but how they did *not* think and how they did *not* speak and how they did *not* behave? Rome and Greece it is *not un*interesting to reflect, elevated human love to a cult, if *not* a religion . . . (685G)

Finally, the judge comments on the theme, the Mythos, of the allegedly obscene book, with repetitive emphasis:

> The theme of this book is the story of a rather attractive young man who is absolutely obsessed with his desire for women. *It is not presented as* an admirable thing . . . *It is not presented* as *a* thing that brought him happiness . . . (687H)

Parenthesis

> Approaching this matter which – let us face it – throughout the ages has been of absorbing interest to men and women . . . (686A)
>
> . . . (particularly at a time like today when ideas and creeds and processes of thought seem, to some extent, to be in the melting pot and people are bewildered and puzzled to know in what direction humanity is heading and in what column we propose to march) (686H)
>
> . . . – literature sacred and profane, poetry and prose – (688D)

Question (Erotesis-Apocrisis)

Then you say: 'Will corrupt and deprave whom?'
to which the answer is:
those whose minds are open to such immoral influences ...
What exactly does that mean?
Are we to take our literary standards as being the level of something that is suitable for the decently brought up young female aged 14?
Or, do we go even further back than that, and are we to be reduced to the sort of books that one reads to a child in the nursery? The answer to that is:
Of course not. (686DE)

Shortly after follows an unusual question that is equally an example of a sarcasm:

If we are going to read novels about how things go in New York, it would not be of much assistance, would it, if contrary to the fact, we were led to suppose that in New York no unmarried woman ... has disabused her mind of the idea that babies are brought by storks or are sometimes found in cabbage patches or under gooseberry bushes? (687A)

Then follows an Antitheton Question:

Really, is it books that put ideas into young heads, or is it nature? (687B)

Towards the end of the Summing-up a further powerful series of questions in quasi-rhetorical form is posed:

'Well that is *sheer filth*'
Is it?
Is the act of sexual passion *sheer filth*?
It may be an error of taste to write about it.
It may be a matter in which, perhaps, old-fashioned people would mourn the reticence that was observed in these matters yesterday, but is it *sheer filth*? (688A)

Finally,

Are we going to say in England that our contemporary literature is to be measured by what is suitable for the 14-year-old schoolgirl to read?

There are also two quotation-questions. The first is special in that it is inter-textual in that it refers to counsel's argument in *Hicklin* (LR 3 QB 360 [1868], at 365): 'What can be more obscene than many pictures publicly exhibited, as the Venus in the Dulwich gallery?' (685B). (The other is a double question with the quotation embedded (686I).) A variant is: '... the Crown say: "Well, that is sheer filth". Is it? Is the act of sexual passion sheer filth?' (*ibid.* 688A). There is also a doubly embedded literary quotation-question:

> If you look at the front page [of *The Philanderer*], you will see the text. It is taken from a Victorian poet, Browning:
>
> > 'What of soul was left, I wonder,
> > When the kissing had to stop?'
>
> I suppose men and women of all ages have wondered that.

Redundancy

This is a form of emphasis.

> ... *obviously and admittedly* is absorbed with sex, the relationship between the male and female of the human species. (At 685D)

Repetitive emphasis

It is a matter of ... importance ... (×4) (684E)
We are not here (×5)
You and you alone ... (684G)
This year or last year ... or next year ... or the year after that ... (685B)
... how they did not (×3) (685G)

There is also concentrated 'We' usage (×7) (×5) (685D–G). Other examples of repetitive emphasis are:

that great mystery (×2) (685DE)
that sex is sin, that the whole thing is dirty, that it was a mistake ... (686A)
the charge is ... (×3) (686D)
filth (×3) 'sheer filth' (×3) (688B)
They have got no ... (×4) (688C)

Slippage

Slippage is not a rhetorical category. It is the subjective ascription of inauthentic communication – bad faith at worst – or an assertion that the 'real' motive of the communicator in some way escapes, or is betrayed.

Given the immense rhetorical freedom available to judges instructing juries, I would not expect to find such evidence in this genre in England and Wales.

The following is put forward not as an example, but as a candidate for readers to consider.

> ... sex ... *I* ... approach that *great mystery* with profound interest and at the same time a very deep sense of reverence.
> *We* cannot get away from it.
> It is not *our* fault that but for the love of man and woman and the act of sex the human race would have ceased to exist thousands of years ago.
> It is not *our* fault that the moment in, shall *we* say, an over-civilised world – ... – sex ceases to be one of the great motive forces in human life, the human race will cease to exist. It is the essential condition ... for whatever ultimate purpose *we* have been brought into this world.

> Speaking to a representative group of people, nine men and three ladies, *I* suppose each one of *you* is of good will and anxious that in *our* approach to this *great mystery* today *we* should achieve some solution which will lead to personal happiness between individuals of the opposite sex in millions of homes throughout this island ...

If this passage is an example of such slippage it is because of the switching between and elision between the first person singular of the instructing judge and the incorporating 'we' which permeates the address in relation to the 'great mystery' with a single second person plural reference to the jury as such. The slippage lies not just in those elisions but in the judge's utilitarian prescription, 'in millions of homes throughout this island. This, after all, is the only possible foundation on which to build a vigorous strong and useful nation' (685D–F). This utilitarian prescription is given without any alternatives.

Trope consciousness

In 1868 the *rhetorical question* was asked:
'What can be more obscene than many pictures exhibited, as the Venus ...' (685B)

Comment on the legal instructions

Burden and standard of proof

Stable J's Direction occurs early (685A, Summing-up commences 684D), which is normal. There are, however, three unusual features. In the introduction (684D–F) the consequences of the verdict for literature are foregrounded. At the same time (684G,H) the prosecution's closing speech was criticized for suggesting that the jury were arbiters of taste. This leads into an unusual inversion: the Standard of proof is presented before the Burden of proof, which is presented colloquially as resting on the prosecution 'from start to finish'.

Structurally, there is a significant final repetition of the Standard of proof:

> Before you can return a verdict of 'Guilty' on that charge you have to be satisfied that that charge has been proved. If it is anything short of that the accused companies and individual are entitled to a verdict at your hands of 'Not Guilty'. (688G)

The Disclaimer

Characteristic of this rhetorically intense Summing-up is the main Disclaimer, including an antitheton and repetitive emphasis:

> It is not what I think about this book; it is the conclusion that you reach. You represent that diversity of minds and ages which represents the public of the English-speaking world. You and you alone must decide this case and if, in the

course of this Summing-up I express my opinion about the matter, you are entitled to ignore it. (684G)

There is a reinforcement at a later structurally important juncture:

I am going to say a few words about the book itself, again reminding you that the determination of this case is a matter exclusively for you. If you do not agree with any view that I may indicate or express, well, you do not agree with it; that is all, and your disagreement is paramount. (687D)

The jury as legitimator

Some Summings-up stress the role of the jury as conferring legitimacy on the legal process. Whether this encourages or awes the jurors is moot, as in:

The important duty rests fairly and squarely on your shoulders. It is not what I think about this book; it is the conclusion that you reach. You represent the diversity of minds and ages which represent the reading public of the English-speaking world. You and you alone must decide the case ... (684G)
... Speaking to a representative group of people, nine men and three ladies ... (685F)

It should be noted in passing that this was the traditional property-qualified jury that was reformed twenty years later.

Consequentialism

Consequential aspects are presented at the outset of the Summing-up:

STABLE, J: The charge against two limited liability companies, and one individual, is a charge of publishing what is called an obscene libel. Everybody agrees here that the two companies and the individual director stand or fall together. There can be no dispute that the verdict that you will give is a matter of *the utmost consequence. It is a matter of very real importance* to the accused and to the individuals who are associated with them. *It is of importance to* authors who, from their minds and imagination, create imaginary worlds for our edification, amusement, and sometimes, too, for our escape. *It is a matter of importance to* the community in general, to the adolescent, perhaps, in particular, *In addition to that, it is of great importance in relation* to the future of the novel in the civilised world and the future generations who can only derive their knowledge of how persons lived, thought, and acted from the contemporary literature of the particular age in which they are interested. *Your verdict will have a great bearing on where the line is drawn between* liberty, that freedom to read and think as the spirit moves it, on the one hand, and licence which is an affront to the society of which we are all members, on the other.

The important duty of deciding rests fairly and squarely on your shoulders. (684D–G)

In the final paragraph of the Summing-up Stable J returns to this mode of argumentation, but negatively:

> They are not literature. They have got no message, they have got no inspiration; they have got no thought. They have got nothing. They are just filth, and, of course, that ought to be stamped out; but in our desire for a healthy society, *if* we drive the criminal law too far, further than it ought to go, *is not there a risk that* there will be a revolt, a demand for a change in the law, so that the pendulum will swing too far the other way and allow to creep in things that under the law as it exists today we can exclude and keep out? (688F)

A distancing method

The structure, tropes and discourse of this Summing-up are my primary concern. However, there is one special feature that should not be passed over.

As it happened *The Philanderer* is an American novel, originally published in the USA. This allows Stable J to insert points that would not have been possible if the book had been an account of British experience, first published in Britain:

> If we are to understand how life is lived in the United States of America . . . the contemporary novels of those nations may afford us some guide. This is an American novel, written by a citizen of the USA, published originally in New York, purporting to depict . . . New York, and to portray . . . New York. If we are going to read novels about . . . New York. It would not be of much assistance, would it, if contrary to the fact, we were led to suppose that in New York no unmarried woman had disabused her mind of the idea that babies are brought by storks or are sometimes found in cabbage patches or under gooseberry bushes? (686H–687A)

This repetitive emphasis on 'America' and 'New York' with the concluding triple sarcasm on sexual ignorance and euphemism has an obvious potential – not available by definition for a British novel – that of distancing the jury from its subject-matter. The presumed impact would be that potentially offensive material reduces in its effect as space (or time) increases, and *pro tanto* acquittal chances would increase.

Conclusion

Because of its accessibility I have analysed this celebrated Summing-up in depth. First I deployed the genre-specific structural analysis that I have developed, which isolated the salience of Krito-doxa – judicial opiniona-tion. Only then did I make a traditional rhetorical analysis of tropes, and how they are deployed within that structure. Even the legal instructions have facets which interlink with the rhetorical structure: the jury as legitimator, consequentialism, and a distancing method. I conclude that this was a 'directional' Summing-up, produced by the variety of methods analysed here to produce the jury's liberal acquittal verdict.

Two doctors are acquitted

Bourne – acquittal of procuring miscarriage

This was a *cause célèbre* test case, acknowledged as such and reported in the Law Reports (*Bourne* [1939] 1KB 687, MacNaghten J).

Mr Bourne was a leading surgeon prosecuted under the Offences Against the Person Act 1861 for 'unlawfully using an instrument to procure miscarriage' of a 14-year-old girl who had been raped and thereby made pregnant.

Mr Bourne	7	-	professional role, nominal
Th. Defendant	5	-	criminal justice role
A man (of the highest skill)	1	-	craftsman role
	(13)		
was acquitted by the			
Members of the Jury	2		
We etc.	2		
	(4)		of this offence against
Th. girl	7	-	impersonal (a legal requirement)

Comments on legal instructions

The judge/jury demarcation
MacNaghten J's Summing-up commences:

> Members of the jury, now that you have heard all the evidence ... it becomes my duty to sum-up the case for you and to give you the necessary directions in law, and then it will be for you to consider the facts in relation to the law as laid down by me, and, after consideration to deliver your verdict.

This introduction involves a simple deictical (temporal) antitheton of function: 'now' ... 'then'. It continues:

> In a trial by jury it is for the judge to give directions to the jury upon matters of law, and it is for the jury to determine the facts; the jury, and the jury alone, are the judges of fact in the case. (At 689)

This is in effect a repetition of the antitheton but limited to role, and is given repetitive emphasis:

> the jury ...; the jury, and the jury alone ...

The judicial Disclaimer on the survey of facts

In this Summing-up there is no express Disclaimer. The nearest is a sentence on jury function:

> You are the judges of the facts and it is for you to say what weight should be given to the testimony of the witnesses ... (At 694)

Appeals to common-sense

Structurally the remark just quoted is sandwiched between two appeals to 'common-sense', a problematic reference in a jury trial where the jury might be thought to embody that quality, or more importantly to construct it in the course of their deliberation (my emphases):

(1) 'the pelvic bones are not set until a girl is eighteen and it is an observation that appeals to one's *common-sense* that it must be injurious to a girl that she should go through the state of pregnancy and finally of labour when she is of tender years ...'
(2) '... of the witnesses; but *no doubt* you will think it is only *common-sense* that a girl who for nine months has to carry in her body the reminder of the dreadful scene ... must suffer great mental anguish, unless ...'

The Burden and Standard of proof

In this Summing-up the Burden and Standard of proof are elided, with the Burden as primary limb, with the legal issue presented negatively and antithetically. My hypothesis is that this is a difficult form for a jury to comprehend and operate, and that it increases the potential for an acquittal (Winter 9 *Law and Soc. Rev.* 1970–71):

> my Direction to you in law is that – the burden rests on the Crown to satisfy you beyond reasonable doubt that the defendant did *not* procure the miscarriage ... for the purpose of preserving her life. If the Crown fails to satisfy you of that, the defendant is entitled by the law of this land to a verdict of acquittal. (my emphasis)
>
> If, on the other hand, you are satisfied that what the defendant did was *not* done by him ... for the purpose of preserving the life of the girl, it is your duty to find him guilty. (At 691)

This is repeated (at 695):

> As I told you yesterday, and I tell you today, the question that you have got to determine is *not*, are you satisfied that he performed the operation in good faith for the purpose of ...
> The question is,
> has the Crown proved the *negative* of that: if the Crown has satisfied you beyond reasonable doubt – if there is a doubt – by our law the accused person is always entitled to be acquitted – If the Crown has satisfied you beyond reasonable doubt that he did not do this act in good faith for the purpose of

> preserving the life ...
> then he is guilty of the offence with which he is charged.
> If the Crown has failed to satisfy you of that, then by the law of England, he is entitled to a verdict of acquittal. (At 695)

Then follows a consequential coda on the considerations for the medical profession of the verdict, combined with a further polarized antitheton against back-street abortionists. Then the Summing-up ends:

> You will give the matter your careful consideration, and if you come to the conclusion that the Crown has discharged the burden that rests on it, your verdict should be Guilty.
> If you are not satisfied of that, then your verdict should be Not guilty.

Consequentialist argument

In the finale to his Summing-up MacNaghten J placed two separate consequentialisms at separate levels, each with repetitive emphasis:

(1) 'But in the case of a normal, decent girl brought up in a normal, decent way, you may not think that Dr Rees was not overstating the effect of the continuance of the pregnancy when he said that it would make her a mental wreck, with all the disastrous consequences that would follow from that' (at 695).

(2) 'The case is a grave case, and no doubt raises matters of grave concern both to the medical profession and to the public ...' (at 695).

Linguistic aspects of the Summing-up in Bourne

Bourne is one of the minority of cases that is largely organized around a single rhetorical trope, the antitheton, actually two antitheta. The first relates to defendant-doctor *versus* professional abortionist. The other holds out this young victim of rape *versus* a 'Dolores' of the 'prostitute class'.

Antitheta in this case do not occur in isolation, but are intensified by other tropes, such as hyperbole.

MacNaghten J constructs a powerful antitheton (which does allow for a broad spectrum between the two poles) around the situation of an abortion event. The negative pole is occupied by a recent case known to the judge in which an unqualified abortionist travelled to London to perform the operation. The effect was dramatic: death in 'time measured not by minutes but by seconds', in which the client 'was dead on the floor' ... This powerful pathos figure manages to combine the condensation of time with consequential bathos (at 690).

Two clusters of metaphor occurred in this Summing-up. The first cluster concerns the consequences to the victim of the rape:

> carry in her body *the reminder* ... (692)
> ... a mental *wreck* (694, 695)

The second is complex and relates both to the structure of the Summing-up and the trial's special features. It is a nominal antitheton by quotation, differentiating the victim from 'a *Dolores* ...' (694).

In the dominant stereotype of rhetoric there is a temptation to privilege the use of literary quotation, but that is in my view a misuse of rhetoric. However, such allusions do occur in *Bourne*. It is structural to one of the antitheta which permeated the Summing-up:

> unless she be feeble-minded or belongs to the class described as 'the prostitute class', a Dolores ...
> '... marked cross from the womb and perverse.'
> (Swinburne, 'Dolores', stanza 18)

There are also crude repetitive emphases.

In referring to the antithetical back-street abortionist the antitheton is thickened by contrasting the positive:

> *she* unlawfully ... *she* did it for money ... *she* used her instruments – (689)

and the negative:

> ... of *no* skill, with *no* medical qualifications, and there is *no* pretence ... Cases of this sort are in *no* way ... (690)

The victim of the rape and patient for the abortion was:

> *a normal decent girl*, brought up in *a normal, decent* way. (694)
> This was a *grave* case ... of *grave* concern. (*Ibid.*)

Comments on Bourne

(1) One of the manifold stratagems set up by MacNaghten J is a running polarized antitheton examplar of a convicted non-professional (female) abortionist. This polarized coupling focuses on the defendants rather than their patients. After the first paragraph on the judge–jury demarcation, the charge under s.58 Offences against the Person Act 1861 is stated:

> ... it is a very grave crime and ... by no means uncommon. This is the second case at the present session of this court ... and I only mention the other case to show you how different the case now before you is ... In that other case a woman without any medical skill or medical qualifications did what is alleged ... here; she unlawfully used an instrument for the purpose of procuring the miscarriage of a pregnant girl; she did it for money: £2 5/- shillings was her fee – a pound was paid on making the appointment and she came from a distance to a place in London to perform the operation. She used her instrument, and, ... the victim of her malpractice was dead. That is the class of case which usually comes before the court.
>
> The case here is very different. A man of the highest skill ... (689–90)

There is discrimination in the comparison itself. The woman is unqualified and subject to condemnation, whereas Mr Bourne, qualified 'of the highest skill . . . in one of our great hospitals', is subject to less rather than more censure. She is at fault for being paid £2 5/-, but Mr Bourne's salary is not mentioned. Both 'used their instruments'. What does not occur in the Summing-up but is reported from argument is that he would not have operated if the patient had contracted venereal disease from the rape (at 688). It follows from that that the patient would have been left by consensus 'a mental wreck', with a baby and possibly both with venereal disease. To whom would the patient have resorted? The response to this need is bracketed out by MacNaghten J.

Deference to doctors remains a problem in jurisprudence (see Robertshaw and Thakker 1 *Med. Law Internat.* (1993)).

(2) The legal point made at page 691 of the transcript is challengeable. The defendant was not charged under the Infant Life (Preservation) Act 1929 s.1(1), which contains a proviso that

> no person shall be found guilty of an offence under this section unless it is proved that the act which caused the death of the child was not done in good faith for the purpose only of preserving the life of the mother.

There is no such proviso in the 1861 statute which refers only to 'unlawfully using an instrument to procure miscarriage'. MacNaghten J imports the meaning of the 1929 proviso into the 1861 statute's 'unlawful'. An express Direction to that effect followed immediately.

There are two difficulties.

The first is the transplantation retrospectively of an express term in a later non-referring statute to a silent earlier statute.

Second, even if this semantic mechanism is ignored and 'unlawfully' is simply interpreted to cover 'the preservation of life of the mother', on the facts of the instant case 'preservation of life' is being given a strained meaning – not congruent with that in the 1929 Act.

(3) The other antitheton between a 'normal' rape victim and a 'Dolores' will not be developed here, except to state that it is similar to the Madonna–Magdalena aspect of the *Archer* Summing-up, in which credibility was constructed through witnesses rather than the plaintiff.

Conclusion

Contrastive rhetorical devices – differentiation, polarization, antitheta – occur 19 times throughout the seven pages of this Summing-up.

Another marked feature is consequential argument (seven times).

Opinionation on non-legal matters (Krito-doxa) occurs six times in the second half of the Summing-up.

Taken together these features in themselves connote a directional statement, which would have been predicated on McNaghten J's jury audience. At that time this was a relatively homogeneous group of middle-class freeholders, largely male. The differentiations he mobilized display an appeal to class ascription rather than medical need: the patient is middle-class ('brought up in a normal decent way'); she is not a 'Dolores' representative of the lumpen proletariat; and the response foregrounds hypothesized psychological harm rather than actual physical damage. Presumably Dolores types were assumed to be beyond psychological damage (see *ex parte Rutty* [1956] 2 QB 109).

I conclude with an Appendix which demonstrates the core feature of this Summing-up as the Antitheton (polarization or differentiation). In addition the deployment of consequentialism is displayed and Krito-doxa occurs in the central sections.

Bourne – Appendix: Structural analysis [1939] 1 KB 687

Page			
689	Trial Mythos and role differentiation		
	Nomo-dogma		
		emphasis	
	Nomo-Mythos and trial Mythos		
690	Nomo-doxa and polarization		
		Pejorative consequentialism	
		differentiation	
	Nomos-role insertion		
		differentiation	
	motivation		
		parenthesis	
		consequentialism	
	Nomos-role conclusion		
	Trial Mythos		
	Nomo-dogma		
	Nomo-Mythos		
	–	proviso	
	Nomo-Mythos		
691	–	proviso analogy	
		differentiation	
	Nomo-doxa		
	Conclusion – nomo-dogma		
	Trial Mythos – emphasis		
692		repetition differentiation	
		consequentialism	
			differentiation
		rhetorical deference	
			anti- differentiation
	Quotation		

Quotation – differentiation
insertion – emphasis
Exemplification
consequentialism
implicature
gloss
Nomo-doxa
693 differentiation
hypothesis
Krito-doxa
differentiation
Krito-doxa
Nomo-doxa
pejorative
analogy
conclusion
694 Nomo-doxa repetition
Nomo-dogma
Mythos
Krito-doxa
analogy
Krito-doxa parenthesis
Trial Mythos
Krito-doxa
psychological consequentialism
forensic legitimation
Mythos
consequentialism
Nomo-dogma disclaimer
Krito-doxa
proviso:
two negative psychological differentiations
Quotation
695 Recapitulation
consequentialism
motivation – disclaimer
motivation – trial Mythos
Nomo-dogma
differentiation
parenthesis
differentiation
repetition
emphasis – repetition
differentiation
parenthesis
differentiation
696 Nomo-dogma

Arthur – acquittal of manslaughter

The trial took place in 1981, but the Summing-up is reported in the BMLR series vol. I of 1988. The BMLR version is considerably edited from the original transcript. Although the reader will find the reported version convenient to read, I shall refer frequently to the transcript which carried important material which was edited out (90 pages compared to the 23 printed pages). I am deeply indebted to my colleague Mervyn Lynn for access to the (battered) transcript.

In this case a paediatrician had to make a decision about a neonate suffering from Down's syndrome, 'mongolism', whose mother and family rejected him at birth. The prognosis was that death would occur sooner rather than later. The consensus in practice for such cases is one of basic care only. However, in this case Dr Arthur prescribed dihydrocodeine DF118. This is an analgesic, pain-reliever – for a baby who was not in pain. The dosage was very high and it was known to have two side-effects: negative consequences for respiration; and the suppression of hunger which in turn would reduce resistance to infection. The jury acquitted Dr Arthur of manslaughter. The modes of jury address are:

Members of the Jury	48	(N and %)
We etc.	45	
You, as a jury	4	
'I' etc.	2	
	99	(Transcript 90 pp.: 1.1 per page)

The jury references are of 'standard intensity' at about one per page.

The defendant references were:

Dr Arthur	98 (transcript)				%
Dr Leonard A	1				
The doctor	7				
The accused Dr A.	1	:	professional	108	97.3
The def. Dr A.	1	:	named	101	91.0
The defendant	3	:	defendant	5	4.5
	111			(111)	

The victim references were:

The child	122 (transcript)				%
The baby	39	:			
The infant	3	:	impersonal	163	70
Th. Baby JP	1				
John Pearson	16		named	17	7
It	55		object	55	23
	236				

The differential forms of address are marked here; the defendant status of Dr Arthur is marginal. The alleged victim has marginal status as a named person; the vast majority of references are impersonal and, uniquely, as an object.

The jury are quite intensively addressed and there is an even balance between formal-distanced mode and cooperative mode. Simply put, 'jury' reference instructs; 'we' usage coaxes or persuades.

Legal instructions in Arthur

Judge/jury demarcation

After an introductory paragraph of praise for counsel, and a further paragraph on the 'enormous importance' of the case, Farquharson J continued, again with repetitive emphasis:

> That question, members of the jury, as every question does in a criminal court, throws up important matters both of law and of fact, and it is important, I think, at the outset of what I have got to say to you, to emphasise the difference in the roles that you and I have to play. It is entirely for you to decide all questions of fact. It is for you to evaluate the evidence and assess its importance. It is for you to say how reliable you find the different witnesses. Few, if any, I think, are alleged here to be in any sense untruthful, but of course, you have important questions in a case of this kind of opinion, and it is for you to say, I repeat, what reliance you place on the opinions of the various witnesses that have come. (Transcript 1E–H)

Jury role

The role is emphasized in this Summing-up. The 'line-drawing' responsibility is stressed. This is a heavy burden to push towards the jury and my supposition is that this foregrounded responsibility is emphasized so as to concentrate the jury's attention on the direction of the Summing-up.

The 'enormous importance' of the case and the role of the jury in relation to it re-emerges briefly later: 'and really this awful problem is now being placed on your shoulders' (17D).

The metaphor then provided for the jury several times is 'drawing the line':

> . . . it is very easy, is it not, to draw the line between those two examples . . . it is very much more difficult, on the other hand, to say where the line should be drawn in relation to this case, and you have got to draw it. (Transcript 19AB)

Then:

> If the prosecution have proved the latter, Members of the jury, so to speak at that point, well, then he would be guilty of murder, or attempted murder as the position now is. (Transcript 20C)

> ... It may be in the end you find the line easy to draw – I don't know – but that is the distinction you have got to make ... (Transcript 20E)

The metaphor occurs again but is qualified:

> ... it is going to be your task to draw the line, whether this comes within the bounds of medical ethics and outside the rules of the criminal law or whether it is, indeed, in breach of a crime, but I should emphasise that when I use a phrase like that 'drawing the line', in one sense it is slightly confusing because one must always keep in the front of your minds that it is the prosecution that has to prove its case and drawing the line might connote in some people's minds that you simply choose between two cases rather than simply saying to yourself: has one side proved it so that I am sure? (Transcript 25E–G).

The jury as legitimator: 'grey areas'

In this Summing-up the jury is implied as the appropriate body to draw the line between the legally permissible and illegal impermissible:

> ... and we as a profession are aware of the grey areas of the law. We are primarily concerned with the patient but we would not wish to feel we are acting above the law ... (Transcript 57C)
> ... He says this: 'There is an important distinction between allowing a baby to die and taking action which will accelerate or cause death'. I think that is really our distinction, the one you have got to draw, and decide on which side of that line this case falls. 'There is an important grey area in between. It is important not only to doctors but also to parents' ... (Transcript 59H–60A)

Then, specifically on the medication:

> If you give an excessive quantity of drugs, more than is really necessary to relieve distress, you would then be accelerating the death of the child? Answer: 'Yes, my Lord'. These are the sort of grey areas I was talking about. It is the point in the spectrum and it is very difficult to draw. There are no black and white situations here, there are grey areas. (Transcript 64CD)

The Burden and Standard of proof

In this Summing-up the stress is on the Burden of proof. The first presentation is parenthetical, and may have been confusing:

> The defence point to the fact that they have called a number of doctors with considerable experience in paediatrics, all of whom have said that while the dosage may be high, it is within therapeutic levels. Once that is established – or rather the prosecution have failed to establish the contrary – I venture to think that you ... (BMLR 4)

Later a series of four questions are put, which are followed by: 'If the prosecution have proved the latter, and you draw the line, so to speak, at that point ...' (BMLR 6).

In the final page of the Summing-up (BMLR 23) Burden and Standard are elided:

> Firstly, has the prosecution made you sure that Dr A ... took steps to bring about the death of J.P. with the intention that he should die? I put it that way to emphasise the Burden of proof. Has the prosecution made you sure that ...

Structurally, one notes that the final enunciation is followed by the Warning that although the defendant had given no evidence, that is any defendant's right: 'there is no point in citizens having rights if one can criticise them for exercising them'. This right is not explicitly linked to the Burden of proof. It is followed by a final positive character reference for the defendant (BMLR 23).

In the *Arthur* transcript another elided Direction on the Burden and Standard occurs:

> It is the prosecution's task to prove that he is guilty ... What does one mean by proving that he is guilty? It means, members of the jury, that they must make you sure that they, the prosecution, must make you sure of his guilt before you can convict.
>
> At the end of the day ... you will have to ask yourself the question: has the prosecution made me sure that Dr A. attempted to kill JP? ... (Transcript 9AB)

The Burden of proof is highlighted on one other occasion in relation to the verdict metaphor of 'drawing the line':

> ... one must always keep in the front of your minds that it is the prosecution that has to prove its case and 'drawing the line' might connote in some people's minds that you simply choose between two cases rather than simply saying to yourself:
>
> has one side proved it so that I am sure? (Transcript 25FG)

The judicial Disclaimer

In this Summing-up there is one overall Disclaimer followed by three special ones relating to particular issues:

> I shall try in this case ... to express no opinion of my own on these matters. It is unlikely that I shall succeed in doing that, but any opinion on a question of fact or the reliability of a witness or the consequence of the evidence that you have heard, that I may express, can be rejected by you instantly if you do not agree with it, because it is not my function, not indeed, my right to impinge in any way on the area where you are supreme, that is to say on all questions of fact. (Transcript 2C–E)

Then:

> If I say it is reduced in importance, I illustrate an example of what I said I must not do. That is a matter for you and not for me. I perhaps should say I merely

> refer to it as representing the case that is now being put before you for your consideration. (Transcription 11G)

Then:

> I repeat again, I am to some extent commenting on witnesses' evidence here. A thing that I will not say I promise not to do because I know perfectly well I will break the promise which I can only do by way of comment in conjunction with repeating the warning I have already given to you that any comments on witnesses, members of the jury, are subject entirely to your view of them, but in as much as I am now putting the defence case on this particular issue it is not inappropriate that reference should be made to the status and the approach of those members of the medical profession. (Transcript 25B–D)

Then:

> ... it was accepted that the child had reached a stage where if infection overcame it, it was going to be left to die. That I suggest is the position although it is for you to say whether it be so. (BMLR 10)

The Direction on emotion

In *Arthur* there were several Directions of significance beyond the normal ones on Burden and Standard of proof. Here is the Direction on emotion:

> Rarely can there have been a case in the criminal courts where emotion had such a pervading presence. You will recall that at the very beginning of this case I asked you whether you had any dealings with handicapped children or membership of any society which may have strong views on this question. None of you had. That was of the greatest importance because, as you have already been told, it is so vital that you approach your consideration of this case on – I was going to say clinical, but perhaps I had better leave that out – a cool objective approach to the evidence. Influenced only by that you have heard from the witness box and your own good judgement rather than by strong feelings. Strong feelings are of no help in this case, and they should be absolutely eschewed and cut out. (Transcript 26F–27B)

Consequentialist remarks

The expression of consequentialism of any kind in judgment or 'objective' conclusion is said to offend formalist and positivist perspectives in jurisprudence. Whatever the value of such criticisms, such remarks are common not only in overt advocacy but in judges' Summings-up to juries.

Here the consequential issue is stated at the commencement of the Summing-up.

> It will by now be perfectly obvious to you that this is a case of enormous importance. It throws up serious questions affecting the practice of the medical profession, as well as matters that gravely affect the interests of the public at large. It really revolves round the question of what is the duty of a doctor when

> prescribing treatment for a severely handicapped child suffering from a handicap of an irreversible nature, whose parents do not want that child to survive. (Transcript 1C–E)

Later in the Summing-up it is developed further by two examples, both leaning towards acquittal. It is taken by quotation from one of the expert witnesses:

> He said: 'I can see no difference in the cases in which I myself have been involved in medical principles and that of Dr Arthur. It was essential that the handicap was of a severe order and irreversible, and the parents must be properly consulted and their instructions taken.'
>
> He gave us, you will recall, in conclusion an example of an experience that he had in America where – well, I hesitate to say that the law is in any way inferior to what it is here, but apparently the terror with which doctors regard it is very much greater – and there was an instance that he gave us of a baby who was born without a brain, and was being artificially kept alive over 20 nominal deaths and revived simply because of the fear that doctors there had they would be held responsible, and yet the future of that baby was a nought. Obviously in the care of Dr Dunn it would have been allowed to die. (Transcript 75A–E)

Then from the President of the Royal College of Physicians:

> He then went on to discuss and, indeed, condemn, the activities of certain pressure groups. I do not think that it is right for me to go into that, members of the jury. He told you that these groups had adverse effects because it created inflexible rules and developed the very unhappy situation where one member of the medical profession might be spying on another. (Transcript 77AB)

Direction on the defendant's silence in court

As has been mentioned there was a Direction and Warning in support of the defendant's right to silence in court (Transcript 51GH, 87–8).

Linguistic aspects of the Summing-up

In this Summing-up the trope rate is not particularly high; sequencing and structure are more salient. Nevertheless the tropes and linguistic figures are worth consideration. These figures include trope consciousness: 'Killing, *or if you do not like the word*, an act of causing death' (Transcript 14H–15A).

There is one colloquialism of extreme poignancy to which I will give full analysis later. It is in quotation form: 'I don't want it, duck' (at 7). In the transcript of *Arthur*, several more colloquialisms occurred. Here is one which relates to that just cited: 'decides to put a pillow over the poor soul's head' (Transcript 26D).

Metaphor
There are two important metaphors in this Summing-up. One concerns jury function: 'It is going to be your task *to draw the line*' (at 6). The other comprises the second part of an antitheton and constitutes part of the judicial frame-setting of Dr Arthur. The facts were that the actual administration of DF118 to the dead child was by the nurses (on Dr Arthur's prescription). When the death was investigated, Dr Arthur took full responsibility, and said that the nurses were merely his agents: 'He did not want any blame attaching to them. As a matter of law and *cold* legal principle that would be right but, of course, as a matter of morality it was *very warming* that he should say such a thing' (at 3).

In addition to the various references to 'drawing the line' the jury have a further difficulty to contend with, a mixed metaphor: '. . . this awful problem is now being placed on your shoulder' (17D) which may have been caused in part by the evidence which had: 'receded and flowed and ebbed' (Transcript 9E).

There are other powerful single-word metaphors to be found in *Arthur*. A part of the consequential scenario in which the trial was located was the possibility that the defendant be '*branded* as a criminal' (Transcript 18C). Even the degree of agreed facts between the parties was expressed dramatically as: 'there was not really much *collision* between the two sides . . .' (Transcript 35E).

A further series of single-word – verb or noun – metaphors related to the deceased neonate mongol in Dr Arthur's case: [There were for this condition] 'ante-natal *detective services*' (Transcript 65H). As a mongol or Down's syndrome sufferer, he ('it') was a '*candidate*' for death (45B, D, D) for whom an *'armoury'* of drugs was available (Transcript 58D), when it was '*relegated* to a side-ward' (Transcript 21G) and its prescription was 'an act *consigning [it]* to death' (Transcript 23B).

In addition there were linguistic methods for constructing a hierarchy of credibility from amongst the expert witnesses that figured so prominently. At one end of this hierarchy were (with a parenthetic apology): 'the *rank-and-file* of the profession' (Transcript 24B), and in contrast: 'the *pinnacle* of his profession' from which 'he has *come down*' (Transcript 75H).

Hyperbole
In *Arthur* there is a reference to the defendant and his professional esteem 'in the highest glowing terms' (at 4). In structural terms this hyperbole, 'glowing', is of significance because it links with a separate description of the doctor described as 'warming'. These are highly positive labels for a defendant.

Euphemism
'Mum feels he will be a strain . . . and her daughter is *not* anxious to keep him.' This, combined with the direct colloquial quotation from the

mother lie structurally at the centre of the Summing-up: 'I don't want *it*, duck.' Another previously cited as an example of trope-consciousness is: 'Killing, or if you do not like the word, an act of causing death' (Transcript 14H–15A).

Appeals to common-sense
There is only one such appeal which is embedded in an exemplification, which was deliberately distanced from the factual situation that occurred in *Arthur* (Transcript 5F).

Exemplification
In his Summing-up Farquharson J states that the fact that a professional body has a code of ethics provides no automatic exemption from the operation of the criminal law. His Lordship then provided a list of four hypothetical examples as models against which to analyse the instant case. (At 5.)

Negatives
Two negative forms are salient in relation to one of the special features of this case: John Pearson's mongolism: 'Even if they *never* do, and *never* can, become normal.' And in euphemistic mode the doctor's note justifying the treatment prescribed (Transcript 16A). 'Mum feels he will be a strain ... and her daughter is *not* anxious to keep him.'

Repetitive emphasis

It is for you ... (× 4) (Transcript 1FG)
Let nobody, nobody ... (Transcript 13)
Yes, he was killing, he was murdering (Transcript 19)
Nursing Care only (Transcript 34–5)
For years and years and years (Transcript 12D)
Easy to recognise, easy to categorise ... (Transcript 19G)
time and time again (Transcript 24A)
based on very, very little experience (Transcript 40C)
besides many, many other appointments (Transcript 65C)

Quotation
In *Arthur* about half the Summing-up in the BMLR version consists of lengthy quotations from the prosecution expert witness (in my view damning) and those for the defence (in my view rather lukewarm).

A different type of quotation also occurs in the Summing-up which I repeat:

[The mother:] I don't want it, duck.
[The doctor:] Mum feels he will be a strain on the family and her daughter is not anxious to keep him. (Both at 7)

However, these do not exhaust the variety. One which occurs quite frequently is the 'implication quotation' in which hypothetical remarks are injected into the jury:

> Then you will say: 'Will corrupt and deprave whom?' To which the answer is . . .

Questions
The issue for the jury was set out as a quintipartite serial question:

> But what is the position here?
> Was what Dr Arthur did in . . . setting out . . . in prescribing . . . in the nature of setting conditions where the child could . . . die peacefully?
> Or, if it revealed any other organic defect, die peacefully?
> Or, was it a positive act on the part of Dr Arthur . . . (within the definition I have given you) accompanied by an intent on his part that it should . . . die?

In the transcript the Standard of proof is posed in question–answer–question form:

> What does one mean by proving that he is guilty?
> It means, members of the Jury, that . . . At the end of the day – . . . – you will have to ask yourself the question:
> 'has the prosecution made me sure that Dr Arthur attempted to kill John Pearson?' (Transcript 9A,B)

Again, much later on the Standard of proof:

> . . . has the prosecution made you sure about that:
> that he took active steps . . . to ensure the baby would die, with the intention to bring that event about? . . .
> you go on to a second question and ask yourselves:
> 'has the prosecution made me sure that the steps that I find were taken by Dr Arthur amount to an attempt . . .?' (87)

Technical terms
In *Arthur* the technical evaluation of DF118 dihydrocodeine was 'delegated' to the battery of expert witnesses for both prosecution and defence. In rhetorical (jury audience) terms there was a further factor involved which I will consider below: that is how the jury was to evaluate the experts.

Semantic slippage
The term 'a holding operation' is used frequently throughout the Summing-up. This refers to the use of DF118 dihydrocodeine and 'Nursing Care Only' once John Pearson's mongolism and his mother's rejection were established. One might envisage this term as 'shorthand'. Alternatively one might envisage it as 'slippage'.

From the latter perspective one must analyse first the two words 'holding' and 'operation'. 'Holding' implies a maintenance of the status quo and by contrast an abstention from any medical treatment or procedure which can or will lead to deterioration in the patient's condition. 'Operation' normally represents an active intervention to produce a positive outcome. One could interpret the word liberally to cover pharmaceutical prescription and possibly acts designed to maintain the status quo rather than an improvement. The slippage asserted lies in the fact that DF118 was never intended to maintain the status quo. Its known side-effects are to suppress hunger and to impair the respiratory system. Given these two primary consequences of prescription the status quo could not be maintained: so deterioration in the quality of life and resistance to infection were the expected secondary consequences, so the one thing it was not was a 'holding operation'.

Special features of the Arthur Summing-up

There are many special features of this trial, some of which are only apparent from the transcript. One example of the transcript's value is that it contains a Warning on emotional responses of jurors, which is absent in the reported version.

Although there are certain aspects of this Summing-up which I consider to be acquittal-orientated, there are special circumstances in the process which may have promoted that; further, Farquharson J quotes at length from the expert witness for both sides and these can hardly be said to favour the defendant:

Expert evidence

By his disclosure of the negative prosecution expert opinion on DF118 (dihydrocodeine) – I would say damning evidence (e.g. Transcript 47, 58, 60C, 80F) – and the rather lukewarm support of the defence's experts (BMLR 21) – one might think that this would tend towards a 'conviction' orientation.

However, there is a subtle factor at play in how the jury are expected to evaluate the various and competing opinions:

(1) The prosecution never called a witness in the same field of medicine as the defendant (Transcript 36E).
(2) There had been problems with the presentation of some of the prosecution evidence: '... it is a prospect that one views with some alarm ... expert evidence ... incomplete ... inaccurate ... then where should we be?' (Transcript 44A).
(3) As in some other Summings-up in relation to experts, there was credibility-weighting by uncritical reference to experience and 'eminence' factors. As it happened this method might have tilted the evaluation balance in favour of the defence, for example the

President of the Royal College of Physicians spoke, in cautious terms, for the defence.

Here are the caveats on the prosecution experts:

(a) 'None of that evidence, that is to say the findings of the pathologists, was tested as to whether in fact that is a correct recording of the cause of death ...' (37F)

(As I understand it that is not exactly the correct question; it should have been whether DF118 actively contributed to the cause (pneumonia) of death because of its effect on respiration and the suppression of hunger, in addition to whether it directly poisoned John Pearson.)

(b) 'He was cross-examined ... along the lines that those are all chemical analyses, that he is not an expert on the effect of drugs on the newly born, or indeed anyone else ...' (Transcript 38C also 39A).
(c) 'Mr Carman (QC) undoubtedly took the view with which the witness to a large extent was prepared to agree, that his findings were based on very, very little experience. Certainly they were not based on clinical or therapeutic experience because that is not his field ... he agrees that he is not an expert on the metabolisms of the newly born babies ...' (Transcript 40B–E).
(d) 'Professor ... He is consultant pathologist to the Home Office, as we know, with very considerable experience ...' (Transcript 41E).
'... If this man had not been represented by those who were in a position to assist him with such skill and thoroughness, it might well have been that there would have been no conceivable basis upon which to challenge ... with all the respect and dignity that his position commands, and then where would we be?' (Transcript 44B).
'... when he did come back, having seen the additional material, made no effort to fudge the issue or to try and maintain an opinion that no longer held water. He frankly came, as a good expert does, to a different conclusion ...' (Transcript 44EF).

Then the defendant: 'The first paragraph sets out his qualifications. The second paragraph his 20 years' experience ...' (Transcript 50G).
Then the defence experts:

(a) 'The first of them was Professor ... His qualifications and the service he has given the community and the committees that he has served on and his academic and medical appointments took an enormous time to recount, as did those of Dr ... So many were they that one wonders how on earth they ever had time to do half the things which they obviously have been able to do, the doctors' practices themselves being demanding enough. But although that perhaps might sound slightly frivolous it does represent somebody, does it not, at the very top of his profession who speaks with great authority, as you may think, although it is for you to say, one of the leaders of the field in which he practises and bearing that in mind you will, no doubt, give appropriate weight to what he says.

I have already remarked to you that you may conclude that these distinguished gentlemen approach their very difficult position with an admirable degree of humility, and that really shone through the evidence of this witness. You will forgive me, I know, and I hope that he will, in not recounting his qualifications. I think that they speak for themselves. He is Professor of Child Health at the University of ... and he told you that he has been involved with some 28,000 babies since beginning his career in paediatrics, including well over 100 of them with Down's syndrome' (52B–G).

(b) 'Dr ... is a Consultant in Perinatal Medicine at the University of ... a Doctor of Medicine of ... University, besides many, many other appointments and distinctions. Another man who (if I may say so) outside the calls of professional duty obviously spends a good deal of his time either in work on conferences or committees or assisting, as we know in one case, the legislature in the pursuit of medicine and medical matters for the benefit of us all. A man devoted, obviously, to a large extent to public work and, therefore, brings all the prestige of somebody who is prepared to devote time like that to the opinions that he lays before you.

He tells us he has dealt with some 35,000 babies before he became a consultant and another 35,000 since. I hope I have got those figures right; they seem so enormous, one hesitates before pronouncing them, but that is the note I have. Like his colleagues, he has dealt with some 100 to 200 Down's babies. He said about one in 600 children are Down's syndrome' (65C–G).

'... I have attended 2000 post-mortems and conducted some hundreds on newly born babies ...' (Transcript 67H).

(c) 'Sir ... Well; his career, of course, spans a wider time than that of any other witness that has been called before you. Apart from teaching in the University of ... for many years, he was also practising in the Royal Infirmary there, and he has been Professor of Medicine in the University for 13 years. He is chief scientist to the Department of Health. Those are all indeed outstanding distinctions for any man in the medical professions. But what puts his position in a different state from the other witnesses is that he is President of the Royal College of Physicians; a man at the very pinnacle of his profession. He has come down to give evidence before you. Another way perhaps of underlining the point that I made yesterday of the importance of this case. The significance of that is not simply that we are being attended by somebody of such importance, but that the President of the Royal College of Physicians, with his colleagues, has a considerable say in

> the ethics of this profession. And so what he has to tell you if you accept it, and I can think of no reason why you should not, must carry great weight. He is a witness, who like the others, you may consider, never allowed his opinions to outrun his thoughts. He was not just coming along to endorse everything that was put to him. The reservations that he made are in some circumstances of some importance, not least in the answers that he gave to Mr Draycot (QC)' (Transcript 75E–G).

From these extracts one can see that however much one may think the forensic opinion favours the prosecution, the credibility/esteem factors weigh in favour of the defence.

Trial process

There had been problems in the handling of the prosecution case. It 'was in total disarray' . . . (Transcript 22D), and they 'switched their case about the drug' (22F). As a result it became clear during the trial that pneumonia might have been caught by John Pearson during the birth passage. In consequence Farquharson J decided to withdraw the charge of murder from the jury during the trial (43F).

Pressure groups

The treatment of John Pearson had been informed to the police by the chair of a pressure group, 'Life' (Transcript 47A–D). Without naming this body, the President of the Royal College of Physicians had condemned the effects of pressure groups, in particular for creating inflexible rules in contrast to the Royal College's guidelines (as in the USA, Transcript 75C–E and 77A–D), including the 'very unhappy situation where one member of the medical profession might be spying on another' (77AB). This links into the general consequentialist propositions put forward by counsel.

'It'

The objective references to John Pearson as 'it' on a large scale, most strikingly by his rejecting mother: 'I don't want it, duck', are unique. This form of address should be considered with the transcript medical account of the stigmata of mongolism (15B–16A and 69F–H) and its social consequences (16A–D), referred to in the transcript by the House of Commons Select Committee on Social Services (69A–D). (See Danet 32 *Semiotica* (1980): 187–219.)

The public construction of the defendant

The initial and concluding frame-setting of Dr Arthur's character references are salient.

There is the initial antitheton between cold legal principle and morality – 'it was very warming' (Transcript 10D) with Dr Arthur's concern with the welfare of patients (13H–14F) in which he is spoken of in the 'highest, glowing terms' (14D).

In the middle of the transcript there is a police statement favouring Dr Arthur's approach in 'battered babies' cases as 'kind and considerate' (48G).

The concluding segment of the Summing-up (88–90) is a paean for several voices for Dr Arthur. One of the nurses gave evidence about his care and concern for her own handicapped child:

> Seldom in a court could one have heard so many testaments to a man's good character, his gentleness, his skill and his consideration for others. (80F)

Then there is his extramural character, as governor of a school for handicapped children; his MP praises him for his work in the local Dyslexia Association, finishing up: 'He is the kind of person who I would put my hand in the fire for' (89H).

Finally the Provost of Derby Cathedral gave an example of Dr Arthur working beyond the call of duty in an emergency case (90A–D).

Conclusion

The report of this Summing-up is more than adequate for legal purposes but omits almost all that would have been significant to jury deliberations by a jury specifically addressed as the legitimating body for the 'grey areas' and policy consequences raised by the trial. The defendant is constructed by a variety of methods, both structural and tropic, in positive terms; the 'eminence count' approach to the Expert evidence was also supportive. The deceased is reduced and marginalized by euphemism and semantic slippage.

Two Serious Fraud Office trials

Naviede – conviction of fraud

The defendant in this trial is the cousin of the Saddiq brothers acquitted in another SFO prosecution, *Seil*, analysed next in this chapter. Mr Naviede was tried of a range of offences under the Theft Acts – obtaining property and services by deception – and of making related false statements under the Act and s.389A(2) Companies Act 1985. The scale of the charges in the indictment (as is necessary for SFO jurisdiction) was large: £3 million credit; £30 million revolving credit facility; £1 million credit; £11 million syndicated loan facility – with intention permanently to deprive. The jury could not agree on the Companies Act charge and were discharged on that count. They convicted on the others. The trial ran for almost six months. The defendant represented himself, as was the case in *Horne*, considered below. It is interesting to note that both defendants based their defence upon a theory of conspiracy against them by regulatory agencies – in *Naviede* the defendant's distrust was of the Bank of England and the SFO.

Despite the complication of the facts, the essential issue, as in most fraud cases, was one of the honesty/dishonesty of the defendant. There was not much technical language. The basic issue was one of business practice. Mr Naviede's business had been one of 'stock or trade finance'; here the money advanced or borrowed to be advanced is underpinned in the first instance by the stock or trade of the person or company to whom money is advanced, but more fundamental is the consistent practice of the advancer to insure against loss. It is this insurance basis of the financing which provided the background confidence for the normal risk of the business. The allegation was that Mr Naviede, who had sole control of the workings of his business, moved into property investment whilst continuing to pose as a trade financier. The point was that property finance is of a completely different nature to trade finance, being a long-term rather than a short-term activity, and in particular those making financial advances to the defendant would have taken mortgages as security, whereas they did nothing believing that their advances were for trade or stock; the insurance cover for these operations never extended – and could not have been extended – to property – completely unsecured – hence these people were duped, since Mr Naviede's business then foundered.

As one would expect in a system where the Summing-up includes a survey of the evidence, it is massive. It covered four days and 450 pages of transcript. There are the normal Directions on the Burden (three times) and Standard of proof; the judicial 'Disclaimer' on selectivity and opinion in the survey of evidence; sample counts; good character; hearsay evidence; and on considering each charge separately. In this context one remarks a unique instance of 'underlining' of the Standard of proof. These are mainly in the early and concluding sections of the Summing-up, 56 uses of the word 'sure' in relation to deliberation and verdict, compared to one use of the word 'unsure' – typically: '... before you can convict you must feel sure of the defendant's guilt'.

In fact the judge is even more insistent on the Standard than that. On six occasions in the first part and three in the conclusion he adds 'all' to 'sure' (29 June 1995: 13, 16, 16, 19, 19, 21; 4 July 1995, 23, 23, 36).

The judge gave guidance on the central issue of dis/honesty, including:

> It may have occurred to you at this point that what the prosecution have to prove in this respect is Mr Naviede's state of mind at a particular time. Of course in the literal sense none of us can see into the mind of another human being and specify a particular intent. However, the law does not require any such supernatural exercise. You are entitled to draw inferences about a man's state of mind from his words and actions or from his failure to act or silence at a time when he might have been expected to have done something or spoken out. This principle applies equally to the other mental states which the prosecution must prove, such as dishonesty.
>
> A deception may be by words or conduct. It includes a deception as to the present intention of the person using the deception. (29 June 1996, 8–9)
>
> ... However, for a deception to be proved, you must all feel sure as to that deception. It would not be sufficient for example that half of you considered that one deception was made out and then consider whether you are sure that he must have realised that what he was doing was by those standards dishonest. (*Ibid.*, 9–10)
>
> ... You must be sure that Mr Naviede acted dishonestly ... you approach the matter in stages. Firstly, consider whether on the evidence before you are sure that Mr Naviede acted dishonestly by the standards of ordinary and decent people. If but only if you consider that he did not so act, then go on to consider whether you are sure that he must have realised that what he was doing was by those standards dishonest.
>
> I should add in this regard, members of the jury, that, although it may seem difficult to envisage a deliberate deception which was not also dishonest, the question of dishonesty is a separate matter to which you must apply your minds. You will, just by way of illustration, remember for example the evidence that Mr Naviede was secretive in his business affairs. There has been a good deal of evidence about that. It is conceivable that the true nature of a business might be concealed by a deliberate deception for the honest purpose of protecting trade secrets or confidentiality. I merely give that to you as an example, members of the jury, about how deception and dishonesty are separate matters to be considered. However, since I have chosen this as an example, I should remind you that it is Mr Naviede's case that he did not deliberately deceive anyone whether for this or any other reason. (*Ibid.*, 9, 10)

Later on the same day another exemplification is given (from counsel's argument):

> Issues of deception and dishonesty are essentially matters of fact for a jury to decide. The issue here is not whether the defendant or the bankers were negligent. There is an important public interest that those who are businessmen and businesswomen do not act in their business deceitfully and dishonestly with those with whom they do business.

Mr Latham, I remember, referred in his speech to a short shoplifting case where obviously dishonesty is at the centre of the issue that juries up and down the land have to decide day in and day out. Sometimes, where the facts are simple, it may be difficult for a jury to decide on questions of deception and dishonesty. Sometimes, where the facts are detailed, the decision itself may not be so difficult. That is entirely a matter for you, because you have now heard all the evidence and you are in the best position to make a judgement on these matters. ... (*Ibid.*, 29–30)

After a brief adjournment one of the three references to common-sense in this Summing-up occurs:

In deciding whether for instance you are sure that an individual offence is made out against NMB, you may take into account the evidence of any of the other banks I have referred to – ... – if you find that there is an underlying unity shown in their evidence as to make coincidence an affront to common sense. ... (*Ibid.*, 31)

Before the judge fully engages with the survey of evidence he explains that he will do so in the form of 'chapters' (introduction; deception of the banks; insurance; inside Arrow (the defendant's company); Binders; accountancy and insolvency; conspiracy to bring down Arrows (*ibid.*, 37–8).

It may be because he anticipates this method that he had anxiety over a similar division of labour within the jury. This may account for the emphatic use of 'all sure'. This interpretation is supported by his Direction:

There has been a great deal of evidence in this case, as I have already mentioned, and of course it is not to be divided up into teams or anything of that kind because it is all evidence for you to consider. ... (*Ibid.*, 37)

This was reasserted immediately before the jury withdrew for the first time to a hotel:

This is a Direction:
there shall be no further discussion about this case ... whilst you are there. There must not be any discussion in twos or threes; you follow the importance of that and that you will come back nice and fresh tomorrow and the discussion resumes once you are altogether (*sic*) in your room ... (4 July 1995 p.m., 24–5)

As far as jury address is concerned, they are not atypical:

		%
Members of the jury	210	75
We etc.	70	24
You the jury/the 12	3	
	283	(0.6 per page)

One cannot effectively compare the forms of address of the convicted defendant with his victims in this instance, because they were all institutions, named as such. The forms of address for the defendant were:

		%
Mr Naviede	380	54
Naviede	184	26
Th. Defendant	142	19
Mr/Muhammed N.	5	1
	711	

collated as 'Mr Naviede, Naviede the defendant', an intermediate construction in terms of credibility-weighting.

Most Summings-up contain some stylistic feature or features which contribute to their uniqueness. I have just mentioned one ('sure/all sure') which combines linguistic repetition with legal emphasis. Many Summings-up comprise quotations extracted from witnesses' statements. In *Naviede*, at 240 pages, they comprise more than half the Summing-up. The judicial interjections are usually brief reminders of who is talking; occasionally they are in question–answer form. It is from those lengthy quotations that another characteristic emerges. These quotations are laced with colloquialisms. When read seriatim they provide a particular kind of gloss to the narrative – from both sides – on the world of trade finance.

Colloquialism

'... those transactions were within the circle – cash up front – the rosy future – a leap of faith – came on stream – it was rubbish – a hands on man – a passive input – £74 million odd – you could not hold your head up high – not given a free rein to wander round – one of the Big Six – a number of cosmetic things – there was no horror story – nothing to cause a panic – go bust – a pack of lies – grab a mortgage – chapter and verse – the proposal was a circle – tittle tattle – a clean bill of health – step off cliffs hoping a ledge is there – make money out of thin air – tangibly unsecured – bargain basement values – sell captive customers stuck with me – gives added kudos – life is a cycle – machine could turn the handle and money would be produced – "get lost" – rent holiday – pushed through summer and winter economic climate – a down market description – a certain kudos – a conversation with pens down – my heart froze – he fudged that – trying to hurt me – it stank – making noises to all my banks – he got into a pickle – to hell with – he felt surrounded – the goodwill had gone up in smoke – belt and braces were necessary – a non starter – on the spot – sowing seeds for the future – on the spot – took you at face value – trying to introduce this into the woodwork without anyone noticing – thrashing around in the dark – it raised alarm bells – raised an alarm bell – alarm bells rang in my head – the picture did not really add up – coloured the mind – the hard core of the business – they went bonkers – would not ask British Airways if they were pig farming – the police were running around – coming on board – the key to the credit – it was the backstop – to the tune of £3 million – they were ripped off – there were shenanigans – a Dear John letter – to pull the rug under me – a squeaky clean report – the insurance long stop – their money was wrapped up in property – wrapped up in property – they could clone the company – a hands on approach – Mr N. looked on Arrows as a man looks at his family – to keep ahead of the game – his main forte – success breeds rumour – at the end of the day – petrified about people learning too much – all went up in smoke – the ultimate say – the pillars of your life – the no hopers – locked into a rollover – moving the goalposts – a clean bill of health – robbing Peter to pay Paul – the police did not want to go cavorting around – better than wandering around like an elephant – others muscling in – a broad brush description – only scratched the surface – down to the last halfpenny – appeared to be okay – I was trotting them out – the Bible for the use of the company – the reverse of the coin – a total revamping – spill the beans – stunned by – call the shots – on the quiet – trying to get a foot in the door – in ballpark figures – in a funny position – he was not my puppet – like headless chickens – living with the company – getting to grips with it – call it £20 million – hopelessly insolvent – recovery through that route – the whole thing collapsed like a pack of cards – they were a huge millstone trying to untangle it all – he lived with the company for all those years – if money had gone outside the net – the key thing is it did not go outside the net – rolled up – you should not touch it with a barge pole – we have the finger on the button – a soft or hard landing – it all seemed to peter out – to collapse the circle – they went bonkers – our relationship was soured – this saga – a file at the Bank of England that is asleep that will be brought to life and destroy you – a clean bill of health – they sort of went off – was sitting down with the police – a pens down discussion – don't touch them with a barge pole – had no axe to grind – he waved the report around – he dropped out of the picture – down like a pack of cards – creating waves – does not make happy reading – to let it lie – sending shivers through the market – a convenient conduit – not to cause shivers – having identified the fact that it contains a fuse and explosive, have failed to call it a bomb – robbing Peter to pay Paul – did not want to go cavorting around – better than wandering around – whittled down to six companies – I was put in a corner – I had to come off the fence – boiled down to bad debt – a Thank you and Good Night letter – using me as a sounding board – ringing me up for old time's sake – all something of a puzzle – it would end in tears – got off on the wrong foot – might end in tears – I was more of a hawk, earlier definitely a dove – to bounce ideas off – we do not sit on the Bill – it came out of the blue – has a meteoric rise ...'

Two questions can be put here. First, as a lawyer I was impressed by the judge's repetition of the Standard of proof as doubt in its approved lay form 'sure'. However, from the perspective of linguistic psychology one wonders whether such marked repetition can leave a trace of 'sureness' rather than 'unsureness'. The obvious way to test this experimentally would be by inverting the quotations to 'unsure' and then testing both versions with matched groups.

The other question is about the general impact of the colloquial language cited above. My personal reflex is that various adjectival – and equally colloquial – images arose on reading it: corner-cutting, dodgy, flash, gung-ho, for example. Again this could be tested experimentally. Since these are overwhelmingly from quotation of evidence, one is cautious to label this Summing-up as directional, unless one extends this description from simple linguistic analysis to analysis of the judge's choice of what to quote in the Summing-up.

On the morning of 3 July the jury sent a Note on counts 1 and 3. After discussion with counsel and Mr Naviede the jury were called back and an elaboration of the Direction on 'permanently to deprive' and 'at the time when the representation was made knew it to be false and intended to deceive . . .' was given.

After three days deliberation conviction verdicts were entered unanimously.

Seil – acquittal of fraud

This was a Serious Fraud Office prosecution of company directors for fraudulent trading under the Companies Act 1985 s.458. The trial lasted more than five weeks; the Summing-up covered several days.

Legal instructions

I have had to be selective in quoting these as they are very lengthy.

The judge–jury demarcation

The style of Summing-up in this Serious Fraud Office trial is in many ways different to the others discussed. For example, the 'demarcation' is not made at the beginning of the Summing-up. The nearest to such a statement is:

> Now we move to that portion of this long trial where you and I have our special parts to play. (4E)
> . . . and I know that you have equally been painstaking and careful in your notes and your underlinings and your highlighting of the references and your jotting down of the page references . . . because I have been watching you do it over all these weeks. (4G) (similarly at 23DE)

There is assistance in a Direction over the approach to be taken to considering the evidence:

> Secondly. Ladies and gentlemen, you must bring to your consideration a dispassionate approach, an even-handed approach either way.
> You see these are very grave matters (× 4) ... (7BC)

The jury role is then given at some length and leads into the Burden of proof:

> I think when I started at the Bar a long time ago there was still some feeling about in the minds of some jurors that the judge was the man who knew about the case, a man who had experience – not many women in those days – and that the judge would give them some sort of hint or indication as to what the proper verdict should be. Ladies and gentlemen, I think that even in those days such jurors who had got such an idea were wrong and I am here to tell you categorically, ladies and gentlemen, that you will get no indication or hint from me. I have put to you as clearly as I may that the verdict is solely for you. That is not my responsibility, I can walk away from this case without that responsibility. That is yours. I think it was Mr Rhodes in his very careful submissions to you who used the phrase that only you the jury stood between his client and the power of the state. I never actually thought of myself in that form of phraseology – I have never really considered I had personified the power of the state, it sounds very impressive – but I do take the point that he was making and there is, ladies and gentlemen, a sort of passing of power, the sharing of responsibility between you and me and it turns upon your verdict. When you come to retire next week these defendants will be in your charge and upon the verdicts that you reach will lie their future. If you come back into court and say in regard to one or more or all Not Guilty I will discharge them. If you come back into court and say in regard to one or more or all he is Guilty then I will proceed to sentence him but that fundamental responsibility, ladies and gentlemen, is entirely, wholly for you. (I 10A–D)

The problem of memory

> ... I'm very conscious, ladies and gentlemen, that in the approximately 12 to 14 hours spread out over 3 days that I have been talking to you and you have very patiently and courteously given at least the appearance of listening to me, I have covered evidence that was spread out over 10 weeks ... They will be matters that will either be in your collective memory, because talking together you will bring together your memories of what the picture was and certainly your memory will be stimulated about all the documentation. (50D)

Burden and Standard of proof

This Summing-up runs the Burden and Standard of proof together, with the Standard of proof occurring first.

> You can only convict if you are sure that they were men seeing what they

judged they could get away with. Ladies and gentlemen that as I say is something to bring your thoughts together on this matter. I turn to try to help you on a different point. I think it is proper that I should explain this ladies and gentlemen. I have to move on now to deal with certain matters of which you will certainly be tempted to say why on earth is Judge P . . . taking up his time, our time by telling us these matters, we know them. Mr Price explained them more than once, other counsel have developed rightly upon them and there are certain matters, ladies and gentlemen, where you may well say, 'Well we have had the good fortune to live in this country. We know about the burden of proof and so on.' Ladies and gentlemen I accept all those points but I make not the slightest apology for dealing with these matters with you because they are of such fundamental importance that each and every defendant is entitled to hear the judge presiding at his trial direct his jury upon them. (I 9B–D)

This is developed further two pages later at some length.

Ladies and gentlemen given that burden lies squarely upon the Crown of course you are going to ask, 'However far does the Crown have to persuade us before we say right we are persuaded, one or more or all of those men whom we have seen day after day, week after week, sitting across the court room from us, they are criminals. They are guilty.' Well, ladies and gentlemen, of course you would not contemplate assuming the responsibility of saying of a man, he is a criminal, he is guilty, unless you are sure now, if you are sure then of course your duty lies plain before you and you accept that responsibility. If you are sure guilt is made out then the verdict is guilty. If you are less than sure then the Crown have failed and the verdict is Not Guilty. I emphasise it I think this way, ladies and gentlemen, because it is of great importance in any matter and it is of particular importance in a case where your attention has been drawn to such an enormous wealth of material and of evidence and where day after day you have had submissions on this point and on that. So I put it to you in this way, that when on Wednesday, as I anticipate it will be Wednesday early afternoon, you retire to consider your verdict when you have discussed it and thought about it together I suggest to you that there are only three states of mind in which you can be. I put it extremely as it were simply to emphasise the point. One of your states of mind might be,
'Oh we have weighed this up, we have considered it, we have had in mind everything that has been urged upon us and it is quite clear to us these are guilty men, we are sure.'
That is straight-forward enough; back you come into court:
'Guilty, Guilty, Guilty';
this one, that one or more, or all but where you are sure where it is clear to you: 'Guilty'.
On the other hand and taking the other extreme, Ladies and Gentlemen, it may be that you will say to each other,
'We have sat here for weeks. These are innocent men, we can't think of how they were brought here. They should never have been put in the dock at all.'
I am putting you at the extreme, Ladies and Gentlemen. Obviously if that was your state of mind clearly you would be only too pleased to hurry back into court to say,

> 'Not Guilty let's end all this.'
> The only third state of mind between those two extremes can surely only be this, where it may be that you are saying to yourselves,
> 'Well this is very odd isn't it. No doubt a lot of money got lost. No doubt a lot of those perfectly respectable looking bankers said well they didn't realise what was happening they wouldn't have dealt in this way. It is quite clear there are one or two little incidents that seem very curious.'
> You might be of a frame of mind where you are saying to each other
> 'This is pretty suspicious. Very likely there was dishonest goings on here, very likely they were deceiving people.'
> Ladies and Gentlemen, if the sort of phrase I have just used that it is suspicious, that very likely there was dishonesty; if that sort of phrase describes your state of mind when you have discussed it and considered it together then once again the verdict is Not Guilty. Of course on the ordinary use of the English language, if you are saying that is very suspicious of course by implication you are saying that,
> 'I am not certain about it',
> and if you say to yourselves,
> 'Very likely that man has committed an offence';
> of course again you are reserving in your own thoughts that possibly he did not and while that possibility is there, Ladies and Gentlemen, you cannot say you are sure and you cannot convict. It comes down I think to something I can put to you very shortly. Although I have emphasised it to you as strongly as I could. All that I have been saying over the last seven or eight minutes can I think probably be summed up in thirty or forty seconds in this way. There are two words in English that come from one word in Latin. The two words are these you don't convict a man unless you are convinced that he is guilty. If you are convinced you can convict him. If you are less than convinced him you throw the case out. (11C-12E)

At the conclusion of the second afternoon of Summing-up a reminder was given (51BC) and at the beginning of the brief finale on the third morning of Summing-up, a further reminder was given of the Standard of proof and specificity of verdicts (1FG).

The judicial Disclaimer

The Disclaimer in the Summing-up occurred during its second day:

> And similarly, Ladies and Gentlemen, never forget your responsibility to find the facts. Why I mention it again is simply this. If as we go through the evidence together I make any sort of comment. Well, if you find it helpful, that is fine because I'm sitting here trying to be helpful, but if you take a different view on a question of evidence or a witness or what you could draw from the evidence; if you take a different view from what my comments suggest, it's your view that counts and if as I have said, if I make a comment and you agree with it and find it helpful – fine – if I make a comment on the evidence on the facts and you say:
> 'No. No. I don't accept that, that's your right.'

> You don't accept anything other than your own decision on questions of the evidence and of the facts. (II 14EF)

Role of the jury as legitimator

In this Summing-up the representative role of the jury in assessing 'dis/honesty' in business practice is made clear:

> ... because, never forget you come into this courtroom to represent the British public. You are sitting there to represent the community and what you think is honest, is honest; what you think is dishonest, that is dishonest. I have no definition of dishonesty or honesty, that is for you. (14A)

and

> ... You as the jury must first decide whether according to the ordinary standard of reasonable and honest people what was done was dishonest. (14G)

The issue of dishonesty

Being a trial of fraudulent trading, the issue of dishonesty was the issue for the jury throughout this trial. There is of course an important difference semantically between dishonesty and lying or falsehood. There is a long section early in the Summing-up on dishonesty in general:

> ... you ask,
> 'Do we think that what was done here was dishonest according to our standards',
> because never forget you come into this court room to represent the British public, you are sitting there to represent the community and what you think is honest that is honest, what you think is dishonest that is dishonest; ... Your first point is this. You weigh up what you find happened and ask yourselves, 'Do we consider this dishonest'.
> If you say to yourselves and to each other:
> 'No that is not dishonest; we are ordinary decent folk, we are ordinary decent business people, we don't think that is dishonest',
> then there is an end of the Crown case. Dishonest according to what you think is honest or dishonest is fundamental and if you don't think that is dishonesty, if you think that is acceptable they are Not Guilty – end of Crown case, but supposing you say to yourselves,
> 'We have weighed this up, we have applied our common-sense and common experience to it, that was dishonest',
> then you have to ask a second question and the second question is simply this, Ladies and Gentlemen, did the particular defendant whom you are considering at that moment, did he in his mind at the time think that what was happening was dishonest? I put it this way, did the thought in his mind run along these lines,
> 'I know what I am doing and I know that ordinary decent business folk will consider what I am doing is dishonest but I am going to go on doing it',

> which as I say there is a two-fold step, first, was what happened dishonest in your view? If you consider it wasn't end of case – end of story. If you think it was dishonest then that second question: was that the state of mind of each particular defendant, and only if you are satisfied that there was dishonesty in that defendant's mind you knew. He knew he was doing something people like yourself would say,
> 'That is not on, that is dishonest'.
> Only if you take those two steps can you begin to move towards a conviction ...
> The way I put it for you, is this a finding of dishonesty, is fundamental before any defendant can be convicted of either count... This is the first leg as I was telling you about a moment ago. If it was not dishonest by those standards that is the end of the matter and the prosecution fails. If it was dishonest by those standards then you as the jury must consider each defendant because of course you are going to be considering them individually and you must consider whether each defendant, each individual man, realised that what he was doing was by those standards dishonest. In most cases where the actions are obviously dishonest by ordinary standards there will be no doubt about it, it will be obvious that the defendant himself knew that he was acting dishonestly It is dishonesty for a defendant to act in a way which he knows ordinary people consider to be dishonest even if he asserts or genuinely believes that he was morally justified. I appreciate the imposition there, Ladies and Gentlemen, if something is dishonest by your standards and is known by everybody to be dishonest it is no good somebody coming forward and saying,
> 'Oh yes I have a particular ideal deep in my heart and I felt I was justified in doing it.'
> That is no answer. If it is dishonest and the person you are dealing with knows it's dishonest, well then that element of the offence is made out. (*Ibid.*, 14–15)

After two more pages of development this is further developed eight pages later and moves into the 'good character' Direction:

> Two questions, Ladies and Gentlemen, that every judge suggests every jury should ask when they come to evaluate the witnesses. Straightforward enough the first question as you go through the list of witnesses, you ask yourselves:
> 'Did we think that this witness was being honest with us?'
> I have already said that there is very little substantial challenge to the narrative of facts here but you will remember that some witnesses have been challenged in cross-examination and if you form the view that any witness had been dishonest with you on any point of course you would want to give time – would you not – to pondering why should that witness have been dishonest. Just a word of caution, Ladies and Gentlemen, do have very much in mind if you were to find that any witness had been dishonest that, if you were to find that, do have in mind there may be different reasons for it ...
> but I am also concerned, Ladies and Gentlemen, with a second question that I invite you to ask when you are assessing each witness and that is if you are sure of honesty you ask whether the witness was in fact accurate. That is a very different kettle of fish isn't it because a witness can be as honest as the day is long, can be trying to do his or her best to help you to the best of their ability

> but they are mistaken and you, Ladies and Gentlemen, have to ponder that possibility in assessing your witnesses as well. (*Ibid.*, 18–19)

'Good character' and 'propensity'

There is a page of standard material on the good character of all four defendants followed by half a page on its relation to credibility, which leads into a further two pages on propensity.

Within this context on the second day, a formal, drafted Warning Direction was given.

There was also a general reminder on 'dishonesty' at the very end of the Summing-up (III 3A–F).

The right to silence

In this major trial none of the defendants gave evidence in court. This was instructed upon both early and late in the Summing-up; the first day:

> The Crown has seen fit to launch this prosecution against these defendants. The Crown has made the accusation. It is entirely up to the Crown to prove it if the Crown can. At no time from start to finish does any responsibility pass to the defendants through the [*inaudible*], and indeed ladies and gentlemen, in the way this case has evolved we have a very good example, we have – as it were – the classic example of the working of that system. Because not one of the defendants has called any evidence and I direct you at once and in the straightest terms that you will in no sense draw any inference adverse to these defendants or any one of them because they did not give evidence. There is no requirement for them to give evidence. Any one of us who is accused is entitled to come to court and say.
>
> 'Very well you have accused me. I have told the court I am not guilty, now you get on and prove it if you can and I will not say a word.'
>
> That is a perfectly straightforward legal position to take any one of us is entitled to take. These defendants have taken it and I emphasise again, you do not for a moment draw any inference adverse, you don't say to yourselves, 'Oh well they didn't explain anything to us did they', they don't have to. It is entirely up to the Crown if the Crown can to make you sure – and I will come to that in a moment – of the case that they bring. I think it proper just to say one further word by way of emphasis, you may well have read in the papers over recent weeks and months that the government has various plans, papers are referred to as threats to the right to silence, the right of silence and so on. Please put any such thoughts from your mind. However whatever the government may or may not do in the future I am telling you the law as it is and that is quite straightforward. No adverse inference to be drawn against a defendant who says, 'You have brought me here. I challenge your case. I am not going to say a word; by my plea of Not Guilty I say to you you are wrong.' (I 10F 113) (also III 1A-B)

Linguistic aspects of Seil

Forms of address

The jury

		%
Ladies and gentlemen	551	67
We etc.	226	27
'We' etc.	30	4
Members of the Jury	5	1
You the Jury	3	–
	815	(130 pp.: 6.5 per page)

This is an extremely intensive example of jury address. The less distanced but courtesy form 'Ladies and Gentlemen' predominates (at 4.3 per page). In addition first person plural forms, both explicit and implicative, are frequent at about 2 per page. This is a model of insistent, polite, cooperative address form.

The defendants
In this complex Summing-up relating to four defendants, one cannot always link nomenclature to person, as in:

The men	3	The Siddiquis	26
		Mr Siddiqui	22
The defendants	60	The Siddiqui brothers	6
	63		54

but one can examine the nomenclature of specified defendants:

Lesley Couzens	3	Maurice Croft	5
Les Couzens	1		
Les	1		
L. Couzens	1		
The defendant Couzens	1	The defendant Maurice Croft	1
Mr Couzens	140	Mr Croft	86
	147		92
Nadim Siddiqui	9	Rehan Siddiqui	14
Nadim	2	Rehan	2
N. Siddiqui	1	R. Siddiqui	1
Mr N. Siddiqui	1	Mr R. Siddiqui	1
	–	Mr Rehan Siddiqui	7
	(13)		25

Although the term 'defendants' occurs frequently (60 times) it is not personalized except once each against the two least significant defendants (Couzens, Croft), and then with their names. They are overwhelmingly referred to as 'Mr'. With the leading Siddiqui director first names predominate, but presumably this is done to differentiate brothers.

Appeals to common-sense
There were seven such references.

> but supposing you say to yourselves, 'We have weighed this up, we have applied our *common sense* and common experience to it, that (it) was dishonest', then you have to ask a second question ... (14C)
> As your *common sense* will suggest, if a crime has been committed, it is still a crime, whether it was done on the Monday, or the Tuesday, or the Wednesday ... (16A)
> There again, ladies and gentlemen, you apply your *common sense* and your experience as to the standards that you expect of ordinary people engaged in business ... (17F)
> You look at all those surrounding circumstances and you apply your collective *common sense* to all of those ... do those surrounding circumstances when we apply our collective *common sense* to them compel us to draw one inference ... (19AB)

These five usages are all connected to the key word 'dishonest' and the jury's role in interpreting it. The next usage, two days later is not in fact the same, since it lacks the appeal to the collective which is the normative basis of *common sense*.

> There it is ladies and gentlemen, it may well be that your *common sense* and experience of life might suggest to you that to dispose of something as a going concern is probably a more profitable thing to do than disposing of it on a break up basis ... (8D)

The final usage again appeals to the collective but it also is not as central as the original group of five usages on 'dishonesty':

> ... ladies and gentlemen you may feel that Mr Shorock was, as it were, simply using Mr Brereton to bring to your attention a matter which your *common sense* would suggest to you Mr Brereton agreed that he would expect Seil to have regard to their auditor's view. (47E)

Exemplification
Fairly early in the Summing-up the trial judge had to deal with the 'joint enterprise' aspect of charges made against the four individuals. He then provided a detailed contrastive example (20C–F):

> I give you an example out of a wholly different field of crime. I have quite deliberately taken it totally remote from here. Supposing we were to have, let

us say, three men and they are drinking in a pub in the evening and they run out of money and they look a bit dolefully at each other because they want to go on drinking, they have run out of money and then one of them says, 'there is a neighbour of mine with a new video set or a new colour television and I happen to know that he is out tonight', and the others say, 'how splendid', and one of them says, 'well I have got my own van outside; if I was round in the back street and you went in and pinched his video or what-have-you, I would be on hand to whip off with it in my van and dispose of it for a few quid and we can go on drinking', and the third man says, 'I know the local CID fellas by sight – I know they are in plain clothes but I know them; I will keep watch on the corner and I will give a whistle if I see a plain clothes man round and about'; and so that is what is done and the man on the corner keeps watch against the plain clothes man or whoever or any policeman coming along, the other man has his van round in the back street and third man actually kicks in the kitchen door of the back of the house goes in and takes the television set. All three of those men are equally responsible for that burglary. The man who stood on the corner to keep an eye out for the policeman, the man in the back street with the van to take the thing away, they are as equally responsible for that burglary as the man who actually kicked in his neighbour's door and carried the TV set out because they were all acting together in the common plan, common agreed plan.

Technical terms

Technical terms must present many difficulties for juries, not least legal technicalities. In general, one can say that they raise the problem of comprehension. In the group of acquittals studied here the most striking set of technical terms occurred in *Seil*. The majority were simultaneously legal terms and the jargon of the finance industry, but they did not appear to be central to the issue of dishonest trading when insolvent. They included five types of company and twelve types of credit.

However, the most potent technical terms were metaphorical colloquialisms: 'A Golden Child' (10F, 23C); and that on which much of the evidence of dishonesty turned: 'Pig on Pork' (5A, 18EG, 19A, 15A, 16C): financial trading without equivalent financial security or other back-up.

Questions

One of the witnesses, a Seil employee, elicited a battery of serial questions, all of the 'Wh-' type, except the two 'did you think' questions:

- *What* did you think of that lady?
- ... competent, you may very well feel – ... but *what* did you think and ... *did* you think her evidence honest?
- *Did* you think her evidence accurate?
- *What* was the picture that she gave?
- *What* was Miss T ...'s position in all this?
- *What* was Miss T ...'s reaction to it all?
- *What* happened then?

Sarcasm

... that lady was not, you may feel *one of the major players* in the banking world ... (8G)

Bathos

There is a reference to the credentials of senior employees of the bankrupt firm: 'were not men who faced a black abyss of emptiness if that job went' (10D).

Repetitive emphasis

The *obvious anxiety, the inescapable anxiety* to have these properly audited accounts. (2E)
There are masses of documents and you may say, we have to look and look and look ... (4B)
Common ground (× 3) (5B)
prepared to risk other people's interests, other people's property, other people's business. (13B)
(Mr Croft) folly, foolishness ... foolishness ... foolishness ... folly ... (5B,F)
(Mr Couzens) baleful influence (× 2) (6C)
No one could fail (× 3) (6C)
the very real mess, the appalling mess ... book-keeping ... (7B)
the sort of thing you have seen again and again and again ... (6B) ... again and again (7C, 8A)
Bills going through and going through and more bills and more bills without any trade underlying them. (21C)
No doubt at all ... (× 2) (22C)
... a careful company with careful businessmen taking careful steps. (30D)

Trope consciousness

... would strengthen the Seil Group if *I can put it that way. I use the word very colloquially* – the Seil business interests, *let's call it* – but which went desperately wrong. (39A)
I use the colloquial 'a brown envelope job' – notes in an envelope. (16F)

Colloquialism

There were twenty colloquial usages. As we have just seen the Judge twice states that he is being colloquial. I shall only cite one of these here, because the other is in fact part of an extended chain of metaphor. The others are:

17A	... payment ... *on the nail*
25B	That is a very *different kettle of fish.*
	... *as honest as the day is long.*
17A	*gone bust ...*
20A	*hopelessly bust*
17A	*pull your horns in*
17B	I am not going to ask you to *heave* too many ...
18E	that *sounded alarm bells*

2B	my blood pressure was *all over the show*
7G	*our old friend* 'pig on pork' (technical)
13D	given *food for thought* as to the necessity of weighing up accuracy
15B	*put it in a nutshell*
36C	*at the end of the day* I believe we would be on *dodgy ground* ...
16F	(Express) I use the colloquial, *a brown envelope job*, notes in an envelope.
32C	Do you *pull the plug on* trade, or trade *on out* (and 34C)
35A	If they had known *the full picture.*
49B	that was *in the wind*
50B	His was a *crass* throwing away of money.

Taken serially these quotations from *Seil* may connote some of the character of the colloquialisms quoted in *Naviede*, but they do not permeate or dominate the narrative as was so strikingly the case in *Naviede*.

Metaphor

In this Summing-up of 130 pages there are a number of metaphors, but what is salient is their interrelationship.

(1) 'The pictures become clearer and clearer with painstaking detail and care. (4F)
... to bring that vast canvas, that large picture into a realistic whole. (14B)

(2) The shipwreck ... (5C)
(*Mixed Metaphor*) ... under whom the banks pulled the rug ... (5D)
... that turbulence in the financial stream (7E) ... ripple (8A)
... venture had failed, the wreckage is strewn all over the place. (27C)
... Don't throw it overboard simply because I haven't mentioned it in my summary. (14D, also 15G, 2D)
... the ship was sinking or the business appeared to be falling apart ... (37E)
... Instead of being something which buoyed up Seil ... it became something that pulled it down. (39A)
Junitext was there, wallowing as it were, in the wash and the waves left behind by the Oakwood failure. (40B)

(3) ... she was no inexperienced cog in the machine ... (8G)
... Siddiqui brothers ... the dynamos within the operation of Seil ... (24A)
... rather a minor cog in the machinery of the office ... (28A)

(4) Mr Croft's business activities can be described as being the vulturous sector of commerce. (35G)
... one final flicker, as it were, of life in regard to this business. (37E)
Junitext was haemorrhaging, just flowing away.' (50B)

The first group (1) concern the relationship between advocacy and jury deliberation and verdict. It is the other three groups which are most interesting. Do they relate to each other, and if so how?

Unlike *Naviede* I am arguing here that metaphor rather than colloquialism is a permeating and central feature in *Seil*.

The charge in this case was fraudulent trading under s.458 Companies Act 1983:

> if any business of a company is carried on with intent to defraud creditors of the company or creditors of any other person for any fraudulent purpose, every person who is knowingly a party to it is committing an offence.

The extended metaphor of shipwreck envisages a ship at the mercy of natural forces in which management does not, cannot control or avoid but of reactive and desperate, futile crisis-management.

However, the next group of metaphor must be mediated with that primary series of natural forces overwhelming the hapless craft. The craft evidently has an engine with cogs, dynamos and machinery. The Siddiqui brothers are certainly in charge of this, but it is the engine they control, *not* the ship.

The last group of metaphor reinvests the situation in nature, as a dying body in raw nature. This group was pronounced in reversed chronological sequence. Here I restate it: 'was haemorrhaging, just flowing away; there was one final flicker of life; the vultures ...'

These powerful images extend over the entire body of the Summing-up. Their salience belies a subtlety: the four defendants are constituted as technical managers rather than as directors of their company, that is as persons of limited responsibility, and as we shall see, were envisaged as being victims of the business cycle as a natural force.

There are other metaphors. One which occurs several times may be better understood as a technical term: 'could not follow/lose the Audit trail' (7B). Also 'within a whisker of a clean audit' (11G).

The heart of fraud is the motive for actions being dishonest. The jury's role is particularly to act as a collective barometer on dishonesty in relation to actions described in court. This is not a technical legal matter and the Directions in *Seil* are clear on that. In a Serious Fraud Office prosecution such as this the great bulk of the business actions and transactions which the jury had to evaluate were quite outside ordinary experience, as was the language describing them.

What the judge does through the Survey of evidence is to contextualize those actions and transactions, in relation to his perception of commerce, including financial trade, and the economic history or 'climate' of the time. Here I focus on that context.

> Secondly, ladies and gentlemen, you must bring to your consideration a dispassionate approach, an even handed approach either way. You see these are very grave matters. They are manifestly very grave matters for the defendants, very serious indeed, men of good character here before the court, been here for

weeks in your charge awaiting your verdict, but of course these are very grave matters from the public's point of view as well. I cannot think that you would for a moment fall into the trap of any sort of over simplification, any sort of simply saying, 'Oh well these bankers they have come up from London and indeed in what we have heard about them and from them, the six million or so that is the sort of figure that is mentioned as loss in this matter is pretty small so far as those men are concerned.' As I say, ladies and gentlemen, I am sure that you would not fall into such an over simplification because on an instant thought it will of course have come into your minds that wherever there is – and I am deliberately seeking a totally neutral word and I will put it this way – wherever there is turbulence or unexpected movements in the finances of the community those unexpected movements, that turbulence in the financial stream – if I can put it that way – has very grave effects on individuals and you may feel but it is a matter entirely for you that you saw and listened to two individuals who were very deeply distressed by financial turbulence. (17C–E)
. . . Mr Rhodes put it to him quite straightly would it not have been, he said, more honourable when Mr Price was asking you those questions to have told us that you were aware that there were errors in what schedules documents you were putting forward. That witness made this quite remarkable reply, and it may well have stayed in your mind as it stayed in mine and you will give that witness credit for the fact that he had then been in the witness box two and possibly into his third day and had been much pressed by counsel, but what he said was honour doesn't come into it. It is a question of judgment. Ladies and gentlemen in this court room honour does come into it. Honour is fundamental to the workings of the law, to you doing your duty and to me doing mine and it is fundamental of course to business transactions. I would invite you to look at it in this way. I say again and I will give you precise directions as to the law in a moment. If you look to that phrase, honour doesn't come into it, it is a question of judgment. In that context wasn't that witness conveying to you, 'You don't have to do what is right, what everyone would think proper, it is a question of judgment, what can you get away with.' Ladies and gentlemen have this in your thoughts, if you are sure that one Mr Siddiqui, the other Mr Siddiqui, Mr Craft, Mr Couzens, if you are sure that their state of mind in regard to what was happening in their business and the way they were conducting it, if you are sure that their state of mind came under that phrase, it is a question of judgment, it is what you can get away with, if you are sure of that then you can consider moving towards convicting them. But if you take the view that in their own minds they were or in your view they may have been behaving honourably doing what they thought was right, doing what they thought was acceptable to the public as a whole, then of course the Crown would fail. You can only convict if you are sure that they were men seeing what they judged they could get away with. (8E–9B)
. . . Well matters moved on into those harder times that you may feel were totally connected with the recession which every one of us in this Court Room knows of our own knowledge was in fact developing through this period and it was early in '91, January of that time when at a meeting between Bullmore and the Siddiquis it was made clear to the Siddiquis that the facility should reduce at a hundred thousand pounds per month, so as it would work down to half a million; and it was quite clear and you could understand it that the Siddiquis were very unhappy about that decision. (III 14D)

> ... He covered some ground that was of course familiar to us, ladies and gentlemen, it's I'm sure unchallenged common ground that of course Seil's customers were vulnerable businesses in time of recession. He knew from the very start of the case, ladies and gentlemen, traders, small businesses went to Seil, paid the expensive rates that Seil you may feel charged because they couldn't get help from the ordinary banks and so of course they were vulnerable when recession came, but it was agreed by Mr Brereton that those customers would be dependent on Seil and would often need repeat bills for on-going trade. Well as I say this is familiar ground, ladies and gentlemen, and in their turn of course Seil was dependent on the discount banks and by early '91 again it's unchallenged the discount banks were anxious to reduce their exposure. (III 46CD)

Conclusion

My contention is that this Summing-up is directional towards acquittal, unlike *Naviede*, which supported conviction but was not directional!

The components of directionality are unusual in that they include the exceptionally lengthy and emphatic nomotic elements, most of which I have had to edit out. Additionally there is a structural relationship between the Directions on dis/honesty, the meta-Mythos of the trading 'climate' in which the issue Mythos is contextualized and the series of metaphors on responsibility. The overall impact of such historical contextualization and particularly the series of naturalist metaphors injected may not go so far as to construct businessmen as victims, but does move them away from a control and responsibility model of directorial behaviour to one of internal and limited authority: of management rather than direction.

The jury at Liverpool Crown Court acquitted.

Two policemen on trial

'Abernethy' – conviction of a policeman

This case is analysed so as to provide a balance to '*Lowe*' (see below), where the Police Constable was acquitted. In other respects the cases are not similar. The accusation was that the driver of a police car had driven recklessly around a car-park – largely empty of cars – scattering the orderly crowd who had congregated to avoid an incident in the town centre. The car had grazed the victim, who went up to the car and told the driver to 'fuck off'. The driver – it was alleged – then smashed her in the face cracking her lip and breaking a tooth, then he drove off. This occurred at about 22.10 in July. The case involved a high level of forensic material for the judge to cover and for the jury to cope with. The defendant exercised his right of silence throughout, but put in a written statement. There was a *Galbraith* application witnessed by the jury for a directed acquittal but the ruling immediately before the Summing-up was that this was a case that could go to the jury. In addition as part of its deliberation the jury had to decide whether the car-park constituted a 'highway', an issue of mixed fact and law, for the purposes of the reckless driving charge.

Linguistic features of the Summing-up

Forms of address

(1) This was an address-intensive and a cooperative mode Summing-up:

We etc.	88	66%
Members of the jury	37	
	125 (41 pp.: 3 per page)	

This was accompanied by precatory form usages (see below (3)).

(2) Defendant and victim differentials

		%			%
Mr Abernethy	15	30	Miss Dwyer	20	80
PC Abernethy	8	20	Claire Dwyer	4	10
Th. man	8	20	Th. girl	4	10
Th. accused	6	15			
Abercrombie	4				
Th. policeman	1				
	42			25	

These can be collated as:

Mr Abernethy – PC Abernethy, the man accused;
Miss Dwyer

(3) Precatory forms
These reinforce the cooperative mode of jury address:

> Can I just say rather more to you, I am afraid, about that. (p. 6)
> Now, can I just say now a word to you please about another matter ... (p. 12)
> Can I just say this to you. (p. 12)
> ... so, please do not forget it. (p. 13)
> Please remember again what I have told you. (p. 14)
> Can we then start please, by ... (p. 16)
> Could you have these, please, in front of you (p. 36)
> Can we look, please at these entries ... (p. 37)

Fixed expressions and appeals to common-sense
The most significant set of terms are appeals to the-order-of-things:

Clearly	1
No doubt	4
Obviously	8
Of course	32
	45

> ... and in the end, you use that well known faculty, your own *common-sense*, and your own knowledge of how your fellow human beings behave, in order to reach a conclusion. (p. 4)

On police car radio CAD entries:

> It may mean that – it must mean at any rate in *common-sense*, members of the jury – at any rate they are 'fairly near', but what that means, unfortunately itself is not altogether certain. (p. 37)

In the context of 'we' (×5):

> Where he was when he got this assignment, again, we do not know, although it is obviously *common-sense* to take the view that he must have been somewhere reasonably near, otherwise they would not have assigned him to go and do it. (p. 39)

Metaphor
The metaphor level is not high, nor are the instances intensive. This single indicator suggests a low 'directionality' in this Summing-up.

(1) The term 'ingredient' (rather than the technical 'element') of a crime occurs twice (pp. 6, 8). This use is so widespread that it may now be a 'dead' metaphor.

(2) The 'shepherding' of crowds away from an incident occurs several times. This image is strongly contrastive of the driver of the police car, which one could metaphorize as 'corgi like'.
(3) 'I think what you have to understand about them [the CAD car radio entries] is this: that they obviously are documents which have *the seeds of danger within them*. The person who made up the documents, that is to say made the entry on computer terminals, is not a witness' (p. 36).
(4) 'Members of the jury, that is one of the problems that arises. It is one of the problems with which you have to *wrestle*. It would clearly have been easier for you to *wrestle* with it had you had before you the actual operator of the machine . . .' (p. 41).

Colloquialism
Compared to metaphor, the level of colloquialism in this Summing-up is high. By this I mean judicial colloquialism rather than colloquialism in witness quotations as in *Naviede*. This level is congruent with the high cooperative level of the jury address form:

> there is nothing magic about being a member of the jury (p. 4)
> you do not lump them together (p. 5)
> no matter how hardened a villain . . . (p. 11)
> to churn over what you have heard (p. 15)
> with some sort of minor disturbance or fracas . . . (p. 18)
> . . . the police had reason to believe that there might be bother . . . the majority of the bother was going to be in . . . (p. 19)
> doing a figure-of-eight in the car park (p. 26)
> . . . told them to move on or they would be 'nicked' (p. 27)
> – I was going to say gung ho . . . (p. 36)
> . . . come from outside determined on getting a piece of the action . . . (p. 36)
> this is another bit of bother . . . (p. 38)
> . . . the TSG, the chaps with the riot shields in transit vans (p. 38)
> Take that or leave it, depending on how you view it (p. 44)
> . . . draw his truncheon and belt Miss Dwyer (p. 44)

Enumeration
There are a number of clusters of enumeration in this Summing-up which I will not discuss here.

Parenthesis
This is widespread.

Exemplification
There is only one exemplification, and it is an important one, though it is not announced as such:

> It obviously needs very careful consideration, and in particular in such circumstances as this where it said to depend upon the evidence of various

> witnesses and documents. Clearly, every witness sees a particular event from a different standpoint, and it is often said that if you put four separate people at four separate corners of a crossroads, and you tell them that two motor vehicles were going to drive along there and collide, and that is what does happen, and you thereafter ask them to describe what happened, you will get four different accounts. That is, of course, because we all see things from our own particular standpoint, and that is particularly so, of course, where events occur quickly, where they are unexpected, where they occur in the hours of darkness and when people are excited; so it is that these matters that the Crown put before you will obviously demand and need careful consideration. (pp. 10–11)

Repetitive emphasis

There are few such tropes, but they are effectively deployed:

> . . . and you will not speculate yourself about those who could, or might, or should, or would, or whatever have given evidence . . . (p. 11)
> . . . do not speculate as to why that man, this man, or that woman, this woman has not come here to give you the benefit of their recollection . . . (p. 12)

Those two instances are supportive and with shared morphology. The next two are antitheta:

> Whether he went to W.H. End, we do not know.
> Whether he acknowledged the assignment . . . we do not know, or whether he was distracted . . . we do not know.
> Where he was going when he got this assignment, again we do not know . . .
> . . . bearing in mind what we know about these entries . . .
> . . . we all know that dog-van went to C. . . We all know that PC X. . . was driving it. We all know that the computer operator got it wrong . . . and we know that in fact that was not the van that went at all . . . (pp. 39–41)

There is a short series of lie-stem remarks against the defendant towards the end of the Summing-up:

> The overwhelming influence (*sic*) the Crown suggest, is that the statement is a lie: a lie in two senses: first of all because . . ., and secondly it is a lie because . . . (p. 44)

However, in terms of structure this is followed by a reprise of the Standard of proof in an implicature first person singular serial question which also combines repetition:

> Secondly, am I satisfied so that I am sure that . . . somebody did drive recklessly, and then say to yourselves:
>
> > 'Well, am I sure either of those offences were committed; am I sure that it was PC A who assaulted her, and I (*sic*) am, sure that it was PC A who drove recklessly? . . .'

... you then have to ask:

> 'well, am I satisfied so I am sure that it was indeed the accused man? ...'

However, if on contemplation, members of the jury, you say to yourselves:

> 'Well it certainly could have been him, might well have been him', then, of course he is entitled to be acquitted ... (p. 45)

Quotations

There are four implicatures which frame the narrative fragments:

Well, it was done in self-defence (p. 6)
Well, that is no good. (p. 7)
You have brought these charges, you go ahead and prove them. (p. 10)
Well, since he has not given evidence, we nevertheless have an account from him of what he tells us he did that night because we have the statement which he gave to the investigating officers. (p. 10)

The others are from witnesses and form the core of the Mythos:

I recognised the driver as a local policeman, or a policeman who has been in E ... from time to time. (p. 13)
... it clipped my leg. (p. 23)
Fuck-off. (p. 23)
He hit me with a long dark object. (p. 23)
All my teeth, fell out. (p. 23)
Skidding about like. (p. 23)
It was a policeman. I've seen him in E ... (p. 27)
He ... has never given me a name, nor have I ever been in a courtroom when I have heard it being given ... I can say this: that that policeman has, if one heard him speak, a Scots accent. (p. 27)
Fuck-off. (p. 30)
There was blood all over her hands, her jumper and her face. (p. 30)
I felt ... I wanted to hide to avoid being hit. (p. 31)
The car ... stopped two car widths away from me, and ... was a Sierra. I only saw one police car in the car park. (pp. 31–2)
It looked ... as if it was trying to split the crowd up, although it did not come near me. But as it came towards the middle of the car park people were jumping out of its way. (p. 32)
I was given a bit of one of her teeth and I gave it back to her. (p. 32)
I saw no signs of any part of the crowd making any sort of attack upon the police car. (p. 33)
You are not obliged to say anything unless you wish to do so. (p. 32)
Well it certainly could have been him, might well have been him, but I am not sure that it was him. (p. 45) (*implicature*)

Questions

The question form is important in this Summing-up, much of it in projected form:

– and you look at it and say, when you are confronted with such a problem, 'Well what did he do?'

When you have worked out what he did, then you say to yourself, 'Well, did that create that obvious and serious risk of danger, physical damage to anybody who might be on the road at that time?' (pp. 7–8)

You have to work out what was in his mind, but how do you do it? (p. 8)

– the real issue which has been raised in this case, of course is, 'Have the prosecution made you sure that it is Mr A who was the driver of that car', and 'have they made you sure he was the man who struck C D?' (p. 9)

... that is something you take into account when you say to yourself, 'Well, what weight do I give to what he says?' (p. 11)

... and you say to yourself, 'Well, is it more or less likely that a man of previous good character would behave in the way in which this man is said to have behaved?' (p. 11)

Can I just say this to you? (p. 12)

... well, really there cannot be any doubt, can there, but that the girl was not only in that car park, but that somebody or something hit her, split her lip and shattered her teeth? (p. 24)

How does that fit, members of the jury, with the rest of the evidence which you heard? (p. 26)

Can you be sure that, whoever it was, I ... D ... did indeed recognise the driver of the car as somebody he had previously seen on the streets in E ...? (p. 27)

You have to ask yourself obvious questions:

Where was the witness when he saw the man he recognised?

What sort of lighting was there?

What sort of state was the witness in?

Was it something that happened quickly and unexpectedly, or was it something for which he was, to a degree, at any rate, prepared?

What did you think of the witness when you looked at him:

did he strike you as a steady, reliable man, or someone upon whom you can say: 'Well this chap, so far as this identification is concerned, strikes me as being a bit dodgy'? (p. 28)

The second question you then have to ask yourselves is this:

'If I am satisfied that he did indeed recognise the policeman who hit Miss D ... as being the one he had previously seen ... am I satisfied so as to be sure it was PC A?' (p. 28)

What could she tell us about the cars? (p. 33)

I suppose the rhetorical questions posed to you is:

'Well how can we be sure that every entry of Y6 is in fact a direction to Y6?' (p. 41)

... because, how, it is asked rhetorically, do we know that A ... was not called off from the call to Ch ... even after it was made and assigned to him? (p. 42)

... secondly, am I satisfied, so that I am sure that in a car park that night in the circumstances described by Miss D and the witnesses somebody did drive recklessly, and then you say to yourselves:

'Well, am I sure it was PC A, who assaulted her, and I (*sic*) am sure it was PC A also drove recklessly?' (p. 45)

If you are sure that either one or both these offences were committed, you than have to ask:

'Well, am I satisfied so I am sure that it was indeed the accused man?' (p. 45)

Antitheton

In this Summing-up the antitheton is not a marked stylistic or rhetorical feature:

> If you think that is a valid chain of reasoning, then of course you are entitled to accept it.
>
> If on the other hand, you feel that, bearing in mind ... really asking you to do too much by way of conclusion, then you will reject it. (p. 40)

Object-subjectification

The central focus of the disputed narrative in this trial was the episode in the car-park. As will be shown later, there was no dispute that at least one police car was there. Since criminal responsibility in the Common Law is very much a matter of individual intentional volition and action, how the narrative recounts the incident is important. We have seen in *Arthur* how important the word 'it' was in reference to the deceased baby. In '*Abernethy*' that object-connoting word is stressed rather than the actions of its driver; *but* in connection with subjective action.

> And *it* was driving around swearing and knocking people; not hitting them, but driving, she felt, towards them. However, she only saw the one police car, and she thought it was a Sierra. It was white, she said, and marked with stripes down the side, and numbers on the top. She felt *it* was going towards people making them dive, she said, over the walls ... *It* turned, went into the car park going up towards S. Road, still in the car park, and then the car came towards herself and AM ... therefore she pulled him across her out of the way, and the car came to a stop. As *it* came to a stop, *it* had, so to speak, reached her. *It* touched her; *it* did not injure her: '*it* clipped my leg.' (p. 23)
>
> ... the car, whichever it was, driving round and round the car park in a thoroughly – I use the word neutrally – what you may think is a thoroughly unsatisfactory manner. (p. 31)
>
> ... she felt that the car was behaving appalling ... (p. 33)

In rhetorical terms this mode of description diverts attention from the driver of the car to the car which becomes subjectified.

One should not assume that this is a rhetorical device to divert attention from the driver's responsibility. It could be that it is psychologically easier to impose responsibility once one has accepted the action Mythos in this form.

Legal aspects

This Summing-up is divided by time into two sections. Pages 3 to 15 were spoken on one afternoon, and the remainder, pages 16 to 46, on the next day. The first section is dominated by the instruction of legal considerations for the jury. It does not entirely avoid reference to the defendant and witnesses, but they are only referred to incidentally in the legal points. These pages are close to the Scottish model of jury instruction, though it is not as systematic. The second day's speech is dominated by the survey of evidence; though there are legal points made on occasion, it is my contention that those legal matters raised in that context are rhetorically loaded, especially by their order and location.

In the first afternoon's speech there are a number of judicial comments and remarks, which I will selectively quote.

> May I then turn to deal with another matter which arises directly, in a way, from what I have just said? Mr Abernethy has chosen not to give evidence. That is his absolute right. Just as when a person is arrested and cautioned, and he is told that he is not obliged to say anything, so it is that no-one who is charged with a criminal offence in these courts is under any obligation to give evidence. He is perfectly entitled – as Mr Abernethy has chosen to do – to sit where he does, and say to the prosecution, 'You have brought these charges, you go ahead and prove them', and under no circumstances must you hold it against him as any indication of guilt in any way, but that is the course he has chosen. You have already been reminded of that by counsel, and I make no apology for mentioning it again because it is of the utmost importance.
>
> You may well say to yourself, members of the jury, 'Well, since he has not given evidence, we nevertheless have an account from him of what he tells us he did that night because we have the statement which he gave to the investigating officers when they came round to interview him'. Well, the position there is this, the contents of that statement are to be given by you such weight as you think it right to do. Obviously, it suffers – if that is the right way of putting it – by the fact that it is not supported by evidence on oath, and nor has it been tested by cross-examination, but that does not mean that it can be disregarded. It can not; you must weigh up what weight you give to it, and you must decide. You can look at its contents, you can look at the rest of the evidence but you must under no circumstances disregard it . . . (pp. 10–11)

Next there are Directions on 'good character' and identification. Then:

> The next thing I want to say to you, and it is almost the last thing I am going to say to you this afternoon, is this: you do not, members of the jury, hold it against Mr Abernethy that efforts were made on his behalf [*Galbraith*] to ascertain whether or not it could be urged upon you that there is doubt as to whether or not the offences were committed, let alone who committed them. It is part of the prosecution case to establish the commission of the offence as well as establishing that it was committed by the accused, and equally, it is part of the defence task to test that evidence and ascertain whether or not the offence was committed, and that is precisely what has been done. Whether the attempts are successful, or not, and if it is successful, to what extent is for you to decide, but you do not hold it against anybody that the attempt was made. If we were to behave in that way, our system, of criminal justice would collapse. [*Slippery-slope consequentialism*]
>
> Finally, I want to say to you this, as well. You will, of course, lay all prejudice aside. You do not hold it against anybody for instance that he is a policeman, or that he is not a policeman. You do not hold it against them that

there were young people congregating in large numbers in town after a football match; it is not in their favour, and it is not against them. What is demanded here is a calm objective consideration of the evidence you heard. I hope that I do not need to say any more about that.

Well, members of the jury ... Please remember again what I have told you ... and you must under no circumstances speak to anybody outside your number about this case, and nor must you let them speak to you. It is tempting, I am sure, to churn over what you have heard today in your own mind, and to try out your conclusions or ideas on somebody else. If that is what you feel, members of the jury, wait until you get back together, and you can try them out together but nobody else has any right to be any part of your deliberations. (pp. 14–15)

The special circumstances of the case

At the heart of this unusual case were two problems of identification, despite the fact that there was no doubt that at least one police car had been in the car-park and one had been driven recklessly, and that Miss D had her teeth smashed by something from within it. The difficulties were: which car; and which occupant had struck her?

Miss D and her companions understandably had difficulty identifying the specific car. The courtroom discourse approached this by reference to manufacturers' models, such as 'Sierra' or 'Rover'. As for the assaulter that too was unclear, as were the number of occupants of the car.

There was a suggested link by one of the witnesses that the driver (PC Abernethy) was known in the area and had a Scottish accent. PC Abernethy did fit this description, but nobody in the police car had spoken.

A forensic approach to the issue was provided by the police Inspector, who gave a detailed account of the CAD system of radio link with police cars, the records for that night being available. This forensic approach had the same limitations in court as it has for the police service. First, police drivers can attend a site independently; second, they can attend under direction but without recording it; they may respond but not attend because of some diversion or new priority – all of these are routine occurrences. In addition the recording is done after the event and the operator has a degree of discretion as to what is entered. It follows that if there is a record it will be of the *last* time at which the incident could have occurred. In this case there was a record for two cars (Y5, and Y6: the Sierra being driven by PC Abernethy). Their despatch was *recorded* as 21.58 hours, 'It does not indicate that they actually got there' (p. 38). The incident occurred not later than 22.10 hours, so these records simply bracket in the *possibility* of Y5 and Y6's presence at that time. So anchoring the forensic narrative deixically was not straightforward. However, there was in addition evidence from a police dog-handler that a further call-away message had gone out at 22.21 and been acknowledged on the channel by PC Abernethy. This was direct evidence, unlike the problematic CAD records.

A further special feature of the case was that the defendant exercised his right to silence both at interview by his colleagues and in the trial itself. This was, as has been shown, alluded to with a standard Direction by the judge twice at the beginning (pp. 10–11) and once at the end of the Summing-up (pp. 42–3).

The Written Statement was in these terms:

> What is said about it is this: so far as the defence say, it is the account of a man who did indeed go to that car park. He did indeed drive round it; he did not hit anybody. Rather it was that his car was peltered (*sic*) with bottles and cans, and chased by a crowd. A number of other policemen turned up, whereupon the youths ran into the terrace, which I think is called G ... Terrace, the whereabouts of which we were not properly provided with. There is a denial of any wrongdoing. (pp. 43–4)

However, the statement included a temporal reference that the incident occurred at about 22.25, a quarter of an hour *after* all the other accounts.

This the prosecution noted was about five minutes *after* his acknowledgement – directly witnessed by the dog-handler – and departure for another district.

This is the final moment in the Summary of evidence, enumerated thus:

> The overwhelming inference, the Crown suggest is that the Statement is a lie; a lie in two senses:
>
> First of all, because he put it at the wrong time in order to exculpate himself; and secondly it is a lie because he did draw his truncheon and belt Miss D (p. 44)

Then follows a reminder to the jury to consider all the evidence as a whole rather than 'one piece in isolation'. Then the final series of questions and implicature questions are given and the Directions on unanimity and appointing a foreman.

Before retiring the jury entered three Notes, seeking the hand-written original Statement by the defendant; the radio record book; and the vehicle records books for cars Y5 and Y8. These requests were granted.

The jury deliberated for 162 minutes then convicted unanimously of the charge of reckless driving. A majority verdict Direction was given then for the charge of assault occasioning actual bodily harm. After a further 25 minutes a majority verdict (10-2) was given for conviction.

No separate verdict was sought or given on the status of the car-park as a public highway.

'Lowe' – acquittal of a policeman

In this trial PC Lowe (altered name) was charged with indecent assault – ejaculating over an informant's breasts – during an interview at her house.

The informant's relations with the police were already established before PC Lowe met her. Those relations were strained and confused.

Legal aspects of the Summing-up

In this Summing-up the judge commenced with the jury's role, stressing their assessment of witnesses. He then continued in classic mode:

> ... the Prosecution bring this charge against this Defendant and what we call the Burden of proof is on the prosecution from first to last. This Defendant, C Lowe, does not have to prove anything at this stage. It is for the Prosecution to prove the case. The Standard they must reach before you could bring in a verdict of guilty is a high one. You only convict this Defendant if the Prosecution have made you sure that he is guilty. The test is as simple to state as that. (1G–2A)

The Standard is reinforced in relation to the issue:

> If the Defendant did what Violet H alleges, that is to say, held her down whilst he ejaculated over her breasts against her will, that was an indecent assault.
>
> The issue in the case is simple enough to state: are you sure that is what happened? (2C)

Jury function and judicial Disclaimer

The judge's style is different to that in '*Sandiland*' (see below). The Direction on jury function, and the 'Disclaimer' regarding judicial opinion, or apparent opinion, on facts is intermingled:

> Now, Members of the jury, those are the matters of law about which I have to direct you. I now pass to the evidence, which as I say, is your sole province ... ... If I remind you of a piece of evidence that you do not think is important then ignore it, because as I say it is your view, and only your view, of the evidence that matters. If I do not remind you of a particular piece of evidence which you do recall and you think is important, give it the weight you think it deserves. If in the course of my summary of the evidence you think you detect a view that I hold on the facts well ignore it, unless it happens also to be your view, because I cannot stress too much, it is only your view that matters. What I am going to do, Members of the jury is to deal with the evidence chronologically and as we go through it I may suggest certain questions that you may care to ask yourselves during your deliberations. (6E–G)

Another difference is the judge's addressing of serial questions on points of detail:

> Do you accept that he had never heard of her before the 25th May?
>
> I invite you to consider that question because Violet H says that in the course of these visits that we are moving on to he made comments based on rumours that he must have heard at the police station about her.

Well, had he? (10D)
... It is a matter for you whether you find that an important matter of detail. Given Violet H's situation would you expect her to raise the question of her clothes? She of course says that the other two visits which the Defendant made were ostensibly to update her about what was happening with her clothes; were they? (10G)

Corroboration and lies

In this trial the Special Directions were necessarily combined. They were on the (then) need for corroboration in sexual offences and on the weight to be given to lies told by the defendant:

> Now, that of course is an allegation of a sexual nature and as has already been anticipated I have to say various things to you about that, because experience has shown that people who make sexual allegations sometimes and for a variety of reasons tell lies and such allegations are very easy to make and they can be extremely difficult to challenge even by entirely innocent people and so it is dangerous to convict on the evidence of the complainant alone unless it is corroborated by other evidence.
>
> Now, what in law is corroboration? Well, it is evidence from a source independent of the complainant which confirms in some important respect not only that the offence has happened but that the defendant committed it. It is not necessary for there to be independent confirmation of everything the complainant says. Now, it is for me as a matter of law to point out to you the evidence in the case which is capable of providing.
>
> There is, Members of the Jury, only one piece of evidence which is capable of independently confirming Violet H's evidence and that is the admitted series of deliberate lies told by the Defendant in interview to the effect that he had only ever been to Violet H's flat on one occasion and nothing of a sexual nature ever occurred between them, but and I stress 'but', to treat those lies as corroboration you must be sure that he lied because he was guilty of this offence and lied to conceal his guilt. If his lie was or may have been for some other reason it is not capable of providing the corroboration you are looking for. Now, why do I say that? For this reason Members of the Jury, the mere fact that a defendant tells lies is not itself evidence of guilt because a defendant may lie for any number of reasons and some of those reasons clearly need to be considered by you in this case. A defendant, for example, may lie to conceal disgraceful conduct short of the commission of a criminal offence. Here the suggestion of a Policeman being involved sexually with a member of the public he is meeting in the course of his duties and fears disciplinary action if that fact comes out. A defendant may lie to bolster a true defence. A defendant may lie out of panic or confusion, and bear in mind the background to the interviews in this case was that he had left a very upset wife at home. So if you think that his lies are explained by one of those or some other innocent explanation you must not treat them as corroboration.
>
> So look for corroboration. If you do not find any, what is the position? Well, the position is as Mr B [counsel] explained it to you yesterday. It is still open to you to convict providing you bear in mind the danger of convicting without it if you are sure that Violet H is in fact telling the truth.

> You heard evidence in this case from, her neighbour William S ... His evidence was to the effect that Violet H ... made a complaint to him about this alleged assault and that she appeared to be very distressed about it. Neither of those pieces of evidence, the complaint or the apparent distress, is capable of being corroboration for the very simple reason it is not independent of Violet H, it comes from her and a false allegation often is accompanied by feigned distress. The only relevance of Mr S's evidence of what Violet H said to him, if you accept that she said it, and accept that it was very soon after the event, is that it may show that her conduct was consistent with her evidence about the incident and that may possibly help you on the question of whether you can be sure that she has in fact told you the truth.
>
> The Defendant a serving Police Officer. It follows that he is a man of good character in the sense that he has no previous convictions. He is 39 and has never committed a criminal offence. Bear that in mind and give it weight in two ways. Firstly, it supports his credibility and secondly it means he is less likely than otherwise might be the case to commit this crime now. In addition, of course, evidence was called as to his positive good character and again you bear that in mind when assessing his credibility ... (3G–5D)

There is one further reference to lying:

> When the defendant was giving his evidence you may recall that his barrister, Mr B ... [counsel] put it to him quite simply, 'You lied'. You may recall the Defendant was not entirely happy with that expression and said, 'I was not totally frank with the interviewing officer'. I do not know whether that answer helps you or not, members of the Jury. (15D)

The right to silence

Here the Warning Direction was factual and simple:

> When the Defendant was arrested he, like any other person suspected of a criminal offence, was cautioned and told he had no need to answer any questions. In two of the interviews which were conducted he chose not to answer any questions. You must not hold his refusal to answer questions against him. (5G–6A)

Consequentialism

Here the only consequential appeal is unusual: the non-penal consequences for the defendant:

> He told you that when he was interviewed he lied; firstly because of the condition in which he had left his wife and secondly he feared that if he told the truth his position as a Police Officer might be in jeopardy. Well, you may well feel there is something in certainly that second point. His future in the Police force probably is in doubt in any event. (17FG)

Linguistic aspects of the Summing-up

Forms of address

The jury

Members of the Jury	9
We etc.	5
	14 (18 pp.: 0.7 per page)

No conclusions can be inferred from these usages.

Defendant and complainant

In this case what is remarkable is the degree of equivalence in naming but not in status between the alleged perpetuator of the indecent assault and the complainant:

The defendant	37	Violet H	36
The defendant C Lowe	1	Violet	1
The aggressor	1	The lady	1
Mr Lowe	1	Mrs H	2
The defendant (38)	40	Violet H (36)	40

What is striking about these nomenclature patterns are the absences from both lists. The defendant is never referred to as Police Constable or PC Lowe, and Violet H is never referred to as the complainant. Instead the predominant images are of an abstract defendant and a relatively intimate Violet H. Does this suggest that the complainant was the more intimate and the defendant, the less?

Colloquialism and metaphor

In reading and re-reading these Summings-up one becomes aware that the split made in usage between colloquialism and metaphor is somewhat artificial. For my purpose I tend to define a figure as metaphor when there is originality in its use, a one-off occasion, whereas a colloquialism is a turn of phrase which, although often metaphoric, is part of a general stock-in-hand of wide usage; also some colloquialisms may be proverbs.

Here are two intertwined examples, the only ones to occur in this Summing-up (at 15A): '. . . that delay was not *down* to Violet, it was simply the procedure *creaking* along'.

After some reflection I categorized both 'down to Violet' and 'creaking along' as colloquialisms.

My concern over these distinctions relates to my speculation about the pragmatic function of the two types of figure. The resort to colloquialism is an attempt to reduce distance, to 'incorporate' the silent jury. It is not the only such method in the judge's repertoire, but it is the most prominent. The metaphor has a different function as persuader (see Robertshaw *Semiotics* (1984) 527–53).

Repetitive emphasis
There are two instances that occur in the Direction on jury function:

> And you ... and you alone, and you ...
> ... who was ... who, though honest ... who was not ... (1C)

Structuration: framing Violet H as 'slag-female'
In this case of alleged (non-rape) sexual assault the victim again presented problems for a jury, quite apart from the non-penal consequences for PC Lowe. The construction of the complainant as 'slag-female' is prominent:

> Now, the story so far as the evidence is concerned, actually goes back to 1984 ... You heard a statement from a Policewoman R that in 1984 Violet H was an informant for her, someone giving her information, although not it would seem a registered informant as you have heard some people can become.
>
> On the 24th July 1984, Violet H in a fit of pique caused some damage to Police Constable R's car. Mrs H was arrested not without a struggle and a flood of obscenities and she was charged with criminal damage. She admitted causing that damage said she would repay the cost of £25 and subsequently £25 turned up in an envelope at Police Constable R's home. Violet H then complained about that arrest and the subsequent procedure. When a Superintendent visited her about the complaint she said she was receiving treatment for cancer of the throat which she believed to be terminal. She told the Superintendent she had consulted a solicitor and did not wish to go through with the complaint. She was cautioned about the damage and made a statement withdrawing the complaint.
>
> In 1986 she obstructed Police Officers who were arresting a drunken man. Again there were obscenities and she had obviously been drinking at the time. She continued to be difficult at the Police Station ... She made a complaint about that arrest. When she was spoken to by a Chief Inspector, she said she was not going to pursue it, but equally she was not going to withdraw it. Later she refused to make a statement saying in effect 'if you won't comply with my procedures, I won't comply with yours'.
>
> In 1988 she complained about an incident that had occurred in December 1987. Various attempts were made to see her. Eventually she went to a Police Station with a solicitor's representative and a statement of complaint was written out. She was then warned by her solicitor's representative about making false statements and she then refused to sign that statement and eventually that statement was treated as withdrawn.
>
> Now, you will recall that when Mrs H in evidence was asked questions about this part of the background she denied that she herself had ever been an informant, although there was a stage when she had associated with an informant. She admitted making complaints. She said it was a lie to say that she refused to go through with them. She said she was still intending to make a complaint about her wrongful arrest for murder, but that this matter was taking priority over that. She said she had not proceeded with the earlier complaints on advice from her solicitors. When it was put to her that on one occasion she had said to a Police Officer, 'I know how to drop you lot in it' she denied

> making that remark but that is part of the evidence that was in the statements that were read which, as you know, the Prosecution has not challenged.
>
> So, Members of the Jury, the background undoubtedly is of a lady well able to complain, knowing not a little about the complaints procedure and putting it fairly neutrally, not entirely frank with you about the background to some of them, and you will have to decide to what extent you think that history of complaints, false or otherwise, helps you in reaching your decision in this case.
>
> On the 8th June 1987, *still some way before this particular incident* [my emphasis], Detective Constable G, at the A Police Station, says he got a call from Violet H. He did not know her. She was offering information and asked to meet him in the ... pub. He went, bought her a drink, she made some incoherent remarks about a charity box. She asked him if he was wired up and then made a grab for his testicles. He knocked her hand away and made some suitable statement as to what he thought of her and then left. He says he never told his colleagues about that because he thought if he did he would become the butt of their jokes. Although he has a reference in his pocket book to the fact that he met a complainant at the [pub] that night there is no reference to that particular aspect of the incident and I do not think we actually heard just how his evidence came out initially, but that was his evidence before you.
>
> In early May 1991, Violet H was arrested following a death. She was held on suspicion of murder. She was interviewed by Detective Constable M on a number of occasions. You have heard him describe, in fairly powerful terms how she was a horrible person to deal with and by September 1991, when he had to take her clothes back to her, he says in effect to protect himself he made sure a colleague went with him and they each made a note in their pocket books of precisely what had happened.
>
> *And so we come to the beginning of the Defendant's involvement with Violet H* ... [my emphasis] (7–10A)

This lengthy framing constructs Violet H:

- as an unregistered (unreliable) police informant;
- as a vexatious complainant against the police;
- as sexually assertive and crude in public;
- and as a murder suspect: a 'slag-female'.

This is constructed entirely from alleged events over a period of time before the incident disputed, none of which involved the defendant.

The jury acquitted PC Lowe unanimously of the indecent assault.

Rape: three acquittals and three convictions

'Mahoney I' – acquittal of rape

Legal aspects of the Summing-up

The judge–jury demarcation and Disclaimer

Here the jury's role is implied from that described for the judge at the outset of the Summing-up:

> Ladies and gentlemen, I have two jobs at this stage. My first job is to tell you what the law is and what I say about that you must accept from me and apply when you come to decide the facts. My second job is to give you a summary of the evidence and, in doing that pick out what seems to me to be the highlights.

After this introduction the Judge continued with the Burden and Standard of proof, and concluded on the judge–jury demarcation:

> Equally, if I comment on this or that aspect of the case, if the comments help you, take it into account. If the comment does not, then ignore it altogether. (61)

The right to silence

Unlike '*Mahoney II*' (see below) the defendant in this trial (name altered) declined to give evidence in court. The Direction was:

> The defendant has not given evidence in this case. The defendant is entitled to go into the dock, plead not guilty and say to the prosecution 'prove the case against me if you can'. The fact that he has done that, you must not assume guilt. The fact that he has not given evidence proves nothing and does not in any way help to establish guilt. (62–3)

Directions on lies and falsehoods

False statements are common in the criminal process and courts have had to develop a position on them, especially when the defendant is isolated, without advice, and surrounded by and dependent on officials. The ensuing Directions are therefore important and relatively standardized. How they operate on juries remains unknown.

In '*Mahoney I*' the Directions on corroboration and lies are intertwined as in '*Lowe*' (above).

> It is for me to say what is capable of amounting to corroboration as a matter of law and for you to say, if you like it as a finding of fact, whether it does indeed amount to corroboration. In this case, subject to the considerations I shall tell you about in a moment, if you are satisfied that the defendant did indeed lie to the police, then those lies which he tells to the police are capable of amounting to corroboration. You may think that what he says to the police falls certainly for a long stage into that interview into two categories. In some instances, of

course, he is saying 'I can't say yes and I can't say no'. He is prevaricating and you may think to prevaricate is as much as a lie – you are purporting to say 'Well, I can't remember one way or the other' but subsequently it emerges that you can remember full well because an admission is made on your behalf that you did indeed have sexual intercourse with the girl – as if you said 'no, I didn't'. In some instances, there are outright denials. Go to pages . . ., if we may for a moment or two, of that interview. Can you recall 14.25 . . . it says: 'probably in a red Peugeot'. You know the type of car in dispute. At the bottom: 'Can you recall going into a pub? I accept the fact that you're saying you have never been in this pub. Can you recall going into a pub in January of this year, the 9th, around 9-ish in the evening, seeing 3 of your friends – Jimmy, Joe, Tom or whatever – seeing 3 of your acquaintances or whatever with 2 girls? You went over to join them. Does that ring a bell at all?'

> I will tell you the truth. It doesn't ring a bell.
> Doesn't ring a bell? Okay. Can you recall at all speaking to 2 girls, one of whom was this Alice, and Alice knows you quite well, then the girl she was with there is quite a long conversation with this girl.
> I do not remember that girl honestly.
> Can you recall but – [*inaudible*] – memory?
> I hear what you're saying. I can't remember.
> Can you recall asking this girl – call her P, is that her name, yeah – can you recall asking this girl P to join you in the car park, sitting in your car and having a chat?
> No, I can't recall nothing like that.
> Would you remember that?
> I can't recall P. I can't even remember the pub. I do not know what you're on about, to tell the truth.
> Then D . . . we're talking about a specific night in January in a pub car park. Can you recall asking somebody, a girl, to go and sit in the car?
> I can't remember. I can't remember anything like that.
> Well would it be fair to say it could have happened?
> To tell you the truth, it couldn't have been because I can't remember anything like and I wasn't around that area as far as I know, know what I mean.

He is asked again a little bit more definite:

> To tell you the truth, I can't say for definite. I know one thing. I do not know a girl, I do not know any of these girls you're talking about.
> Somebody's got it wrong when they say that you have got in the car and you raped the girl. Would that be wrong?
> That would be very wrong.
> What about taking a girl for a ride in the car and then having sex with her?
> No.
> Is that not . . .
> No, I can't remember no girl in no car.

The matter is entirely for you, but you may think that that was an outright lie.

So what is the effect of that? The effect is this; if you need a lie in itself proves

> nothing because you may think that that is self-evident. But what you do need to bear in mind is the fact that a lie may be motivated or told sometimes because a young man may panic, sometimes he may lie to bolster up what is in fact a just cause because he thinks that if he tells the truth he may not be believed or sometimes he lies because he wants to conceal perhaps disgraceful conduct falling short of lies.
>
> But if you are sure, on the other hand, that the lie is a deliberate lie and it is a lie not told for some of the reasons or any of the reasons I have suggested to you, but is told because he knows he is guilty and fears the truth coming out then, if you are satisfied that it is a lie and that it is a deliberate lie – that the lie relates to a material issue, you may think in this case that passage I have referred you to clearly does, because a material issue is whether he had sexual intercourse with a girl in the car – and that it is shown to be a lie by the admissions made on his behalf, namely, that he did have sexual intercourse with her in the car, then it is capable of amounting to corroboration.
>
> What does not amount to corroboration is the girl's distressed condition and the complaint she makes afterwards. They only go to the consistency of her account. They are not corroboration ... (65–8)

These points are reinforced at the end of the Summing-up, before the Directions on appointing a foreman and majority verdicts:

> It is nonetheless dangerous to convict in the absence of corroboration. I remind you, as I said yesterday, the only evidence capable of amounting to corroboration is in what the defendant said to the police and that can only amount to corroboration if you are satisfied, firstly, that he lied and he lied deliberately, Secondly, that he lied not for some innocent reason such as panic or fear that his proper defence would not be believed or to cancel discreditable conduct short of crime, but only if he lied because he knew of his guilt and feared the truth coming out.
>
> If you are satisfied that he did lie, then of course also as I said yesterday you must be satisfied that the lie goes to the material issue. Clearly, in this case it does because material issue or one of the material issues is whether he took P S in a car from the Masons Arms public house and had sexual intercourse with her at the end of the blue line on her plan.
>
> Also, of course, you must be satisfied that what he said to the police has been shown to be a lie by evidence other than the evidence of P S. In this case, it is clearly shown to be one by the admission that he did indeed take P S to that field and had sexual intercourse with her. (93–4A).

Linguistic aspects in 'Mahoney I'

Forms of address

The jury

Ladies and gentlemen	5
Members of the jury	1
We	<u>1</u>
	7 (33 pp.: 0.22 per page)

This is a very low intensity form of address.

The defendant and complainant				
The defendant	18	The Witness	1	
The man	2	The girl	2	
		P S	8	
		P R	3	
The defendant (90%)	20		14	P S/R (80%)

The usual imbalance between impersonal defendant address and named complainant address occurs. All that is unusual is that the complainant is denoted as having changed status.

Colloquialism
The defendant's quoted police interview is peppered with colloquialism.

Quotation
This is a frequently used method of developing the contested Mythos. Because the defendant exercised his right of silence in court, there was much quotation from his police interview.

Proverb and adage
There is one: 'But hindsight is a wonderful thing' (17). These are not as common as I had anticipated.

Repetitive emphasis
Quotation from the defendant in his police interview: 'No' (× 5) (67), also '. . . she was not only angry, she was not only ashamed, but . . .' (70) and 'again, it is a matter entirely for you' (× 4) (70).

Special features of 'Mahoney I'

In this Summing-up the judge uses flashback to the forensic Mythos of the police station interview. It is live narrative by Erotesis–Apocrisis Quotation in which the defendant's responses comprise 19 serial denials and negatives incorporating five appeals to veracity. There is no termination marker for the series with the judge leading via disclaimer:

> The matter is entirely for you

into a single robust projection:

> but you may think that was an outright lie

followed by six lie stems in the ensuing Nomo-doxa. Structurally the lie stem recurs in the finale.

What has not been quoted in the excerpt is the reason for the defendant's admission: DNA testing demonstrated that the sexual intercourse alleged had been with him; this left the issue of consent for trial (91).

As presented here the directionality is against the defendant.

There are, however, comments on the alleged victim which might have prompted a 'date-rape exoneration'. These are:

(1) There was the alleged victim's previous sexual relationship with another, originally denied by her.

(2) Her admission that that was not a serious, long-term, relationship (at 60). Although the judge is balanced in his refutation of these 'criticisms', the fact that they are made may be used by a jury to exonerate.

(3) She is criticized for beginning to talk to the defendant in the car-park: 'You may think she is not the first nor she is not the last 20 year old girl who has been happy to be chatted up by a man in a car park or even in a car, but you may think equally the fact that a girl is prepared to go outside to be chatted up, perhaps even to be kissed, does not mean that she is instantly inviting sexual intercourse with the person concerned.'

(4) Then there are two qualified points: 'It is said that she does not scream for help. There are indeed moments, for instance, like the car park at H Common where the CB band radio fans go, where she might have screamed and shouted out or whatever. When she does start protesting, on her account, look what happens to her – she gets slapped. You may think in a frightening situation people react in a different way.

'So you must make up your minds about her evidence, assessing it as you find her to be, not upon the basis of how in that situation you might have reacted in a different way to her because you are not her.'

(5) She is criticized for the fact that she does not go to the police right away. 'But hindsight is a wonderful thing. You will recall she was not only angry, she was not only ashamed, but she described herself as crying and shaking. You may think that this is a description of shock and you may ask yourself – again, it is a matter entirely for you at the end of the day – do we logically in that kind of condition, does anyone always behave logically or do some people – again, it is a matter entirely for you – perhaps sometimes tend to run for the cover of their homes, not perhaps in the first instance thinking things through logically. You may think, again it is a matter entirely for you, that that is more so in those cases in which she says she had worries or fears from what she says this defendant said to her little brother who she had been looking after since the death of her mother.'

(6) Then, of course, she was also criticized because there was no physical injury to her. 'There is no doubt about that, but again you may think, because she had made the point herself, it was a slap with an open hand when she was slapped so there was no bruise and she was not a

virgin. You may think in the case of a virgin, perhaps injuries to the vagina, it is a matter entirely for you, are more likely than injuries in someone who is not a virgin. Again, that is a matter entirely for you. It is a matter of comment for you to consider.

Clearly, on her own admission, you are dealing with a girl who, in an established relationship, has had sexual intercourse before and has enjoyed them or not necessarily dealing as might be the case sometimes. That is why I say perhaps in this case no real reason for her needing to lie has emerged as, when I said to you in relation to corroboration, that is sometimes the reason why stories of this kind are invented. It never comes out but she has had previous relationships.' (69–71)

The 'slag-female' construction of the complainant relevant to a 'date-rape exoneration' comprises the following elements:

- Her lie. The jury might trade-off one liar (multiple liar – the defendant) against another (single liar – the complainant). Her lie, however, if it was such, did not relate to the alleged rape.
- She was not a virgin and she had an on-off relationship with another.
- She was sexually forward in talking to the defendant in the car-park.
- Subsidiary points: she did not scream or go to the police immediately.

'Mahoney II' – acquittal of rape

Legal aspects

The judge's role (1A–C)

The judge–jury demarcation (1C)

Burden and standard of proof (1DE)
These are all in the same formulation – by the same judge – as in '*Mahoney I*' above.

Corroboration and lies
Although the complainant and allegations were different the defendant's behaviour when apprehended was basically the same as in '*Mahoney I*' with the following Directions: 'All we have capable of amounting to corroboration in this case is the lies that the defendant tells in the first interview . . .' (4F).

The right to silence and lies
In '*Mahoney II*' the Direction on the right to silence during police interview occurs during the general Direction on Corroboration:

All we have capable of amounting to corroboration in this case is the lies that the defendant tells in the first interview, for you will remember that in that first interview for a large part of it he made no answer. He was perfectly entitled at all stages to make no comment if he so chose because he had been cautioned. He had been told that he was not obliged to say anything unless he wished to, but what he did say would be taken down and given in evidence. That means exactly what it says. If he chooses to make no comment, it must not in any way be held against him if her is exercising the right that the law gives to him. (4F–H)

... But at the end of the interview – this is a matter which, subject to the qualifications I shall come to in a moment, is capable of amounting to corroboration – he was asked this question: 'Do you know this girl? Can you remember her?'

'I can't remember her to tell you the truth. I don't live in S ... Two years ago I lived in L ...'

He admits to you, in his own evidence, that that was indeed a lie and that he could indeed remember. You may not even have had to have waited for his evidence for that matter to come clear, because you remember on the identification parade held on 6th August, she was the wrong-side of a two-way mirror – I say the wrong side – so that he could not see her and she could see him. He accepted that fact and he said in his second interview he hadn't seen her, that he was able to comment to the man next to him:

'She should be able to recognise me. I used to go out with her.'

If you are satisfied that he lied and that he says that he did in fact remember the girl in the first interview, then in the circumstances which I will now come to that is capable of amounting to corroboration. I want to make it clear to you at the outset in what I have to say about lies, is that a lie in itself does not prove anything, but it can corroborate. Before you even consider it as corroboration, you will have to bear in mind that a defendant may lie for many reasons, short of the fact that he has committed an offence. The most obvious reason that he has given to you; that faced with a terrible accusation, he panics and feels that the easiest way out is to lie because were he to tell the truth he would not be believed.

Another reason is sometimes people lie to conceal distasteful conduct short of crime. But really, in this case, it is the first reason, that of panic, that you need to concentrate on because that is the reason he gives to you. Before you have even considered the lie as corroboration, you have to be satisfied so that you were sure that he had not lied out of panic, but had lied because he was only too well aware of his guilt and feared the truth coming out.

You will, of course, have to be satisfied in addition too that that the lie was deliberate. In effect, he has told you that it was deliberate because he said 'I knew the girl', it was not something where his memory had played a trick. You have to be satisfied that the lie is material to the issue before you. Clearly, knowing that interview (*sic*) is material to the issue before you. You have to be satisfied that it is shown to be a lie by evidence other than that of E P. In this case, that is the case because he admitted to you on his evidence that it is a lie. Provided you are satisfied of those criteria and, above all, you are satisfied that the lie was not given for any innocent reason such as panic, but that he was lying because he knew of his guilt and feared the truth coming out, then you are entitled to consider whether, in your view – it is for you to decide – it amounts to corroboration.

> I have referred already to the fact that in interview he was entitled at all stages to say nothing and that you must not hold that fact against him. But where he does choose to answer, the other side of the coin then is this; you are entitled to take his answer, what he said, into consideration in deciding where in this case the truth lies, bearing in mind, as I have indicated to you already, it is for the prosecution at all times to prove the case against him. (4H–7A)

Linguistic aspects

Forms of address

The jury

Members of the Jury	3	
We etc.	5	
	8	(61 pp.: 0.09 per page)

In this Summing-up there is minimal address contact with the jury.

Defendant and complainant

The defendant	23			
The man	3	The girl	2	
		E P	4	
		E	23	
The defendant (90%)	26		29	E (90%)

As in '*Sandiland*' (below) in both '*Mahoney I*' and '*Mahoney II*' the defendant is never personalized. The alleged victims in both '*Mahoney I*' and '*Mahoney II*' are neither named as such, nor as complainants. Instead in both cases there are dual nominalizations. These do differ. In '*Mahoney I*' the first name remains constant, whilst the surname changes: she is available. Here in '*Mahoney II*' the predominant reference is the intimate mode of forename alone (80%).

Special features

Again, the difficulty of rape trials without witnesses is apparent. Also apparent are the risks in references to alleged victims.

Here the judicial disparagement of the complainant and her public construction as 'slag-female' comprises:

- Sarcasm:
  'He asked me to have sexual intercourse with him and he kept on and so I had sexual intercourse with him. This took about 10 minutes. We all got into the car and they drove us home.' –
  Hardly the longest seduction scene in the world, you may think. (7–8)

- Her previous abortion:
  'Dr B. saw her at 5.30 p.m. She dealt with the fact that E had had a termination of pregnancy in 1990 ...'
- Her on–off relationship with her existing boyfriend, and
- The casual site for intercourse with him.
  '... her boyfriend ... she had seen this man again for the first time the night before the events you are concerned with and she had sexual intercourse, you remember, in a derelict house with him that night ...' (15)

'Sandiland' – acquittal of rape

Legal aspects

Here the judge's opening remarks are simple:

> Members of the jury, it is now my duty to direct you as to the law; you must accept and apply that direction. It is your duty to decide issues of fact, that is your exclusive province. (26B)

Then follows immediately the 'Disclaimer'. As with the Direction on jury function it is equally brief and to the point:

> So, if when I refer to fact or express or seem to express an opinion of my own, please disregard it, unless you happen to share it. My opinion about fact does not matter. (26B)

Lies
As is so often the case in sexual assaults, such as rape, the trial tests two starkly different accounts of a past personal encounter with all the over- and undertones of gender conflict. Until recently this involved the special Direction on corroboration of the putative victim. In '*Sandiland*' this necessitated further warnings on lies:

> Having given you that Warning, about the desirability of corroboration, and the danger of convicting without it, I must add this; it is open to you, in law, to convict on the evidence of the girl alone, if you are satisfied that her evidence is true. Only two persons know what really happened, each has given evidence and the accounts are irreconcilable. If you conclude that Rikke C has lied or may have lied, you must acquit.
>
> If you conclude that the defendant has lied, both to the police and to you, that fact does not, of itself, prove guilt; there can be innocent explanation for lies and if any innocent explanation can be the proper explanation in this case, you take no notice of the lies. If you are sure there is no innocent explanation for lies and if any innocent explanation can be the proper explanation in this case, you take no notice of the lies. If you are sure there is no innocent explanation for lies by the defendant, then the fact that he has lied, if you find that established, can support the prosecution's case. (29B–F)

Burden and Standard of proof

Here there is an elision, but with the Standard preceding the Burden of proof. It occurs immediately after the brief statement of judge and jury roles with which the Summing-up commences (26C–E):

> The first thing I tell you about the law is something you have heard already, it is a fundamental principle of great importance, please keep it in the forefront of your minds as you examine the evidence and it is this; before you can convict the defendant of either of the charges brought against him, you must be satisfied, by the evidence, satisfied so that you can feel sure, that the prosecution has established guilt. The defendant does not have to prove anything. From beginning to end, the prosecution must prove the charge which the prosecution brings, prove it by evidence that you find acceptable. Prove it to the extent that each one of you is satisfied and sure. If you are then not satisfied you must acquit. If either of you are satisfied, it is your duty to convict. (26C–F)

At the conclusion of the Summing-up (prior to the usual Directions on majority verdict and choosing a foreman) there is a repetition in sequence:

> Let me finish as I began, the defendant does not have to prove anything. Before you can convict on either Count the prosecution must satisfy you by the evidence, satisfy so you are sure, that guilt is proved. If that has not been done you must acquit; if that has been done it is your duty to convict.

In '*Sandiland*' the final emphasis is on conviction, but 120 minutes later an acquittal was delivered.

Linguistic and other aspects of the Summing-up

The jury is only addressed once at the commencement of the Summing-up, as 'Members of the Jury'. There are no other forms. It is therefore (at 1 of 13 pages 0.08 per page) a model of distanced address.

'The defendant' was addressed as such throughout (× 23), so that mode of address also is impersonal.

The complainant is predominantly 'Miss C' (× 13) but her Danish forename enters the description (× 4).

It follows that there is a typical loading in favour of the complainant in terms of credibility-weighting by address form. However, it is important not to take this rhetorical indicator on its own.

Apart from this there is almost nothing of significance: some use of parenthesis; some repetitive emphasis: 'she' × 6 (33E), 'lies' × 7 (29D). However, there are two examples of tropes that are not often found in criminal trials: euphemism and innuendo. These are involved in the construction of the complainant as a variant of 'slag-female'.

'*Mahoney I*' and '*Mahoney II*' may have demonstrated the risks of jury exoneration where court construction of the 'slag-female' has occurred, especially where they express their social level by mixing with marginal, outcast males ('travellers'). Sandiland raises a variant: Danish sex-tripper.

This occurs in the preliminary sections and comprises four elements:

Euphemism
'... if violence was *offered* to her' (27F): violence denoted as a gift or choice.

Innuendo
Or she was 'feigning reluctance' (28A) in eighteenth-century linguistic usage, with connotations of 'Moll Flanders'.

Construction as sexually assertive
'... within 48 hours she telephoned him' (30C).

Post-incident behaviour
(1) She did not run away (33C,E), especially when he left the keys of the house with her (35C).
(2) In the finale of the survey of evidence: 'she became pregnant and this was aborted' (38G).

Conclusion

The three Summings-up on acquittal for rape – in this case and '*Mahoney I*' and '*Mahoney II*' – and in '*P.C. Lowe*' – allow one to suggest that there is a possibility of acquittal, even in cases where the evidence is strong against the defendant, where there is denigratory material concerning the complainant, even when reference to her sexual history is absent or marginal. In the concluding chapter of the book I shall suggest a method for reducing these possibilities. Such denigration is out of place in a legal system which today gives protection to prostitutes against rape (Smith 1989).

'Mynah' – conviction of rape

In this trial the

'Members of the jury'	2 (in 10 pp.: 0.2 per page) convicted	
Th. Defendant	29	
Th. man	1	
	30	
of raping		
Th. Girl	16	
Miss C	12	
The young woman	1	
The young lady	2	
	31	

after a deliberation of 38 minutes; it was a 'short but obviously important case'. The judge paid particular emphasis to the jury's verdict being

> on the evidence you have heard in the course of the last day or so, and on that alone. You approach that evidence fairly, impartially, without sympathy, without prejudice, but you apply to the evidence your common sense and your knowledge of how people behave ... you are not in any way concerned with the consequences which may flow from a verdict of guilty, because all matters relating to sentence are my responsibility, not yours.
> You have been brought here to do one thing, and one thing only: to decide whether this allegation has been proved as against this defendant on the evidence you have heard.

There was also a standard 'good character' Direction because the defendant (whose name is altered) had no previous convictions.

There was one special circumstance present in this trial. The allegation was of a double rape by two men, the defendant following immediately after the first man H ....

On this the judge gave the following Direction:

> In considering that question, of course, you have to take into account all the circumstances of the case. Those circumstances include the fact that very shortly before she had sexual intercourse with this defendant, she had been raped by the other man. The other man, H ..., was arrested; he has not yet been prosecuted; you do not have to trouble about his position. You may well think that he ought to be in the dock with this defendant. Quite obviously, he is not. You are trying this defendant on the evidence you have heard and you will not, as I say, be troubled by the position of the second man. (5)

The DNA evidence 'confirmed beyond any doubt that the defendant had had sexual intercourse with the girl and there was on the same scientific evidence a very high probability that that H ... also had done so' (10).

In this Summing-up, structure is more significant than the deployment of tropes, but I draw attention here to two sets of tropes. First there is the acceleration of narrative through abbreviation of sentence length, combined with contrastive repetition of she/he (H ...) in the episode *before* the rape itself. The lack of consent is established at that time:

> ... the defendant ... came back wearing what she described as a sort of skirt, but which is properly described as a lungi, and H ... changed his trousers.
> *She* became alarmed ... *she* had better go.
> She tried to leave ... *she* got to the front door.
> *He* blocked off the front door.
> *She* screamed,
> *he* pushed
> – as she put it –
> then H ... took her to the bedroom ...
> – and indeed according to the defendant – then H ... undressed her and raped

> her and the defendant was there watching.
> He said to Miss C that he was sorry but he did nothing whatever to help her.
> The defendant then joined them on the bed one on each side and the defendant took his turn ... she just lay there ...
> Members of the jury, I repeat again:
> submission is not consent.

H ... and the defendant then let her go, the defendant giving her £3. The complainant's behaviour was then consistent with her general allegations. She returned to her hostel, at 3 a.m., told her friend G ... B ... what had happened; the police were called at 4.15 a.m. She went with them and pointed out the flat where she said the rapes had occurred. She was medically examined at 7.15 a.m. and the bruising confirmed. At 8 a.m. the defendant was arrested.

This brings us to the second tropic element – repetitive emphasis in abbreviated sentences – and their place in the narrative structure.

Again short sentence structure is used, and occurs twice:

> *That was a lie.*
>
> It was admitted that the defendant had originally told the [police at the flat] that 'no woman had come to his flat'. *That was a lie.* Later on he said, and I quote: 'There was a girl. She wanted to come here for food and tea.' (9)

Then he was interviewed at the police station where 'he denied having sexual intercourse with the girl at all, but said that his friend did. *That was a lie.* He said he was confused and frightened. It is only right to say that his solicitor was there and so was an interpreter. When the question was repeated, he then said he did have sexual intercourse with her after H ... had done so, but it was with the girl's consent' (*ibid.*) so the issue for the jury was whether that too 'was a lie'.

The judge concluded his Summing-up thus:

> Therefore, on his own evidence, you have this situation:
> H ... rapes the girl on a bed in the defendant's flat while the defendant watches. The defendant then gets on the bed and has intercourse with the girl but that second act of intercourse, according to him, is with her consent.
>
> If that account is, or might be right, then he is not guilty.
>
> If you reject that account as wholly unbelievable, then she was raped both by H ... and by this man, and the defendant accordingly is guilty. (11)

Comment

The jury are confronted with two narrative layers:

(1) The defendant lied about Miss C's existence then lied about sex with her.
Did he also lie about her consent to sex?

(2) The defendant's sex with her followed immediately after her rape by H, which he watched passively.
Was his sexual intercourse with her consensual?

Rhetorically the discourse is loaded by the two sets of short sentences regarding, (i) submission as consent, and (ii) sexual intercourse.

(i) as 'That was a lie'
and (ii) as 'wholly unbelievable'.

The contradiction within these narrative layers is that the jury were, as has been cited, specifically instructed not to assume that H . . . had raped her first. Once this assumption is removed the logic of (2) falls apart, as does its relationship with (1).

A Summing-up without reference to H . . .'s alleged rape could have been constructed. It would have covered the defendant's lies; it would have covered the DNA evidence; and it would have covered the complainant's corroborative behaviour following from the alleged rape by the defendant. It would, however, have lacked the direction towards inevitability of conclusion which this Summing-up so effectively creates.

'Dargento' – conviction of rape

This trial concerned an attempted rape, followed shortly by a rape. The defendant's name has been altered. The jury convicted unanimously of both offences after 197 minutes' deliberation, committed against

Miss C, the complainant	1	
Miss C	13	
Justine	9	
Justine C	6	
th. young lady	3	
th. girl	1	
	33	: Miss C . . ., Justine C . . .

who had moved into the apartment of an acquaintance:

th. Defendant	31	
D the defendant	1	
	32	: The Defendant

partly because she wished to escape the unwelcome sexual advances of her stepfather, and also because the defendant led her to believe that he was shortly to go abroad thus leaving her as sole occupier.

On the night of her arrival they had sexual intercourse, and this occurred from time to time over the following month. Miss C decided then that the defendant was becoming more emotionally involved with her than she wished, so she moved into another bedroom.

The defendant said this was because she had cystitis or thrush but that some sexual intercourse continued. Miss C said that once she had moved no further consensual sex took place.

Apart from this disagreement of fact, it was mutually agreed that the defendant would sometimes knock on her bolted door and ask to talk to her. She would usually agree and they would sit talking until early morning, since neither was in work.

One day she found a note pinned with a dart to her bedroom door. This made her uneasy; she noticed that the defendant seemed to resent her friendships with other men, especially

Simon H : 9

a friend of the defendant.

'That in a way, is all background but it is background that you bear in mind when you come to consider', as

Members of the Jury	7
We/us/our	3
	10

(in 16 pages of Summing-up 1:1.6; 0.6 per page: low intensity address)

'... the events of the following two days'.

'Miss C went out to dinner with female friends, arriving back at about 3 in the morning. She knocked on the sitting room door to let Mr Dargento know that she was back. She went to bed. She then heard a knock on her door. She got up, put on a dressing gown and went to the sitting room.

'She was tired but she listened to him for about three-quarters of an hour. She then said she really had to go to bed. Mr Dargento followed her; he hugged her; she hugged him back because she was sorry for him because he seemed upset and depressed, and had fits of crying.

'He was suffering from cocaine withdrawal symptoms and had committed robberies and was considering giving himself up to the police.

'His story

He asked Justine if they could make love but she said

"No"

and so he didn't pursue the matter.

He told her about his robberies and that he intended to give himself up to the police, but he did not want to because he would almost certainly be imprisoned.

Then he asked her again if they could make love and this time she said

"Yes".

Hand in hand they went into the bedroom and with her complete consent and cooperation they had sexual intercourse. He did not use a condom and he did ejaculate inside her.

After, he said that he could no longer trust her to look after the flat. Then he went to sleep in the living room.

He woke about midday and Justine was still in her bedroom. He dressed and left the flat with her inside it, leaving her a note saying he was sorry about the argument they had had. On top of the note he put the flat keys, so that she would know he was leaving the flat for good and that he had changed his mind and that she could remain.

That afternoon he surrendered to the police in respect of the robberies.

'Her story

He would not let her go. He pulled her, resisting into the bedroom, pushed her on the bed and got on top of her.

She said:

"Don't do it, let me go."

He persisted.

She felt his penis against her vagina.

She said:

"You know what this is called."

He stopped and began to cry.

[Members of the jury, if that account is the truth that, you may think, is plainly an attempt to rape her]

She went to the kitchen, got a drink and returned. Mr Dargento was still sitting on the bed, weeping.

She said:

"It's all right".

They returned to the sitting room. There Mr Dargento told her about the robberies and that if he did not go abroad he would probably go to prison.

At about 7 a.m. Miss C said that she was very tired and was finally going to bed.

Mr Dargento again said he wanted to make love to her. He picked her up, put her over his shoulder, took her to the bedroom, pulled down her knickers and ejaculated inside her, without using a condom.

He got off her and she was able to go back to her own room.

[Again, if that is a truthful account, that is rape.]

She lay down and went to sleep.

She woke at about 1 p.m. in the afternoon, finding the defendant lying beside her. While he slept she dressed and left the flat.

'She then went to the flat – in the same block – of her friend

Louise G (3), Miss G (1)
Then she phoned Simon H
Later they, with Simon H's wife
Karen H (1), Karen (1)

returned to Mr Dargento's flat and collected all her belongings from it. She found another note from him saying that he was sorry. She never returned.

'At 10 p.m. she went to the police.
Just before midnight she was examined by
Dr K (3), the Doctor (1)
[she is an experienced doctor – particularly in this sort of case].
The medical evidence is neutral.
It does not help the Prosecution to prove there was a rape;
it does not help the Defence
– the defence do not have to prove anything –
that there was no rape;
it is neutral.
– this is a matter entirely for you, not me –
that his account of events does leave two questions unanswered:

'First, he said more than once that
Justine C ... did not want him to give himself up and go into custody for the robberies.
If that is right, you may wonder why on the same day she made a false complaint of rape which would ensure that into custody he would go?

'Second, Justine, on any view, you may think wanted a flat on her own away from her parents, particularly away from her stepfather.
On the 4th August she went back to that flat; she knew that is what she had got because the defendant had left his keys ...
Why then did she collect her belongings and leave the flat never to return?
The defendant says nothing happened;
she says she was raped.
Members of the jury ... that is a summary of the evidence ...'

Then follow further the usual concluding Directions on:

- separate verdicts on each count
- majority verdict not available at this stage
- foreman/spokesman
- papers and exhibits, but not witness statements may be taken.

Linguistic aspects

Forms of address

The differential in the address forms for defendant and complainant is typical. The defendant is never addressed by name and the complainant is only addressed as such once.

Parenthesis

Parenthesis is common, with 27 occurrences.

Emphasis

They are only occasionally devices of emphasis; usually they are glosses or reminders:

> 'and this is the crucial issue in this case'
> 'this is common ground between both parties'
> 'and this is the defence case'
> 'again this is common ground'
> 'and she was an experienced doctor, particularly in this sort of case'
> 'the defence do not have to prove anything'
> 'this is a matter entirely for you, not me'
> 'because separate verdicts on each count, and the verdicts do not have to be the same'

Quotation

Quotation is rare in this Summing-up. It takes two forms: implicature and direct. There is an interrelationship between two of them:

> Rape occurs whenever a woman says
> 'No'
> to sexual intercourse and means it, and the man, knowing that she means it, nevertheless goes on and has that sexual intercourse. It matters not that the same woman may on previous occasions have said
> 'Yes'
> to the same man. (p. 7)
>
> ... He said he asked her again if they could make love but she said
> 'No'.
> And so he did not pursue the matter. The he said he asked her again if they could make love and this time she said
> 'Yes'.

The other implicature is:

> The defendant gave evidence. He did not have to, he could have stayed where he was in the dock and said in effect to the Prosecution:
> 'You go ahead and prove it, I am not saying anything'. (p. 15)

Three other quotations are from the complainant. One relates to her reaction to the defendant's weeping: 'It's all right' (p. 2). The others are in direct conflict with the defendant:

> 'Don't do it, let me go', or words to that effect ... (p. 11)
> ... something to the effect 'You know what this is called' (p. 11)
> At no time did I rape her. (p. 15)

Questions
There are seven questions in this Summing-up, including two serial pairs, the first of which emphasizes the issue:

> The issue in this case becomes:
> Did these events happen in the way she says?
> Or, to put it more starkly:
> Is that young lady telling the truth when she says that what took place was without her consent? (p. 6EF)

Two questions isolate the contention between the defendant and complainant; both are in projected form:

> You will ask:
> 'Could she reasonably be sure about details such as that? (p. 13C)
> You ask the same question about it as you ask of any other witness; in particular:
> 'Is he telling the truth?' (p. 16A)

However, these comments must focus above all on the other serial questions whose significance lies in their location as the final points in the survey of evidence, with the concluding antitheton:

> However, you may also think this is a matter entirely for you not me that this account of events does leave two questions unanswered:
>
> First, he said more than once that Justine C did not want him to give himself up and go into custody for the robberies. If that is right, you may wonder why on that same day she made a false complaint of rape which would ensure that into custody he would go?
>
> Second, Justine on any view, you may think, wanted a flat on her own away from her parents, particularly away from her stepfather. On 4th August when she went back to that flat, she knew that that is what she had got, because the defendant had left his keys; he had gone and he had left his keys to indicate he was not coming back. Why then did she collect her belongings and leave that flat never to return? What had happened to make her leave? The defendant says nothing had happened; she says she was raped.
>
> Members of the jury, that is a summary of the evidence ... (p. 18)

Comment

These final questions appear devastating to the defendant's case as it is represented. They are presented in question form, though that may amount to 'rhetorical' questioning statements, and they are also introduced by a strong antitheton disclaimer: 'entirely for you, not me . . .'.

Nevertheless they illustrate the risk of the survey of evidence in the Anglo-Welsh Summing-up as an occasion for role confusion between judge as advocate and as judge, and between judge as judge and as potential sentencer.

The first comment is to demonstrate again the importance of location in structure, in this instance as an example of Mythos layering at the micro-level. It relates to the attempted rape.

If we consider the micro-context of the complainant's remark: 'You know what this is called', we find it in this context: 'He pulled at her knickers and she felt his penis against her vagina.'

In this micro-adjacency context a linguistic ambiguity is possible, as an ironic remark in sexual foreplay by the complainant. That ambiguity is removed because of its deixis diachronically in a wider context.

> 'Don't do it, let me go . . .'
> He persisted.
> He began to pull her dressing-gown apart.
> He pulled at her knickers and she felt his penis . . .

The second comment is intended to demonstrate the risk to balance between defence and prosecution that is always present in any Summing-up, regardless of the Disclaimer. This relates to the matter-of-fact, taken-for-granted, account of the complainant's post rape behaviour:

> Then . . . he pulled down her knickers and had sexual intercourse with her. He ejaculated inside her, he was not using a condom. He got off her and she was able to go back to her own room. Again, if that is a truthful account, that is rape. She lay down and went to sleep. She said she woke up about 1.00 p.m. in the afternoon to find the defendant lying beside her. She was able, while he slept, to get dressed, and in effect to creep out of the house. (p. 12)

The questions which I suggest could have been entered on this evidence might have been in addition:

> On the other hand if, as is alleged by the complainant, the defendant ejaculated inside her without using a condom, you may ask why did she simply go back to her own room and go to sleep? Members of the jury, given that she had just been raped, why was the complainant able to go to sleep for six hours and then exhibit symptoms of distress after that sleep? Remember, that the medical evidence in this trial is absolutely neutral.

However, my position does not actually support this type of appeal-hypothesized reformulation. My position is that the narrative is redundant in that counsel have already put their versions to the jury and neither the judge's words, nor my alternative, are relevant to instruction on this legal issue.

'Matchman' – conviction of rape

In this case

Th. Defendant:	22	was convicted by a 10–2 majority of the
Members of the jury:	1	
We	5	
	6	(13 pp.: 0.45 per page: very low intensity cooperative mode)
of the rape of		
Miss G	22	
Rose G	2	
Th. lady	2	
Th. woman	1	
	27	

The defendant (whose name is altered) had previously been acquitted of one rape upon her and the same jury had 'hung', been unable to agree on a second alleged rape, which was retried in the instant case. This background was known to the members of this jury.

The previous relationship between the defendant and Miss G ... was encapsulated in one of the five antitheta in the Summing-up:

> ... sometimes they lived together, sometimes they lived apart ... (p. 8)

The other four antitheta were typical: the judge–jury demarcation; the verdict-sentencing demarcation; and two on the Standard of proof:

> ... If you are so satisfied, the right verdict is guilty; if you are not so satisfied, then the right verdict is not guilty. (p. 5)

As far as the previous relationship was concerned the judge made the first of a number of Erotesis–Apocrisis pairs which with single questions were the only stylistic features of this Summing-up.

> What bearing does that have on your consideration of this case?
> Members of the jury, very little. (p. 6)

Then followed immediately a Krito-doxic coda infusing with Nomos:

> Even in 1992, there are some people who seem to think that rape can only occur if some total stranger jumps out of the bushes on to a girl, knocks her about and has intercourse with her. Of course, that is rape. That is not the only occasion in which rape occurs. Rape occurs when a woman says 'No' and means it, and the man, knowing that she means it, nevertheless goes ahead and has sex with her against her will. The fact that she has said 'Yes' to the same man on other occasions has nothing to do with it. (pp. 5–6)

At the time of the trial, the Corroboration Direction was still in force for allegations of rape. The judge gave this as required then followed it with a declaratory sentence; two Erotesis–Apocrisis pairs: an implicative question with repetitive emphases: with its answer; a further 'Wh'-question, and its answer.

> That is the position here; there is no independent evidence which supports the evidence of Miss G. You might say: But what about her complaints; her complaint to her sister; her complaint two days later to the doctor and to the police? Members of the jury, what those complaints show is that from an early stage that lady was consistent in what she was alleging. Those complaints cannot amount to corroboration. They cannot amount to independent evidence supporting her evidence. Why? Obviously, because they come from her and they are not independent of her. (p. 7)

This is followed by the usual Warning on such evidence.

Then follows the statement of issue with its embedded antitheta:

> The issue in this case, members of the jury, could not be more simple. It is this: Either Miss G is lying or the defendant is lying. There is no room for honest mistake. If you are sure that it is the defendant who is lying, you will convict him. If you think it may be Miss G who is lying then you will acquit him. That is the issue in this case.

The survey of facts was 'a very short summary' (p. 8). In quantitative terms five pages covered the Prosecution (Miss G) version and three pages that of the defendant.

The context of the incident was Miss G deciding to end 'the relationship, you may think, was very much on and off' (p. 8). The relationship had produced a son 'who is now four and a bit years old'.

> You may think that Rose G. had a good deal to put up with: The defendant would arrive at her flat at all hours of the night, having spent the night or the previous night at clubs and in the company of other women. She had a job to go to. That being so, she resented being woken up in the early hours of the morning.
>
> Who could blame her?
>
> She says the defendant on occasions could be violent and threatening to her.

He says he was neither of those things.

Accordingly on Tuesday 17th September, after a discussion, she told the defendant she wanted to finish. At that point, after that discussion she had bagged up his clothes and put them in the hallway.

At 5 p.m. on Saturday the 21st he phoned her, but she put the phone down on him. That evening she went to her mother's with her son. She returned at 1 a.m. on the Sunday morning, put their son to bed and then went to bed herself. Around 3-4 a.m. she heard breaking glass from the French windows into her sitting room. She got up and found the defendant in the hall.

From this point the Prosecution and Defence narratives diverge in the Summing-up:

'*Her story*
... the defendant was ranting and raving. He seemed to be high on something; drink or drugs or both. He was saying ... he could have her any time he wanted. He was ... as mad as hell and she was terrified. He was making threats of physical violence to her ... the defendant then told her to go into the other bedroom ... he continued to rant and rave at her. Then he took his clothes off ... it was obvious what was going to happen next. She told him not to do it, but he ignored her protests ... sexual intercourse began with the defendant on top of her. It is a matter for you, not me, but this may be of some importance when you are considering whether that woman is a truthful witness or an untruthful witness, who from malice has invented a story of rape because what she said was this: She knew what turned this defendant on, she realised that the sooner she could get him to climax the sooner the whole thing would be over, and in any event he was at that point threatening to bugger her. So she turned herself over and she guided his penis into her. She said she did this to get the whole

'*His story*
The defendant gave evidence. He had exercised his right to silence when arrested. [You will not hold that against him because nobody is obliged to answer police questions if they do not want to. He chose to remain silent as he was entitled to.] [*The language of the Summing-up is not totally clear here but I interpret it as stating that the discussion about the future/ending of the relationship was caused by the defendant's use of heroin. He said she used it as well; she said she did not.*]

After she had put the phone down on him on the Saturday afternoon, he was desperate to collect his clothes because he was going off to a rehabilitation centre ... because of the heroin. It seems that he actually arrived into the rehabilitation centre very nearly two months later, but that is what he said; he was desperate for his clothes ... [an] associate – he would not give his name – agreed to drive him to Miss G's flat ... and because there was too much of it for him to move on his own ... he and the associate went to the flat and knocked on the door. There was no reply, so he assumed the flat

thing over with, and she did not do it because she was in any sense consenting to what was going on. You must make up your minds about that piece of evidence; decide whether it has the ring of truth; if it does then you will ask: ... (10)

After the defendant had ejaculated he fell asleep and after some time so did she. Next morning ... Then she woke the defendant up. She said he made her swear that she would not tell anyone, particularly the police, what had happened.

She went to her sister's house, taking the little boy with her. Her parents were also there. She said she told her father that the defendant had broken into her flat, but she did not go on to tell her father about the rape. However, a little later she told her sister and a friend of her sister's called again, that the defendant had raped her.

Then, two days later, having considered the matter very carefully, having considered what she would have to go through if she did report it to the police, she went to the police and made her report.'

was empty. Therefore, he climbed ... dropped down on to the balcony outside the living room, and at this point his associate drove off leaving him, of course, without transport. He had no money and so he could not get a minicab, but he was so desperate to get his clothes that he forced the door ... he found, not that the flat was empty, but this Miss G and the little boy were in there. They went into the bedroom, and he suggested that they should have a smoke of heroin because he had two, obviously very small, bags of heroin with him ... They chatted perfectly friendly, amicably together. They smoked a couple of joints together. The heroin obviously agreed with Miss G because when he suggested they should have sexual intercourse, she readily agreed at once, although she did say it would be for the last time. Therefore ... with her complete consent and cooperation, they had sexual intercourse together. In the morning ... after she had gone he left her flat. He did not take any of his clothes with him but a few days later, by arrangement, he collected them from her mother's flat.'

After reporting to the police Miss G was medically examined. Her account to the doctor was marginally inconsistent with the one she gave in court. She told the doctor that she had slashed the defendant on the back; in court she said she had not.

> There were no injuries on her. As the doctor said, and as you may think is plain commonsense, that does not prove anything one way or the other. The medical evidence is absolutely neutral ... the medical evidence takes the case no further one way or the other. (p. 12)

Linguistic aspects

The questions in 'Matchman'

Erotesis–Apocrisis

(1) 'What must be proved to establish an allegation of rape?
Three things:
First, that there was sexual intercourse ... any penetration by the penis of the male of the vagina of the female ...; in this case it is agreed that sexual intercourse took place.
The second thing ... sexual intercourse took place without the consent of the woman in question. That is the issue in this case,
The third thing ... is that the defendant either knew the woman was not consenting, or was reckless as to whether she was consenting or not ...' (p. 6)

(2) '– a long standing previous relationship ...
What bearing does that have on your consideration of this case?
Members of the jury, very little. Even in 1992 ...' (p. 6)

(3) 'You might say:
But what about her complaints; her complaint to her sister; her complaint two days later to the doctor and to the police?
Members of the jury, what those complaints show is that from an early stage that lady was consistent in what she was alleging.' (p. 7)

(4) 'Those complaints cannot amount to corroboration. They cannot amount to independent evidence supporting her evidence.' (p. 7)
'Why?
Obviously, because they come from her and they are not independent of her.' (p. 7)

Rhetorical question

(5) 'That being so, she resented being woken up in the early hours of the morning.
Who could blame her?' (p. 8)

Implicative questions

(6) 'You make your minds up about that piece of evidence; decide whether it has the ring of truth; if it does then you ask:
"Well, would a malicious woman inventing a false story of rape have invented that little detail?"' (p. 11)

(7) 'I repeat again:
Is she telling the truth, or is she, or may she be, a malicious woman who out of spite and to get rid of the defendant, is inventing an untruthful story?'

(8) 'You ask the same questions about him:
Is he trying to give a truthful account of what happened or is he trying to mislead you in his own interests?' (p. 13)

Comment

This case presents a puzzle that has not been alluded to so far, though the reader may have noticed it. It raises two issues which are not rhetorically based. The first is comprehension:

> Did the jury comprehend what was required of them?

The other is pragmatic:

> How do juries cope when uncertain as to what is required of them, beyond the knowledge that they must give a verdict?

The facts alleged by the complainant, non-consensual buggery, do not fit the indictment nor the judge's clear direction on the first limb of the definition of rape (prior to reform in the Criminal Justice Act 1994) which he gave as 'sexual intercourse. In the eyes of the law, that means any penetration by the penis of the male of the vagina of the female' (p. 6)

From the allegation, there was attempted rape converted into non-consensual buggery by the complainant – to get it over quickly. Given this hiatus between fact and law, it is interesting to note that after 68 minutes the jury sent in a Note to the judge. This did not raise that issue, but sought further clarification of consent, which was given. One hundred and forty minutes later the majority verdict was delivered.

That verdict was formally sought on 'rape' (p. 19). This raises a number of issues:

(1) Whether there was a misdirection on law since buggery was not an offence on which an alternative verdict could be given under s.6(3) Criminal Law Act 1966.

The clear terms of the Direction on 'the vagina' may not have been noticed.

(2) Alternatively a form of jury 'equity' might have occurred, in which rape and non-consensual buggery were elided. Legally, at that time, this would have been a perverse conviction.

(3) That does not exhaust the possibilities. Another possibility is that the jury did consciously convict of rape. If this – literal version – was indeed the case, the jury would have accepted that the complainant was malicious, but also that the defendant did rape her.

(4) On this possibility a further comment can be attached. Usually in cases of this type one learns whether the defendant purportedly wore a condom or not. Here there was no information, yet it was alleged that he was 'ranting and raving' and might have been high on drugs, or drink or both. If that was the case the 'collusive' buggery can be perceived as a rational prophylactic response to an impossible situation. That this was not mentioned in the prosecution case might be suggestive of the 'malice'

theory of the defence. The jury's verdict, however, avoids the dichotomous approach put forward by the judge; the victim may have been malicious in inventing the buggery, but not in alleging the rape. (5) It is not surprising that this was a majority verdict.

Two assault convictions

'Hill' – actual bodily harm

It was important to find some 'ordinary' trials. I have obtained one case of violence that is not in the same category as the depressing series of murders and rapes that I have read. '*Hill*' (name of defendant altered) is a case of actual bodily harm, bruising caused by falling when the victim Miss Mack was pushed by the defendant in an altercation over loud music from his flat.

Because the Summing-up is only six pages in length I will present its structure produced by the usual analysis. The structure:

Page	**Lines**		
4	(1–11)	*Nomo-dogma*	judge–jury roles (Disclaimer)
	(12–26)	*Nomo-dogma*	the charge
5	(1–14)	*Nomo-dogma*	the charge – a.b.h.
	(15–27)	*Nomo-doxa*	Proportionality Example –
6	(7)	*Nomo-doxa*	Proportionality Example +
	(8–16)	*Nomo-dogma*	application to this trial
	(17–26)	*Nomo-dogma*	method regarding the law
	(27)–7(1)	*Nomo-dogma*	Burden of proof
7	(1–6)	*Nomo-dogma*	Standard of proof
	(7–13)	*Nomo-dogma*	Majority verdicts
	(14–22)	*Nomo-dogma*	The Summarizing function (Disclaimer)
	(23)–8(6)	*Mythos I*	Crown Prosecution Service case
8	(7–18)	*Mythos II*	Defence case
	(8)–9(7)	*Nomo-dogma*	Status of lies
9	(8–13)	*Nomo-dogma*	Foreman selection

There is a relatively intense, formal referral rate to the jury at 1.3 per page:

8	Members of the Jury
1	Ladies and gentlemen
1	We etc.
10	

The imbalance in addressing defendant and victim is typical:

9	Th. Defendant	5	Miss Mack
2	N Hill	1	J Mack
2	Th. Accused	1	Th. lady
13		7	

Linguistic aspects

There were three Questions:

(1) 'Really, the question for you to decide here is: has that allegation been proved?' (p. 4)
(2) 'You would not be entitled, would you, to take out an axe and strike her on the head?' (p. 6)
(3) 'If in fact he did push her, thinking she might have stopped him, was that a reasonable thing to do in all the circumstances, because if it is reasonable and he was acting in self-defence, why then, members of the jury, it would not be unlawful, would it?' (p. 6)

The Exemplifications, negative and positive, were

> The force used in self-defence must be commensurate with the threat. Let us take an example way away from this case:
> an angry little old lady advances upon you with an umbrella and threatens to whack you on the head with it. You would not be entitled ... strike her on the head? That would be absurd.
>
> You have to use reasonable force proportionate to the threat you are faced with. On the other hand, faced with an armed robber with a sawn-off shotgun, you may well be entitled to shoot him dead ... (pp. 5–6)

Legal aspects

The legal Direction on the judge–jury demarcation is striking (and relevant):

> You are the 12 judges of fact. There are not 13 judges.
> I have nothing whatever to do or say with regard to the facts; that is your province. (p. 4)

The special interest of this case exemplifies the link between tropes and their location in structure. The structure is itself unusual. The Burden and Standard of proof are given at the end of the legal Directions, followed by that on unanimity. Unusually the unanimity/majority verdict Direction immediately precedes the Direction on foreman selection and the jury's withdrawal for deliberation – though there is no legal requirement for this routine. Having given the Direction on unanimity the judge then says that he will summarize the case. This contradicts his opening remark that 'I have nothing to do or say with regard to the facts'.

He commences 'let me summarise the case for the Crown and the case for the defence'. The summary for the Crown covers 14 lines, and that for the defence 10 lines. However, there is an important slippage here as the 'defence' summary concludes with Prosecution points and a Nomodogma on those points:

> He says that, if he had not pushed her, she might have slapped him, and agrees

> that in the interview he said – in what he described as 'the heat of the moment' – she had in fact slapped him but now he agrees that that was a lie. Indeed he admits that when he was arrested and was asked had he an explanation for what occurred, he again lied by saying: 'I don't know what you are talking about. I have only just got in. Anyway she is probably drunk.'

Then follows a typical Warning on lies (and the Direction to choose a chair for the jury's discussion).

The statement of the lies and the Nomo-dogma on lying cover a further 19 lines and conclude the survey of evidence and the Summing-up. In tropic terms this concluding segment carries a simple form: repetitive emphasis. There are twelve uses of the 'lie' stem.

The slippage consists of the ratchet mode of adding substantially to the Prosecution account within the category of Defence account. In addition that method enables the strongest Prosecution points undermining the defendant's credibility to be the final and emphatic topic which the jury took out with them.

The jury deliberated for 55 minutes and convicted unanimously.

'Bowen' – trial as quasi-mediation: murder acquittal: majority manslaughter conviction

In this case

Th. Defendant	39
Th. Defender	5
Th. Accused	1
	45 : The Defendant/er

was acquitted of the murder, but convicted by a majority of 10–2 by the

Members of the jury	5
You the jury	3
'We etc.	3
	11 (in 24 pages: 0.45 per page: low intensity)

of the manslaughter of

Th. Man	24
Th. Deceased	17
Th. White guy	6
Th. White man	5 : 11
Th. deceased man	3
Th. aggressor	2
Th. instigator	1
	58 : Th. deceased man, the white

The second witness was a friend of the defendant who had been attacked immediately before the deceased fatally attacked the defendant. The defendant's name has been changed.

Michael	18
Michael S.	3
th. Black guy	3
th. West Indian	3
Th. Coloured one	2
Th. Black boy	1
Th. Black man	1
Th. chap	1
	32 : Michael, the black

The structure of the Summing-up will not be given at this point, but its themes appear as an Appendix at the end of this chapter.

The basic facts were not in dispute. They appear in quotation form from witnesses known to the defendant, to the deceased, and to neither.

Quotation and the Mythos

The Mythos, the disputed event at the centre of this trial, is reported almost entirely in quotation form, with some judicially interjected parentheses. These cover six pages (pp. 14–20). They are in order: Lester B, aged 17, a friend of the defendant; Michael S, a friend of Lester B and the defendant (he, Michael S, was attacked first); Miss S who was walking her dog in the park, the site of the action; Mrs R, another dog walker; Mr L who had been returning from a fete at his old school, to play football in the park; Mr E another dog walker and friend of the deceased and Mr B who was with Mr E.

Matters subsequent to the death were reported by the judge in direct speech. The defendant gave no evidence in court but the jury had a 102-page transcript of his interview by the police in the presence of his solicitor.

I shall paraphrase the incident because the witnesses quoted are not in conflict and corroborate each other in different respects. The issue in this trial was the legal interpretation to be put upon these events.

The Mythos

Three young men were walking in a park. One of them Michael S was black. Suddenly he was accosted in a hostile way by a white man (the deceased) who was walking his dog. A series of short questions were shouted at Michael S including 'What are you staring at?' This was followed by 'You are one of those leery ones, aren't you?'; then punches, one of which landed, the other, a heavy one, Michael S avoided. Lester B intervened. The deceased then uttered obscenities and moved on to the defendant. The defendant ducked the first blow and closed up with the deceased's second blow. The defendant had taken out a knife. It entered the deceased, who shouted 'He's stabbed me'. The defendant then ran off evading Mr E.

The forensic evidence was that death was due to a single stab wound to the abdomen, which (although the knife was shorter), because of the movement, penetrated 13 cm. There was no clear evidence as to whether the wound was caused by the forward momentum of the defendant, the deceased or both, but it was not in dispute that the knife wound was the cause of death.

The legal issue

The issue was whether the defendant was guilty of murder or manslaughter or Not Guilty because of reasonable self-defence (provocation was not raised as a defence).

In this Summing-up a number of features appear to favour the defendant:

(1) *Diminution of the murder charge*

'... there are three possible verdicts. They are guilty of murder; although as I understand it the Crown are not suggesting that you should return that verdict but it is open to you on the evidence' (p. 5).

'As I have indicated, it rather seems, from what learned counsel for the Crown has said in his speech to you just now – although it is entirely a matter for you – that the Crown do not feel able to argue, at any rate strenuously in favour of intent for the requisite of murder' (p. 12).

'If the answer is yes – although the Crown do not invite it – then you find him guilty of murder ...' (p. 22).

(2) *Disparagement of the deceased*

(a) The first method is one of comparison (antitheton) with the defendant:

'He [the defendant] was then, I suppose, what one might call a lad of 17. The deceased man was nearly 22; he was going to be 22 in the July. The defendant was tall, 6 foot 1. Again, you may think he was not far out from being a lanky school boy. It is for you to judge.

'However, as you know from the evidence according to Dr H ... the deceased was a big man: well nourished; about 13 stone: 6 feet tall.

'You will have to consider those aspects' (p. 10).

(b) The second method is factual and evaluative:

'... the Crown, in effect, concede that the deceased man was in effect, the aggressor ...' (p. 8).

'On the evidence here, it was the deceased who was the instigator of the abuse [there are eight 'Fuck offs' in the evidence cited] and violence in the first place ...' (p. 10).

There is further comparison:

'What is the background? The defendant is aged 17. He lived at home with his father, mother, his elder brother ... and his younger brother. He left school in the previous year. He was having some training to become a quantity surveyor. He has been in no previous trouble with the police. On the evidence he was a peaceable lad; not given to quick temper or to violence' (p. 13).

(c) The third is by the introduction of negative but irrelevant information:

'Although there were traces of alcohol and cannabis found in the deceased man's system, the forensic scientist says that it is clear that there was nothing like sufficient to have affected his conduct that evening ...' (p. 13).

'... scientists were able to say that there was nothing like sufficient trace of alcohol or cannabis to affect his behaviour at that particular time' (p. 20).

(d) The fourth is contextual:

'The poor man, he has gone forever and he is not here to tell his side of the story ... We are not here to judge him, save only insofar as your judgment of him may be relevant to the issues which you have to try in this case.

'In this regard, I say this, and I think no more: it is an old adage that a man is often judged by the company he keeps.

'You have had an opportunity in this trial of observing some who, on the evidence, were his friends. You have heard evidence of the events of the following day, which otherwise are wholly irrelevant; events, no doubt, brought about by the actions of certainly one of the deceased man's friends. You may think that if anything the evidence as to his friends – and if you look at that old adage – tends to support the evidence of those witnesses who speak of the deceased man as being the aggressor' (p. 14).

also:

'Members of the jury, I do not think I need remind you of his [Mr E ..., the deceased's friend] behaviour in cross-examination; you saw it and witnessed it and I let it be seen, it is quite proper you should' (p. 19).

(e) One other method is via the comparative nomenclature of the defendant and deceased. Subsidiary modes for each are complementary:

Th. Defender 5 The aggressor/instigator 3

'Defender', uniquely used here has the same stem as defendant, but its semantic weight is morally loaded in favour of the defendant.

The contextualizing of the wounding

(1) *Negatively*

At its strongest the facts admitted or agreed to would allow for a conviction for murder.

The strongest point against the defendant was the temporal context of the attack upon him. It was not the defendant but his black friend who was attacked without provocation first. The attack consisted of hostile words, obscene words and punches. Michael S ... simply evaded the attack once he realized what was happening. The attack on the defendant was not unforeseen and was no more violent.

> The Crown make these points for your consideration and you heard them this morning. First of all, the defendant simply was not going to back down, although he was capable of jogging off; he proved that by evading the two would-be arresters later on. Secondly, this was not a case of him standing in a dark alley with his back up against a wall; here was an open park where he could have run off and disengaged. Thirdly, if he was only having the knife for protection, why not show it to the man and threaten him first? Fourthly – this is again said – the defendant had no injury upon him whereas the other man died. Of course, those are factors which you take into account.
>
> The Crown for their part point out that the defendant agreed – at page 44 (of his interview) – that he had never been threatened. Also, he agreed that – page 75 – he had not backed down. 'I am not the sort of person to run.' It is also a matter for you to take into account. (p. 21)

(2) *Positively*

> ... but the possibility remained that he [the deceased] may have had some weapon, just as he, himself, had: who was to know?
>
> The defendant had in the back of his mind the injury suffered by his brother in the attack the month before. May he instinctively – and one has to consider all these matters because it happened in seconds and instinct is an important aspect – have been anxious for his own protection? There is reference to this talk of violence at page 44 of the interview. May this have been at the back of his mind? ... (pp. 10–11)
>
> As you know, the defendant was carrying a knife in his pocket. In the event, of course, it was an unwise thing to have done. He tells you that he had done so for his own protection, in case there was or may have been an attack upon him, such as was on his brother the previous month, which resulted in the wounds to the face – as you have heard and seen in the photographs – requiring 29 stitches. (p. 13)

Linguistic aspects

The use of Questions

Page		
4	And ask yourselves: 'where is the truth'?	method – wh
7	The first question is: at the material time was there any necessity for self-defence in the particular circumstances?	
7	In particular, have the Crown proved that there was no such necessity?	
8	How do you, the jury, decide what is or might have been reasonable?	method – wh
9	Thus, what circumstances do you look at on the one hand and on the other?	method – wh
9	Thirdly, if he was having the knife only for protection, why not show it to the man and threaten him first?	motive – wh
10	... did the defendant have the maturity of a man?	
10	But the possibility remained that he may have had some weapon just as he, himself, had: who was to know?	rhetorical – wh
11	may he instinctively ... have been more anxious for his own protection?	
11	... May this have been at the back of his mind?	
11	How does one prove intention?	method – wh
12	What is the background?	Initiator – wh
14	What do the witnesses say?	Initiator – wh
14	'The man was saying: "What are you looking at?" '	'Quote – wh
15	... ask yourselves is he trying to tell you the truth as he saw it and observed it?	
15	Then I heard ... 'What is your problem?'	Quote – wh
	'What are you staring at?'	Quote – wh
Or	'What's wrong with you?'	Quote – wh
	'Have you a problem?'	Quote
16	'You are one of those leery ones, aren't you?'	Quote
19	'What's happening?'	Quote – wh
22	the second issue: have the Crown proved that at the time he was acting with an intention to kill or at least to cause really serious bodily injury?	
24	Do you understand?	
	Does that answer your question?	
25	The first revolves round the question: was this an unlawful killing?	
25	The second question: was this unlawful killing murder or was it manslaughter?	

25 Firstly, was this an unlawful killing . . . a killing not done in necessary and reasonable self-defence?
26 Ask yourselves this question: whether in a moment of unexpected danger the defender had done only what he honestly and instinctively thought was necessary in those circumstances? method – wh
27 Did he in producing that knife and striking with that knife, surely go beyond what was reasonable? . . . Are you sure that he went beyond what was reasonable in the particular circumstances?
28 Does that answer the question that you asked?

The 'Wh'-questions in this Summing-up fall into five categories:

(1) reportage-quotation: pp. 14, 15, 15, 15, 19.
(2) as segment initiators: pp. 12, 14.
(3) as introductions to instruction on jury method: pp. 4, 8, 9, 11.
(4) in relation to the defendant's motive: pp. 9, 10.
(5) in posing a rhetorical question: p. 10.

Direct questions are largely raised in relation to the legal issues: pp. 7, 7, 10, 11, 11, 15, 22, 24, 26, 27.

Appeals to common-sense

'You are a body from the outside world, bringing with you your own individual *common sense* and powers of judgment . . . you pool your collective wisdom, *common sense*, and powers of judgment so that it becomes the *common sense*, judgment, and the wisdom of the jury as a whole' (p. 4).

'As to the first matter, both the law and *common sense* recognise the natural instinct and right of a person to defend himself . . .

'. . . immediate defensive or avoiding action may be necessary in the particular circumstances: that is *common sense*' (p. 7).

'Again, the law and *common sense* dictate that a person may do, but only may do what is reasonable to defend himself when the necessity arises' (p. 7).

'If you are a frail woman and you are being attacked by a strong man then, of course, you could go to substantial lengths to beat him off. It is again *common sense*' (p. 10).

[The effect of 'good character']

'Yes, members of the jury, I think it is again a matter of *common sense*, as so many things are' (p. 23).

'Do you understand? However by all means take it into account as far as *common sense* allows you to do so . . .

'As I mentioned to you before, the law and *common sense* do dictate that a person may do, but may only do, what is reasonable to defend himself' (p. 25).

There are two types of usage of 'common-sense' here, and they may be contradictory.

The first and penultimate instances exemplify common-sense as a particularistic construction by the jury. Since this cannot occur without deliberation, even conflict, it cannot be taken for granted as a pre-ordained category.

The second and third instances elide law and common-sense, an elision of the Nomo-dogmatic and the Krito-doxic, since it is an empirical and contingent issue whether and in what circumstances individuals do actually defend themselves. This is illustrated well by the next exemplification (p. 10): it is highly contingent whether a frail woman would beat off an attack by a strong man, however morally and legally justifiable that might be.

Exemplification and instantiation

'Let me explain:

the killing of one person by another is not necessarily unlawful.

'Evidence of this is when death tragically results from an accident, whether on the roads or in the factories or elsewhere.

'Also, death sometimes tragically results from a person properly defending himself or his home or his family against an aggressor or intruder' (pp. 5 and 25).

'If the unlawful blow was struck, not with such an intention but for instance, an intention to frighten or hurt, then that is not murder but it is manslaughter . . .' (p. 6).

'If the attack is serious, so that it puts someone in immediate danger, then immediate defensive or avoiding action may be necessary in the particular circumstances; that is common sense. If a person is attacked he does not have to stand there and take a pasting, of course he can defend himself. However, if there is no attack, or if any attack is over, then no further defensive action is necessary; that is obvious' (p. 7).

'What is reasonable varies infinitely according to the circumstances of any particular case. If you are faced with, and threatened by, a ruthless man armed with a shotgun, the action which you might be disposed to take would be totally different from that if you were threatened with assault by an elderly lady with an umbrella: two extremes, but between those extremes the circumstances vary infinitely . . .' (pp. 7–8).

'If an attacked person is a weaker one than the attacker, then it is a factor which one may have to take into account in all fairness, especially in the dark alley situation. If you are a frail woman and you are being attacked by a strong man then, of course, you could go to substantial lengths to beat him off. It is again common sense' (p. 10).

'... for instance, the defendant may have intended to frighten or to hurt, no more than that; even to injure but not seriously; or even striking out blindly, he had no particular intention at all ...' (p. 27).

The function of these examples and instances is to provide parameters, outer limits in different directions within which the jury will have to make closure in one or other of the two directions dichotomized by the examples.

Some legal aspects of the Summing-up

Discounting sympathy

'In a case of this nature it is you who are the important people to consider the evidence and ask yourselves where upon the evidence does the truth lie. Each one of you is sworn to return a true verdict according to evidence. I emphasise "according to evidence" because you do not act on speculation or on suspicion and you do not act out of sympathy, wherever sympathy may lie; sympathy for the deceased man who has died at an early age or sympathy for the defendant in his present predicament. You have to look at the evidence as dispassionately as you can; and it is not easy to be unemotive in these matters. Look as dispassionately as you can and ask yourselves: where is the truth?' (pp. 3–4).

Disclaimer – counsels' submissions

'By all means take account of the submissions of learned counsel on the one hand and on the other. If you feel that you agree with one learned counsel rather than the other, as to the submissions he makes, by all means follow them; so long as they are founded upon the evidence. On the other hand, you are equally free to disagree with the suggestions or submissions that learned counsel has made to you, because it is not learned counsel any more than I who decide this case but it is you' (p. 4).

The Standard of proof

'The Crown have to prove guilt so that you are sure; you must be satisfied beyond a reasonable doubt, that is an expression with which I am sure most of you are acquainted. That means this, no more and certainly no less, that if a jury in considering the evidence say to themselves with a good conscience: We are sure this charge is proved, then they say so by their verdict of guilty. On the other hand, if the jury, equally with a good conscience, say to themselves: We cannot be sure, they deliver a verdict of not guilty' (pp. 4–5).

'Did he, in producing that knife and striking with that knife, surely go beyond what was reasonable? That is the whole nub of the question. Are you sure that he went beyond what was reasonable in the particular circumstances? If you are not sure then he is not guilty. If you are sure that the production of a knife and the use of the knife in those circumstances go beyond what was reasonable, then, of course, he is guilty of an unlawful blow ...' (pp. 26–7).

Jury deliberation of reasonableness

'What I have pointed out to you is this. You do not just carry out an analytical study as of now in the cold light of day, you have to pitch yourselves back in your mind's eye to wherever the confrontation occurred and put yourselves in that position, considering all the circumstances surrounding the situation. One of the factors is the length of time which it all took, which may be no more than seconds in actual fact; a lot can happen in seconds. However, put yourselves in the position of the defender and ask yourselves this question: whether in a moment of unexpected danger the defender had done only what he honestly and instinctively thought was necessary in those circumstances? If the answer is yes ...' (p. 8).

'How do you, the jury, decide what is or may have been reasonable? You ought not simply in the cold of light of day, or in the lesser light of the courtroom, draw up some form of balance sheet, judging to a nicety the balance between the force and means of aggression on the one hand and the force and means of defence on the other. It may be easy for us to say this, that, and the other, sitting where you are, sitting where counsel is and where I am, but that is not the point. You should project yourselves in your mind's eye, as far as you possibly can, into the position of the defender, wherever he was: in the dark alley; in the pub brawl; in the park, wherever it happens to be. Put yourselves in the position of the defender and ask yourselves whether in a moment of unexpected danger the defender had only done what he honestly and instinctively thought was necessary in the particular circumstances. If the answer is, yes ...' (p. 26).

Jury deliberation of Intention

'The next question is whether he be guilty of murder or manslaughter. I remind you that the distinction between the two lies in the intent with which the blow was struck. How does one prove intention? You cannot split a man's head open to see what was going on in his mind at any particular point of time; you can only gauge a man's thoughts, his beliefs and his intentions by fair and proper inference from the proved facts. That is to say, you have to consider what facts are proved before you and ask yourselves what inference you can properly draw from those proved facts' (p. 11).

Conclusion

At first glance this case appears to be one of a racial attack, diverted to an attack on the victim's friend who overreacted with death ensuing. There is, however, what I call 'layering' as an ante- and post context: an attack on the defendant's brother before the incident leading to the death, and the (unexplicated) trouble in the neighbourhood after the aggressor's death, and then the loutish behaviour by the deceased's friends in the court itself in which 'The Story in the Trial' became part of 'The Story of the Trial'.

The prosecution and judge are clearly torn between removing the murder charge and leaving it to the jury; in short, everything short of a Direction to acquit on that charge occurs. The jury, however, took their task seriously and after two hours of deliberation, through their forewoman sent in a Note for further elucidation of manslaughter and reasonable force. A further Direction was given on this (pp. 25–7). The jury were called back by the judge an hour later to be given a positive majority verdict Direction. An hour and a quarter later the jury returned to enter an acquittal on the murder charge and a majority verdict (10-2) conviction of manslaughter. This was immediately *preceded* by a second Note to the judge: 'We have reached a majority verdict of 10 to 2 on manslaughter, but the whole jury have great sympathy for the defendant.'

The special difficulty confronting the prosecution was that the behaviour in court of the deceased's witnesses put the facts as pleaded in an altered perspective, by adding a further narrative layer witnessed by the jury, as a result of which a conviction for murder appeared remote. It looks with hindsight as if the episode was not one of racial attacks, or even homophobia ('Aren't you one of the leery ones?'), but of turf-assertion by bullies over a period of time. From a purely academic viewpoint, murder was a (non-*Galbraith*) possibility. If that verdict had followed, the judge in turn would lose control of the sentencing, since the mandatory 'life' sentence and 'tariff' procedure would have to follow. The jury in its turn read the situation as it was presented to them and signalled that it comprehended the problem with its unanimous Note. This was expressly taken into account and a 'wholly exceptional' non-custodial sentence ordered.

'Bowen' – Appendix: Themes of the Summing-up

Page		
4	Introduction to judge/jury demarcation	
	Judicial trial function and Disclaimer	
	Jury role:	evidence *versus* sympathy
5		common-sense
		counsel
	Burden of proof	
	Standard of proof	
6	The charge and three possible verdicts	
	unlawful homicide	
	unlawful blow	
	unlawful intention	
	self-defence	
7	Examples +/–	
	Examples +/–	
8	Deciding on reasonableness	
	the deceased the aggressor	

9	The circumstances of the killing
	The Prosecution perspective
10	Comparison of defendant and deceased (antitheton)
	wider context of the incident
11	The question of intention in murder/manslaughter
12	The evidence
	Defendant's right to silence
	The defendant
13	The walk in the park (the knife)
	forensic evidence for deceased
	The deceased
	The witnesses
14	Lester B, defendant's friend (Quotation)
15	Michael S, defendant's friend (Quotation)
16	Michael S ... (Quotation)
17	Miss S (dog walker) (Quotation)
	Mrs R (Quotation)
18	Mr L (school fete) (Quotation)
19	Mr E, deceased's friend (Quotation)
	– Judicial interjected parentheses –
	Mr B (friend of Mr E) (Quotation)
20	Judicial narrative of ambulance, hospital
	Postmortem
	Forensic evidence
21	PC A ... (jailer)
	Defendant's interview 102 pages
	Defendant's admissions
22	Conclusion: jury verdict on the evidence
	Burden of proof – self-defence
	Murder (Crown not inviting)
23	Majority verdict Direction
	Foreman, appointing
	Exhibits
	Defence counsel's interjection
24	'Good character'
	12.57 – 3.02 p.m. Jury Note
25	Manslaughter or reasonable force
26	Jury projection into the situation
	Reasonableness
27	Murder/manslaughter intention

6 Three alternative models

In this chapter I introduce three models of judges' trial speech to the jury at the conclusion of a trial.

In the USA, there is no survey of the evidence, except in a handful of states and in federal criminal process.

In Canada, an extended – reformed if you like – version of its Anglo-Welsh ancestor occurs in trials, under the federal aspect of the Constitution.

In Scotland, whose relevant law has been outlined earlier, as in the USA the legal instructions dominate (not in such extreme legalese) but the evidence is not eschewed. That evidence, however, is not 'surveyed' in a rhetorical narrative of narratives, but averred to within the context of the relevant legal instructions.

Jury instruction – the USA states' model

In the USA the practice and court-rulings during this century have in most states removed the survey of evidence from the trial judge's instructions to the jury. It is also clear that the instructions themselves emerge from a differently constituted legal culture in which the adversarial principle is writ large by advocate control of proceedings, and appeals are a routine part of process. This has had an impact on judicial discretion in two ways (in addition to the lack of surveys of evidence).

First, appeal-court approved 'Pattern Instructions' are universal and rigorously followed. To that extent the judge is no more than a selector and regurgitator. Second, either or both attorneys may collaborate to a greater or lesser extent to dictate the terms of particular instructions.

I was unable to obtain any state pattern book in Britain, and was also stymied in the USA because the international inter-library loan service does not handle loose-leaf volumes.

Because it is readily available – and subject to penetrating analysis – I shall refer readers here to Stygall's *Trial Language* (1994: 182–90) which includes a tabulation of the Final Instruction in a *civil* trial (Fig. 5.4) with some examples of actual instruction.

There were 15 instructions, of which ten were from the Indiana Pattern Instruction (e.g. 3.01):

2. (3.01)	Sets responsibility for judging evidence and manner.
3. (3.03)	Defines the term 'preponderance' – *repeats* Preliminary Instruction.
4. (3.05)	Gives the manner of resolving conflicts in evidence – *repeats* Preliminary Instruction.
5. (3.07)	Gives type of evidence that diminishes credibility.
6. (5.81)	Defines the term 'proximate cause' – *repeats* Preliminary Instruction.
7. (7.01)	Sets Standard of proof (in civil proceedings) – *repeats* Preliminary Instruction.
11. (3.15)	Informs jurors that they must consider the evidence as a whole.
12. (3.17)	Tells jurors to ignore testimony and exhibits not admitted into evidence.
14. (29.03)	Gives jurors the possible verdicts.
15. (3.31)	Selecting a foreman.

Two instructions were agreed in collaboration between the judge and attorneys for both parties (not relevant to criminal process): 1 and 8.

One instruction was put forward by the plaintiff's attorney (not relevant to criminal process): 9.

One was put forward by the defendant's attorney (not directly relevant to criminal process): 10, but this is similar to the British judicial 'Disclaimer':

> The fact that I have instructed you as to the proper measure of damages should not be considered as intimating in any manner any view of mine as to the amount of damages the Plaintiff should recover. Instructions as to the measures of damages are intended for your guidance only.

One instruction only was put forward by the judge at her own initiative. Regrettably, this was not reproduced:

13.	Explains how jurors are to deliberate.

This is a typical set of (civil) jury instructions in the American legal system today. It provides one model at a particular pole of how the judge should relate to the jury in relation to the facts at issue in a trial. This I call the Fact Abstention model. It is characterized by abstract definitions and a lack of exemplification. What it does not constitute is a 'hegemonic tale' in the terms of the sociology of narrative put forward by Ewick and Silbey (29 *Law and Soc. Rev.* (1995) 197).

In federal criminal jurisdiction the position in law appears to be nearer that in England and Wales but since I have obtained no instructions from such a court, I am not in a position to comment on specifics.

I have obtained the *Manual on Jury Instructions in Federal Criminal Cases* – the 'pattern book'. It was produced by the Seventh Circuit Judicial

Conference on Jury Instructions, chaired by The Honourable La Buy J in 1963 (La Buy 1965 edition).

In his foreword Chief Judge Hastings stated that it 'will be the basis for a lasting and valuable authoritative guide for many years to come'.

In his Introduction (p. vii) Judge La Buy stated that '... in composing these instructions – we pursued the objective of clarity, conciseness and simplicity'.

The largest part of the book (pp. 87–314) covers law relating to federal offences: anti-trust law; bankruptcy; conspiracy; counterfeiting and forgery; food and drug law; income tax; kidnapping; labour law; mail fraud; narcotics; perjury; thefts of government property; thefts from interstate shipments; thefts from the mails; transportation interstate of stolen motor vehicles; stolen goods; forged securities.

Part I contains seven chapters:

1. Scope and procedure of jury instructions
2. Orientation of the jury
3. Persons criminally liable
4. Elements of the crime
5. Defences
6. Evidence evaluation
7. Mechanics of the verdict

Of these one can see that chapters 1, 2 and 6 might be relevant to this study. Chapter 1 para. 1.01 states:

> The federal trial courts also include summarizing and commenting on the evidence in an impartial, dispassionate and judicial manner.
>
> The court must clearly indicate however that the jurors may disregard such remarks or come to a different conclusion in the exercise of their own individual untrammeled judgment in determining the facts.

In chapter 2, para. 2.03 states:

> The function of the jury is to determine the facts. (*McLanahan* v. *US* 292 F2d 630 (5th Cir 1961)). This should be done without prejudice, fear or favor, and solely from a fair consideration of the evidence. The evidence should be considered and viewed by the jurors in the light of their own observations and experience in the affairs of life. (*Holland* v. *US* 348 US 140 (1954), *Daniel* v. *US* 268 F2d 840, 853 (5th Cir 1959)). If during the trial, the court has intimated any opinion as to the facts, the jury is not bound by that opinion. The jury alone is the sole and exclusive judge of the facts. (*Quercia* v. *US* 289 US 466 (1932)).

It is submitted that the position for federal criminal process is not dissimilar to that in England and Wales, but it does not represent the position for the State trial courts where surveys of the evidence are not acceptable.

There was some jurisprudence on such surveys of evidence.

In *Blunt* v. *US* 244 F2d 355, 365 (DC Cir 1957) the court exceeded fair comment in stating that a psychologist's testimony was not based on observation or fact. It is doubtful that an English court would have made the same ruling.

Nearer the Anglo-Welsh approach were *Heinecke* v. *US* 294 F2d 727, 729 (DC Cir 1961), *Franano* v. *US* 310 F2d 533, 537 (8th Cir 1962), and *US* v. *Kahaner* 317 F2d 459, 479 (2nd Cir 1963) in which it was emphasized that courts were reluctant to reverse a judgment due to alleged unfair comment unless the trial judge clearly became argumentative and assumed the role of an advocate. In that respect the courts were not required to comment on every titbit of evidence that each litigant considered most favourable (*US* v. *Benevena* 319 F2d 916, 980 (2nd Cir 1953)). Also there is no requirement that time spent reviewing Government and defence testimony should be equally apportioned (*US* v. *Laurelli* 293 F2d 830, 833 (3rd Cir 1961)); neither can the right to summarize be circumscribed by the defendant's failure to offer evidence (*Wayne* v. *US* 318 F2d 205, 209 (DC Cir 1963)).

This leaves chapter 6 of the *Manual on Jury Instructions* – 'Evidence evaluation' – which is confined to legal pattern instruction on the whole business of evidence: presumption of evidence; Burden of proof; reasonable doubt; evidence and judicial notice; statements of counsel; inadmissible and stricken evidence; direct and circumstantial evidence; credibility; accomplice and informer testimony; reputation of defendant; flight or concealment; confessions and admissions; exculpatory and accusatory statements; Expert evidence; missing witnesses; publicity.

Canadian 'Charges to the jury'

I was privileged to obtain through students two Canadian Charges to the jury for two cases in the Superior Court of the Province of Alberta at Edmonton in 1995 and the Supreme Court of British Columbia at Vancouver in 1996. In the first, *R* v. *Damon Horne*, the accusation was robbery of a bank. In *R* v. *Daniel Starr* the accusations were of sexual assaults (rape) on two women known to the defendant.

There were a number of special features of both trials, notably *Starr*. Horne represented himself; one man had already been convicted and a woman involved became a Crown witness. He alleged a conspiracy against him by law enforcement agencies and that the evidence was 'cooked'.

With *Starr* the basic issue was consent and in this the evidence and narrative were to a considerable extent outside British courtroom experience. This was because of the intertwining of Native Canadian 'Plains Indian' culture throughout the action, including the trial itself. I have to say that I was very impressed by the way in which the parties and the Court handled these matters which were not easy.

Nevertheless, having written complete analyses, I have decided not to include them. There is a simple reason for this. Canadian Charges to the jury are in one overriding respect the same as those in England and Wales, in that judges provide a full survey of the evidence.

I will not go so far as to ignore the Canadian cases, but will focus largely on those matters that relate to the form of the Charge, especially where they differ from the Anglo-Welsh pattern.

The form of the Canadian Charge

Induction statement

Both the Charges commence with an induction statement.

Horne

This statement occurs immediately after the opening remarks on the judge–jury function.

> Your duty to your community is to ascertain if crimes have been committed and whether the accused committed those crimes. You have a responsibility to the accused to ensure that he is not improperly convicted. (1080)

This statement on the nature of the jury obligation is followed by a specifically Canadian warning on the influence of press reporting, and then a brief judicial 'Disclaimer':

> In my Charge to you, I may express an opinion about certain evidence or state that something has been proven or more likely, state that you will have little difficulty in finding something has been proven. If I do so, you're not bound by any opinion which I may express. Nothing is proven as a fact until you as the jury find it to be so. (*Ibid.*)

This is followed by a 'semi-Disclaimer' on the submissions made by counsel for the Crown and Mr Horne, the defendant appearing in person.

There are specific Directions on a number of issues, which I shall only mention here:

The defendant placing his character in evidence (1082); previous convictions, and corroboration (1086); flight as evidence of guilt (1095); and alibi (1115). An important one which occurs at the very end of the Charge is the Canadian Direction on unanimity of verdict (1134–5). There is also a very brief consequentialist Direction immediately after: 'You should not consider the question of penalty or punishment. You're not involved in the matter of sentencing' (1135).

Starr

In this trial Smith J had made an induction speech to the jury at the commencement of the trial. The Charge also commenced with a brief induction statement:

> The first thing I want to say to you is that you will decide the case on the evidence adduced in this courtroom, and nothing else. You will try it without prejudice against or sympathy for any person involved in the proceedings. Consider the evidence rationally, and do not let your emotions affect your judgment. (208)

The Burden and Standard of proof

Horne

In this Charge the Burden was stated four times:

> There's a very important rule of law which applies in this case as it does in every criminal case. This rule is known as the presumption of innocence. The accused is presumed to be innocent until the Crown has proven his guilt beyond a reasonable doubt. The presumption of innocence and the burden of proof in a criminal case are inseparable. The burden of proving the guilt of the accused person beyond a reasonable doubt rests with the Crown and that burden never shifts. (1080–1)

This Direction is repeated with emphasis as an antitheton:

> There is no burden on the accused to prove his innocence. There is no burden on the accused to prove anything. The burden is on the Crown to prove the guilt of the accused beyond a reasonable doubt. (*Ibid.*)

In the context of a particular presumption, the doctrine of recent possession, the Direction is given again in short form:

> Furthermore, the doctrine ... does not relieve the Crown of its obligation to prove its case beyond a reasonable doubt. (1093, repeated at 1094)

The first Direction on the Standard of proof occurs, as one would expect, in conjunction with that on the Burden of proof:

> The Crown must prove each and every element of the offences with which the accused is charged beyond a reasonable doubt.
>
> What is meant by proof beyond a reasonable doubt?
>
> When I speak of a reasonable doubt, I use the words in their ordinary sense and not as a legal term having some sort of special meaning.
>
> By reasonable doubt, we do not mean an imaginary or frivolous doubt which may be conjured up in one's mind. Reasonable doubt is an honest and fair doubt. A doubt based on reason and common sense. A real doubt which arises from evidence and not from any conjecture or speculation. It is the degree of proof which convinces the mind and satisfies the conscious (*sic*). It is the degree of proof that permits you, as a conscientious juror, to say: I am sure. (1081)

Again the Standard of proof for the doctrine of recent possession is repeated in conjunction with the Direction for the Burden of proof:

> As I explained to you earlier, the requirement for proof beyond a reasonable doubt in criminal cases is a fundamental principle that must govern your decision in this case. (1093)

Finally in relation to the robbery charges and their seven 'ingredients':

> I must remind you that the Crown must prove each of these ingredients beyond a reasonable doubt. You must return the verdict of Not Guilty of the offence of robbery if the Crown has not proved each of these ingredients beyond a reasonable doubt. (1105)

There are two aspects of Direction on which a comprehension test might be helpful, even though they may present no problem to lawyers:

> The Crown must prove each and every element of which the accused is charged. (1081 – l.7)
> You must avoid applying the reasonable doubt test to proof of individual facts. (1081 – l.39)

One matter that is put forward early in the Charge must be mentioned in conclusion: legitimation:

> You bring your collective experience from your contact with people into the juryroom. Simply use your good sense in deciding these issues. (1083)

Starr

The Burden of proof and Standard of proof weave in and out of the entire Charge at appropriate moments.

Here is the main statement of the Standard:

> You will note that I have said that the Crown must establish the accused's guilt beyond a reasonable doubt, not beyond any doubt. A reasonable doubt is exactly what it says, a doubt based on reason, on the logical processes of the mind. It is not a fanciful or speculative doubt, nor is it a doubt based upon sympathy or prejudice. It is the sort of doubt which, if you ask yourself, 'Why do I doubt?', you can assign a logical reason as an answer. A logical reason in this context means a reason connected either to the evidence itself, including any conflict you may find exists after you have considered the evidence as a whole, or to an absence of evidence, which, in the circumstances of this case, you believe is essential to a conviction. You must not base your doubt on the proposition that nothing is certain or impossible, or on the proposition that anything is possible. You are not entitled to set up a standard of absolute certainty, and to say that the evidence does not measure up to that standard. In many things it is impossible to prove absolute certainty. If, after careful consideration of all of the evidence in relation to each count in this case, there remains in your mind a reasonable doubt as to the guilt of the accused on any count, the Crown has failed to meet the standard of proof which the law requires, the presumption of innocence prevails, and you must, not may, acquit on that count or counts. (209)

Advice on deliberation

At the conclusion of the Charge in *Starr*, there is advice on deliberation, which I have not seen elsewhere:

> It is your duty to consult with one another and to reach a just verdict according to the law and to the evidence. Your foreman, Mr Loaka, will naturally preside and assist you in the orderly discussion of the issues. Each of you should have the opportunity of expressing your own point of view, without being unnecessarily repetitive. When you are discussing the issues, you should, of course, listen attentively to the arguments of your fellow jurors, approach your duties in a rational way and put forward your own points of view in a calm and reasonable way. (258–9)

There is also an unusual coda on the Standard of proof:

> If you have any reasonable doubt concerning his guilt on any count, you must give the benefit of that doubt to him and find him not guilty on that count. You are doing him no favour by doing that; you are merely doing the duty that is cast upon you by the law.
>
> On the other hand, if you do not have a reasonable doubt concerning his guilt on any count, you must find him guilty as charged. That, too, is your plain duty and the law requires that of you. (250)

The survey of evidence

I will first deal with the location of the survey of evidence.

Its location in the Charge

In *Starr*, apart from the judicial 'Disclaimer' made very early in the Charge, the location of the survey of facts is significant. It only occurs after a lengthy consideration of the general and specific law relating to the alleged offences. It may be therefore that any 'advocacy' efforts will be diluted by its subordinate context. On the other hand, it is the segment which jurors receive nearest to their time of deliberation, and could have the most impact.

The survey of evidence has its own heralding statement, including a further Disclaimer:

> I'm now going to mention some of the more important evidence that you've heard during this trial in order to consider your verdict. Keep in mind that what I'm relating to you comes from my longhand notes so there may be some inaccuracies. As I told you before, it is your memory of the evidence that counts and not the memory of counsel or my recollection of what the witnesses said.
>
> As well I may neglect to mention some portion of the evidence you consider important. Again, it is your view of the evidence that counts. At the end of the charge I will tell you how you may have parts of the evidence read back to you if you have difficulty recalling an important piece of evidence ... (1116)

In *Horne*, too, the survey of evidence has in its own discrete segment after the legal Directions.

(This trial was unique in my experience of reading such transcripts in that it had an all-female jury – given the alleged offence and offenders one speculates that counsel saw no purpose in challenging on that ground. In terms of modes of address that is not, however, what was significant in this Charge.)

I will now deal with the survey of evidence in connection with the 'Theory of the cases'.

The survey of evidence and the 'Theory of the cases'

The 'Theory of the case' forms a distinct segment of the Canadian Charge which is not woven into legal issues. In this respect the Canadian Charge does constitute a separate model of jury instruction, though it shares the Anglo-Welsh feature of having a full survey of the evidence.

This segmentation is made more pronounced by the inclusion of sections on the 'adversarial theory' of each side at the end of the survey of evidence. In *Horne* the defence theory followed straight on from the survey of defence evidence (1132–3) and contained five elements.

The theory of the Crown followed:

> There were 32 factors or elements which the Crown submitted has a cumulative effect of establishing guilt of the accused beyond reasonable doubt. (1133)

Ritter J then noted twelve of these elements.

I am not arguing that this more formal and lengthier mode of instructing the jury escapes the problems I associate with the Anglo-Welsh Summing-up. In crude quantitative terms – having omitted here virtually all the rhetorical analysis – the Crown's case was given more weight with 23 witnesses considered in 14 pages compared to the defence case with seven witnesses considered in three pages. Further the defence case and theory with five elements is sandwiched together between the prosecution case and its concluding theory section with twelve of its 32 elements highlighted.

In *Starr*, the 'Theory of each side' also occurred straight after the survey of evidence; first for the Crown (252–5) and then for the defence (255–8), which was followed by the advice on deliberation mentioned earlier.

Rhetorical aspects

Imperative and precatory forms

Horne

Judges instructing juries are usually cautious not to overtly dictate to them even when directing on law. In this Charge there is one example of a peremptory imperative. This is unusual, but I should not be taken as being critical of it. It is:

> *Examine* all the evidence when you're deciding whether the alibi is merely untruthful; or was a fabricated or concocted story designed to hide guilt. *Keep in mind* that a person may tell an untrue story for reasons other than trying to hide guilt. (1116)

Equally unusual is the use of the precatory form that occurs five times in this Charge. The first is combined with a repetitive turn to the first person plural.

> *Please* bear in mind, however that we sometimes make mistakes when we try to recognize people we know quite well. (1089)
> *Please* understand that these three things I've mentioned . . . are questions of fact which you must decide.
> *Please* remember that guilty knowledge is not the only reason someone might take flight after an offence has been committed. (1095)
> [However,] *Please* remember that it is up to you to decide whether or not the Crown has proved this ingredient. (1102) [and again]
> *Please* remember that the question for you to decide is what did the robber in fact intend. (1103)

Starr

There are no precatory forms in this Charge, but there is one imperative, which is also emphatic:

> *Remember* that a criminal record does not necessarily mean that someone is a liar, in the same way that a clean record does not necessarily mean that someone is truthful. (214)

Nomenclature and forms of address

Horne

'You, as the jury'	3
'Ladies of the jury'	4
'We' etc.	30
	37

Although the intensity of non-second person address is not above average at 0.7 per page, the resort to the cooperative (first person plural) form is high at 83 per cent.

As for the nomenclature of parties, there is no significant victim (the bank) form of address for comparison. The defendant and alleged co-offender (already convicted) are addressed:

		%			%
Mr Horne	160	58.0 >	Mr Turko	26	32.5
Damon Horne	61	22.1 <	Ken/neth Turko	53	66.2
The accused	47	17.0 >		0	
Damon	4				
The offender	3				
Horne			Turko	1	
	275			80	

The other offender, turned Crown witness, fared differently:

Betty Ann McKenzie	38	92.7%
Ms McKenzie	2	
Betty Ann	1	
	41	

as did the principal police witnesses:

		%			%
Det. Tutt	21	84.0	Const. Buckley	9	75.0
The Det.	2	(92.0)	The Constable	2	
Mr Tutt	2		Const. Richard B.	1	(100.0)
	25			12	

In terms of formality-credibility scale the two police officers have the highest ranking and the Crown witness the lowest. The accused's nomenclature is flawed by three references to 'the offender'.

Starr

Jury address forms are extremely sparse in this Charge, but they are nevertheless of interest in that the foreman receives unique treatment and is even named, which might be unlawful in the UK:

Mr Foreman and Members of the Jury	1
Your Foreman, Mr Loaka	1
We	3
	5 (minimalist)

The naming of the accused differs from that of the two complainants and the corroboration witness:

		%				%
The accused	57	62.6	>	Th. Complainant	8	16.7
Mr Starr	27	29.7	>	Miss Champagne	3	6.2
Daniel Starr	1		<	Diane Champagne	33	68.7
Daniel Lloyd Starr	1					
Starr	1					
Dan	1					
The offender	1			Th. Witness	4	8.4
	89				48	

		%			%
The complainant	3				
Miss Ryan	1		Miss Narcisse	3	
Pamela Ryan	33	80.0	Iona Narcisse	11	55.0
Pamela	3		Iona	6	
The witness	1				
	41			20	

Conclusion

The Canadian mode of instruction to juries does differ in detail from that in England and Wales. In particular it appears to show consciousness of the problems inherent in the survey of evidence and to provide attempts at correction or balancing of the problems. On this small evidence one cannot say that these methods – induction, advice on deliberation, theory of each side – are successful.

Scotland – two convictions and their judges' Charges

Through the good offices of the Crown Office at Edinburgh, I acquired two 'Charges to the jury' where convictions followed. One was by Lord Caplan and the other by a Sheriff, both with Glasgow jurors. The first trial was over paternal incest and sexual abuse of three daughters. The other was of robbery and breach of the peace by two defendants. As in England and Wales, transcripts of acquittals (both Not Proven and Not Guilty) are notoriously difficult to obtain – usually because they are only required for appeal purposes – so I was unable to acquire either type.

Nevertheless this sample of two has proved invaluable in providing an alternative model of Summing-up to juries.

Neither Charge is particularly lengthy: *M* was 22 pages (with 50 minutes deliberation) and *Mitchell and Kelly* was 35 pages (with 213 minutes deliberation).

In both the normal address is 'Ladies and Gentlemen': once in *M* and

16 times in *Mitchell and Kelly*. In both 'we' is used four times. Thus, jury address is not stressed, but it is in formal tone.

Emphatic conjunctives do occur but are not stressed:

	M	*Mitchell and Kelly*
Well	4	6
Indeed	0	2
Now	13	22
	17	30

In *M* alone there are twelve appeals to the 'order of things':

Of course	8
Common-sense	2
At the end of the day	2

The typical address of the defendants was the correct, Scottish, term 'the accused':

	M	*Mitchell and Kelly*	
Th. accused	21 : 84%	Th. accused	84 : 93%
Th. perpetrator	1	Stephen Mitchell	2
Th. father	3	Mitchell	1
		Anthony Kelly	3
	25		90

There was more variation in references to the victims:

M		*Mitchell and Kelly*	
Th. daughter/s	6	Mr. Maxwell	17
Th. girls	7		
Th. witnesses	1		
Th. young persons	1	Th. man	1
Th. complainant/s	8	Th. victim Mr M	1
A/D/M	14	Th. victim	4

From this one can construct a polarized duality of address in both Charges:

M

'The complainant/s, girl/s, daughter/s (A/D/M) "*versus*" the accused.'

Mitchell and Kelly

'Mr Maxwell, the victim, "*versus*" the accused.'

The use of colloquialisms, metaphors and other tropes is much lower than in the English Summings-up.

M

There is one, typical, antitheton on the judge–jury demarcation with repetitive emphasis:

I and I alone (2B).
You will decide (× 4) (2D–3A).

There is another repetitive emphasis in the Direction against bias: 'try and act ...' × 3 (6B). Also one combined with a double appeal to the natural order in the Direction on the Standard of proof:

... at the end of the day ... [× 2] ... commonsense ... (4F)

There are two serial (Wh-) questions:

How does it stand up to critical analysis?
How do you evaluate the evidence of a witness against the evidence of other witnesses? (8E–9A)

There are two, adjectival metaphors:

... at the *root* of our system of law that a person is presumed to be innocent ... (3C)
... cannot be proved with *mathematical* precision ... (4B)

There are three colloquialisms:

Now, as far as oral evidence is concerned, that doesn't mean the questions *coming out of counsel's mouth* ... (5A)
... but that is *neither here nor there* ... (16B)
You have to listen to a lot of *speechifying* in these cases. (24B)

There is one significant exemplification bracketing out acceptable from unlawful behaviour:

... a caring parent discharging normal duties of care, for example undressing a young child ... (14B)

Finally there are two implicatures:

> ... and to enable you to say ...
> Well, I can accept 'such and such' a piece of evidence because it gains support from another piece of evidence ... (7C)
> If there is any witness ... you do not accept, you think:
> 'Well, I can't take anything from that, it is unreliable.' ... (10A)

I suggest that on this evidence the rhetorical volume and intensity of this Summing-up is low, and much lower than all of the English ones analysed.

However – and this may be a partial explanation of this low intensity – there is an even more striking difference. There is no formal survey of the evidence, and the Mythos elements that do occur are largely present by necessity within the legal orientation and structure of the charge.

Here are the Mythos elements:

> ... the three complainers were all daughters resulting from the marriage of the accused to E B (16A)
> The father is said to have abused the girls in the family home ... and abuse ... is said to have begun with certain acts of indecency involving mutual touching, and then through time the behaviour is said to have deteriorated to become sexual intercourse ... accompanied by a degree of threatening conduct ... (19A–C)
> ... that the motivation of the complainers could be a hope for compensation ... or also jealousy arising from the birth of a stepsister ... the complaints were initiated by M who was at the time away from her family and living in Germany ... (20A–C Trial Mythos)
> ... the three girls never confided in anyone over all the years that have passed since the alleged incidents. Well, you heard them. They gave explanations for that. They said they felt isolated and threatened, and you will have to weigh up the arguments that were put to you for and against and decide what your view is about that matter. There is the fact that, until M raised her complaint with the police, A, and D in particular, and even M to a limited extent, seemed to have preserved a family relationship with their father. You will remember the evidence you heard about visits and babysitting and the matters of that sort, the fact that D allowed her father to take her daughter to school. (21A–D)

These Mythos elements comprise about two pages of the 22 – about 9% – and commence two-thirds of the way through the Charge. It is also clear that they do not comprise free-standing narrative, but are imbricated in legal issues. In other words, the Mythos elements would not have been recounted at all except to illustrate or give function to the legal issues. At most a further page – about 4% – is given to linguistic and semantic figures. In short: about seven-eighths – about 88% – of the entire Charge text is given over to legal issues.

Mitchell and Kelly

The low intensity of trope usage is even clearer:

There is some repetitive emphasis:

You and you alone; for you ... (×4) (2DE).
Indeed. It is your ... (×2) (4BC).
quite/fairly robust questioning (×2) (18A).

There are a few euphemisms:

This unfortunate young man (12C)
... slightly difficult concept to grasp ... (20A)
... the fruits of robbery (31AB)

There are two achrologisms, which are also terms of legal technique, which might raise problems of comprehension, and require interpretation:

exculpate (8E and 17D).
Evidence of concert (30B).

There is one colloquialism:

... something of a question mark over it ... (12D).

There is one (negative) exemplification:

... as an example, evidence which should not in fact have been given by Inspector McQuade about what someone he interviewed had said ... Well, you disregard that. (16BC)

The above amount at most to a page, about 3%.

The Mythos elements are also much reduced on the typical Anglo-Welsh Summing-up:

... the constables say the accused persons were shouting on this night before they arrested them. They gave them a warning to desist and they persisted in it. (10C)
... the accused persons were subject to questioning by the police which you may think was quite robust ... the accused were faced with fairly robust questioning. (18A)
... the fractured skull and of the multiple injuries and bruising which took place ... (21E)
... the signs of kicking ... Mr M's jacket and waistcoat and his wallet and contents were removed ... (22A)
... if it should be that the fracture of the skull was sustained as a result of Mr M falling when he was being assaulted, rather than directly as a result of being kicked ... (22D)

> ... the first accused ... was found shortly after ... the time of the assault and robbery was committed ... wearing the waistcoat belonging to the victim of the assault and robbery ... keys belonging to the victim were found in his possession. (24AB)
> ... the second accused ... is in possession of stolen goods or goods which are the fruits of robbery rather at the same time as the first accused ... he was present at the scene of the crime ... (31C)

These amount to about a page and a half – less than 4% of the total. However, there is at least the same volume tacked well within the survey of disputed facts and legal issues. So, again, about 88% of the 35 pages is taken up by Nomos, legal issues.

Analysis of M

I present in conclusion the themes of the Charge in *M* with some illustrative quotations:

2A	Introduction: Roles
BC	The judge's role
CDE	The jury's role
3AB	Disclaimer:
	'... and I must make it absolutely clear that although I direct you in law I have got no right, nor indeed any intention to influence you as to what verdict you arrive at, and if I seem to be doing that then either you are misunderstanding me or I am not expressing myself clearly enough. It is your function to make the decisions about the facts, not mine' (3AB)
CD	Burden of proof
E	Standard of proof
–4F	'Now, you must note that you only need to take account of a reasonable doubt. Human affairs are complex and I think, as has been suggested to you, cannot be proved with mathematical precision, so if you had a doubt that could be described as a strained, fanciful, capricious, remote doubt, that kind of doubt you don't need to take account of. It has often been said that if you have a doubt that would cause you to hesitate before you took a decision about your own affairs then that certainly would be a reasonable doubt, but at the end of the day it is really a matter of commonsense as to whether a doubt could be described as reasonable, but certainly if the doubt is so remote from plausibility that it could be described as ridiculous, then that kind of doubt you should certainly reject, and if at the end of the day you were not left with any reasonable doubt about guilt, then it would be your responsibility to bring in a verdict of guilty' (4B–F)

5A	Evidence
B	Evidence – Joint Minute
CD	Jury's note-taking
E	Warning on bias etc.
–6B	Warning on bias etc.
CD	Consequential Warning re punishment
EF	(Scottish) Corroboration Warning
–7D	Implicature
E	Non-corroboration and evidence in favour accused
–8D	Non-corroboration and evidence in favour accused
E	Reliability and credibility of witnesses
9B	Questions
–D	Questions of reliability
E	Warning on discrepancies
10B	On rejecting evidence; implicature
C	The charges – intent
D	separate consideration
11	two charges per (three) daughters; one statutory charge
12C	Incest
D	s.5 Sex Offences (Scotland) Act 1976
13C	Consent not material
DE	'lewd'/'lascivious'/'libidinous'/'indecent'
13	Motivation
B–E	Example – 'caring' bracketed
15	Incest Act 1567
CD	'sexual intercourse'
E	degrees of relationship
–16D	the daughters – consent immaterial
E	The Prosecution case
17A	Judge's selection and problem of emphasis/omission
B–E	Corroboration – *Mooroy* principle: mutuality
-18D	
E	Common features in the three complaints
19B	Common features in time . . . behaviour
CD	Jury decision and *Mooroy* on 2+ daughters
–20C	Complainers' motivation: compensation/jealousy
DE	Defence case
21A	The three girls never confided in anyone
B	Their explanations
C	The family relationship preserved
D	D allowed father to take her daughter to school
E	Conflict between prosecution and defence
–22A	Conflict between prosecution and defence
BE	Absence of forensic evidence – not available
23A	Directions on choosing verdict
B	Separate verdicts on each charge

CD	three verdicts available: the two types of acquittal
E	Majority verdict
24A	Majority verdict on conviction (8+)
B	Spokesperson

Conclusion on the Scottish Charge

On this evidence the Scottish Charge to the jury provides a cousin to that of England and Wales. It is not restricted to purely legal Directions, but it operates a principle of relative and relevant factual parsimony. This is reinforced by a lower level of rhetorical intensity. This minimalist model correctly, in my view, privileges the advocates as fact-urgers and the jury as fact-finders. Pragmatically it does not eschew fact surveys entirely but locates them on a basis of necessity in relation to the overall structure of legal issues to be considered.

Conclusion on models of jury instruction

In this chapter I have surveyed a variety of judicial final speeches in jury trials. In the USA the federal courts appear to operate in a similar manner to the Crown Court in England and Wales. The state courts, however, usually avoid surveys of the evidence; they reflect their extreme adversarial process in which the advocates' 'Summations' comprise the final versions of the facts for the jury, so the trial judge's legal instructions involve a Fact Abdication model. In Canada there is a reformed traditional model in which the survey of facts follows some elementary jury induction and is succeeded by a 'theory' section for each side. In Scotland the position is as summarized above, a 'factual relevance and parsimony' model is the norm, and is embedded in the caselaw considered earlier.

7 Modest proposals

In what follows there is no attempt to echo Swift, no sarcastic equivalent of suggesting that mothers reduce the population by cooking their children. I shall conclude with modest and constructive prescriptions. Logically, however, before one can prescribe one must be satisfied that there is a problem that requires intervention.

In this book I have not surveyed even in a superficial way the historical emergence of the trial judge's Summing-up at the conclusion of a jury trial – especially the survey of evidence. In England and Wales one can see a typically fudged settlement around 1700: the jury are the undisputed deciders of 'the facts' and the related 'guilt or innocence' of the defendant by the means of a general verdict; moreover, although the judge may/must direct an acquittal in certain circumstances s/he cannot direct a conviction. However, the judge is not removed from that verdict entirely. Not only does the judge – as in all Common Law jurisdictions – instruct on the law relevant to the verdict, s/he additionally in England and Wales (and Canada and US *federal* jurisdiction) surveys the evidence adduced by Crown and defence for the jury, a narrative of narratives, fragmented by law.

It is a trite point, but relevant, that all our judges progress to the Bench on the basis of merit as advocates; the judiciary is not a separate legal profession as on the continent of Europe. This 'mental set' is not necessarily easy to slough off, and the fact that many counsel and therefore judges take on cases from both Crown and defence perspectives is neither here nor there, as the constant is advocacy.

In conducting a trial the judge, as can also be said for individual jurors, may reach a preliminary conclusion at the end of counsel's final speeches. This may not always happen, but when it does the judge's own sense of justice can come into play; it would be odd if it did not. The point, however, is that there is a terrain available on which it can come out to play: the survey of evidence within the Summing-up. The law does set parameters on the way in which that survey is presented, under the vague rubric of 'unfairness'. Beyond that there is almost nothing in the law or the Benchbooks about the structure and weighting of a Summing-up. All the judge has to do is enter the standard 'Disclaimer' at least once. In Chapter 2 where I dealt with 'Unfairness', I have shown the situations in which a Summing-up may be challenged.

I have attempted to demonstrate how the survey of evidence tends to be 'directional'. Frequently – though not universally – surveys of evidence lean one way or another, and there seems to be a strong correlation between such direction and the jury's verdict.

Additionally in the first chapter of this book I suggested a considerable number of ways in which the jury is situated so as to be receptive to the trial judge's Summing-up at the conclusion of the trial. In particular it is only in its survey of the evidence that the jury are likely to receive anything resembling a normal narrative of the dispute's events and their context. If it were not for this the jury would have to construct the Mythos from the series of segmented, disrupted and non-diachronic fragments that counsel and witnesses produce in examination and cross-examination. This has an effect on my choice of the positive prescriptive model I suggest below.

For what it is worth my reaction to what I have read (in some instances, many times) is that the judge's sense of the justice of the case is usually one I share, however much I may have deconstructed how the judge arrived at his expressed view. I would then add more robustly, that my view, like the judge's, is worth nothing, because we are both trespassing on the jury's domain: the twelve people who heard the trial from start to finish with all the virtues and risks of being almost certainly totally new and naive to their role, and having been set up by the situation, as I demonstrated, to be influenceable by directional surveys of the evidence. This structural position of weakness is, however, balanced by the opportunity to test evidence and individual views through eleven other individuals' experience of life.

In addition the cases surveyed here could never be called a representative sample. There are far too many missing offence types: robbery, grievous bodily harm, burglary, for example. There is not a single Welsh case and few from outside London. However, there is one mitigation: as far as *convictions* following trial and Summing-up are concerned I read and analysed many more Summings-up than those presented here, which did cover those offence types just listed. I was in fact torn by some of the omissions, but on pragmatic grounds I had to limit myself, particularly by entering those which balance convictions and acquittals: serious fraud; policeman defendants; and rape. Those excluded Summings-up are not different in any significant respect from those entered here.

We now also have the interview research for the Royal Commission on Criminal Justice, drawn from a large number of former jurors (Zander and Henderson 1993), that one notional juror per jury found the evidence 'fairly' or 'very difficult' (8%, 1%: 9%) (*ibid.*: T8.3); similarly with scientific evidence (9%, 1%: 10%) (*ibid.*: T8.4); and that it would have been 'much harder' without the Summing-up on the facts, especially as the length of trial increased:

1 day	13%
1–3 days	17%
3–5 days	22%
Over 1 week	34% (*Ibid.*: T8.13)

This shows a rise from one to four notional jurors.

Against this we can see what this book has demonstrated:

16% of jurors (two notional jurors per jury) thought that the judge's Summing-up pointed 'strongly' or 'slightly' towards acquittal (4%, 12%: 16%) and the same number thought it was towards conviction (3%, 13%: 16%). So in all a third of jurors felt there was directionality (*ibid.*: T8.16). It is not clear whether those beliefs ever occurred in the same jury.

Of these 32% felt that the pro-acquittal directionality was against the weight of the evidence; and 10% for the pro-conviction directionality (*ibid.*: T8.17).

The effect of directionality was marked: where it was 'strongly' or 'somewhat' for acquittal, acquittal almost always followed: 94%, 89%; similarly where the directionality was towards conviction 'strongly' or 'somewhat': 91%, 87% conviction rates occurred (*ibid.*: T8.18).

Jurors clearly believe and appear to act on the belief that the Summing-up on the facts does and should influence them. Incidentally, as far as conviction directionality is concerned the interview research contradicts experimental research (Sealy and Cornish 1979). Whether such 'covert advocacy' should have this effect is moot (Gold 1987), especially as interview research from Northern Ireland found that 32% of jurors (four notional jurors per jury) found it impossible to follow 'disregard' directions (Jackson, Kilpatrick and Harvey 1991: 5.9.7).

Having suggested, and hopefully demonstrated, the directionality of the Summing-up genre – in both directions – a further generalization can be made. There is no evidence of routine resort to tropic cliché by the judges as a whole. Indeed, when I have been able to consider more than one Summing-up by the same judge, the same holds true. Of course there are repeats of standard Directions on law from either the Benchbook or the judge's own variant, but the survey of evidence is very much a unique response to the unique arguments and parade of evidence of unique trials. So, the antitheton may dominate in one, metaphor in another, and so on; and how these are sited in structure will also vary in each instance. To summarize: the Anglo-Welsh Summing-up can hardly be accused of formulaicism, though it may be charged with attempted manipulation.

If one wished to replace manipulation through the survey of facts with formulae, one would evangelize for the American State jury instructions. With rare exceptions they are limited to the law of the case; largely derived from appeal-approved pattern books and when not so derived, are delivered with an appellate court in mind. So the jury is spared the manipulative re-presentation of the stories in the trial but instead force-fed with often incomprehensible legal instructions in lawyerese dialect

(Charrow and Charrow *Col. L. Rev.* (1979)). I should not be taken here as hinting that we should dispense with legal instructions; that would be to replace cooking the baby with throwing it out with the bathwater. Nor am I hinting that judge's discretion to instruct on the law be trammelled into routines, unless the Court of Appeal clearly so rules. It should be clear from the preceding chapters that the variety of strictly legal instructions gave me little trouble – they are cited simply to demonstrate the range of possibilities.

We can instead consider the other transatlantic jury jurisdiction, Canada. The form of the Canadian jury Charge appears to show recognition that there is a problem in the survey of the evidence. However, instead of eschewing it as was the case with their neighbours, they have attended to it by two additions. One is by a greater degree of jury induction; the other is by a concluding section on the 'theory' propounded by both sides. The survey of evidence itself remains in Anglo-Welsh form. My sample of two suggests that theory sections may not subtract from the problem of the survey of evidence.

In Scotland, there has developed, in law and practice, another model. This does eschew the 'survey' of evidence, but does not evade the evidence in its entirety. In the Scottish Charge to the jury the Mythos elements are sited on the basis of appropriateness into the relevant segments of legal instruction, operating what I have termed a principle of parsimony: no more and no less than what is required at a given point. The consequence is a marked reduction in but no absence of Mythos. Further, the jury actually receive assistance in that the relevant evidence is re-placed before them at the point where they need it, with a much lower incidence of rhetorical tropes. In the Anglo-Welsh model the legal instruction tends to precede the much lengthier Mythos survey, which therefore demands a degree of mental back-tracking during the Mythos survey which, even in a textual version, can be difficult.

So what is to be done? As I wrote at the outset, this is a modest proposal. I make no call for legislation nor for slavish copying of other's practices from other jurisdictions often with subtle, and not so subtle, legal and cultural differences from the UK. My prescriptions are as follows:

1. The pedagogic luxury of krito-doxa, judicial opinionation off the facts should be avoided.
2. Exemplification, especially the combining of examples, positive and negative, may be helpful to jurors; the fact-abstention model in the USA may be unhelpful in this respect.
3. Consequential argument is risky. It appears to trespass on the jury domain; this should be considered in the light of frequent warnings to juries against penal consequentialism by them.
4. Enumeration may appear to be helpful, but unless its critical paths are kept simple, confusion may be caused. Experimental testing might be helpful in this.

5. Standard forms of address should be adhered to:

   'Members of the Jury', or
   'Ladies and gentlemen';
   'The defendant';
   'The complainant'.

6. The first person plural should be avoided in advising juries, as should implicature statements.
7. I shall not catalogue those blatantly persuasion-orientated tropes, starting with metaphor. Instead I suggest that trial judges individually and in consultation with their colleagues, perhaps through the medium of the Judicial Studies Board, review their practice.
8. Whilst it will be clear that I am impressed by the Scottish model with its policy that judges be deliberately abstentionist in regard to the jury's role and function, I am not convinced that an immediate Practice Direction, new edition of the Benchbook, let alone legislation is required, though something *is* required. Instead it would be invaluable if some judges experimented with a Scottish approach to their own Summing-up. Whilst the Anglo-Welsh Summing-up in trials resulting in conviction verdicts would be appealed in Scotland time after time – and probably with success – I can see nothing about the Scottish model that would be *in ipso* appealable in England and Wales. This could in time be generalized in some way, informally by the Benchbook, or formally by Practice Direction. What matters is the move towards harmonization of this procedural moment. Of course, if one does not trust juries to 'get it right', or believes that counsel need extra support, or that juries should not be in Court in the first place, one will continue as at present.

   Another experiment would be to follow American State trial practice and provide no assistance on the facts, perhaps in short, straightforward cases (Zander *NLJ* 28 February 1997). In *'Hill'*, the 'a.b.h.' trial considered earlier, it is apparent that the trial judge originally had that in mind, but could not resist the habit both of a survey of the evidence, and within it of directionality.

I conclude with an illustrative anecdote followed by a constitutional point and a final prescription. Recently a friend of mine was tried in England in the Crown Court before a jury including nine 'New Commonwealth' persons and four women including the Afro-Caribbean forewoman. The complainant was a Central European male. The accusation was of extreme embarrassment, quite apart from the stress and stigmatic element of any trial. I along with 20 others put in a written positive character reference. My friend was not only well served by excellent counsel, the judge's Summing-up was, as my friend put it, 'loaded' in his favour. The jury took five minutes to acquit. For someone acquainted with the narratives (Mythos) of the case and the events in the trial this was hardly surprising: justice was done, my friend's reputation was resoundingly vindicated. But, one may ask whether the fact that the judge appeared to lead the jury horses to water, in a subtle way, reduced that cathartic sense of social delivery? The defendant was deprived of knowing that the twelve had done it on their own.

There is a constitutional point lurking in this anecdote. The current law and practice in England and Wales reflects rather well that fudged 'unwritten' settlement at the turn of the seventeenth/eighteenth century: a fluid, shared power between aristocracy and burghers, gentry and yeomanry. What it does not reflect is the modern democratic spirit of the Juries Act 1974, with jury service based (by and large) on adult suffrage. In this context the legitimation of the legal verdict lies in the lay persons who are (by and large) drawn by random sample into court.

If one makes comparison with the USA it is interesting to note the differences that stem from its main constitutional settlement of the period of Independence at the end of the eighteenth century. Because of the immigration of William Penn of *Penn and Meade* and especially its aftermath *Bushel's Case* (1690), Americans were wary of judicial power in the trial. Further, there was the homegrown anti-colonial case of *John Peter Zenger* in 1735. The consequence of *Zenger* in particular is that to this day the jury debate in the USA takes place on different ground (I ignore here the issue of race). In the USA the debate is not over the judge–jury relationship, but over the scope of the jury function. In the UK we are aware that juries can deliberately get it 'wrong' legally, for 'good' moral reasons, even after the judge has summed up and surveyed the evidence for them. When this happens – probably rarely, although historically of great importance – we call it 'perverse' or, more charitably, 'jury equity'. In the USA there is different jargon: 'nullification'; there the jury is seen in a quasi-legislative capacity as having the power, even constitutional power, to strike down a law in certain circumstances. Of course this is controversial, but my point is that the terrain for debate is different. (See Abramson 1994: ch. 2.) Nevertheless this comparison enables one to see the constitutional implications of the jury's role and relationship with the judge. It would be very interesting to discover whether that different relationship between Scots judges and juries was present at the time of the Act of Union in 1707, or whether because of the special subsidiarity for the legal system in the Act of Union that relationship crystallized later; for example 'perversity' or 'equity' are far less likely with the different voting system by different numbers of jurors in Scotland, which also empowers the 'Not Proven' acquittal.

I conclude with an empiricist prescription. I have drawn attention throughout to the correlation between directionality in the Summing-up and the eventual jury verdict. That suggests rhetorically that the correlation is somehow causative. That is indeed my suggestion, but it is not a grounded assumption. Of course such correlation does not occur in every single instance; one should consider here the rape trial of

'*Mahoney I*' considered above where the very strong directionality against the defendant appears to have been counterbalanced by the negative construction of the complainant. It would be of great value to know how – or if – the Summing-up figures in, or permeates, the method of deliberating juries. At the time of writing one skirts around this space by statistical studies of verdicts, or as here, by pointing out correlations. In the last resort these are interesting speculations. The time has come for some hard data, not least because these would enable further debate and further research and modest proposals. In that context I welcome the Lord Chancellor's decision that he will introduce the necessary legislation with the backing of the Lord Chief Justice (F. Gibb, *The Times*, 5 December 1996; HL Debs, *Hansard* 19 February 1998, cols 307–309).

Bibliography

Abramson, J. *We the Jury: The Jury System and the Ideal of Democracy* (1994) New York: Basic Books.

Ashworth, A. *Criminal Law Review* (1995) 533.

Baldwin, J. and McConville, M. 48 *Modern Law Review* (1978) 544–58.

Bennett, W. and Feldman, M. S. *Reconstructing Reality in the Courtroom* (1981) London: Tavistock.

Billig, M. *Arguing and Thinking: A Rhetorical Approach to Social Psychology* (1987) Cambridge: Cambridge University Press.

Blackburn, J. 48 *Australian Law Journal* (1974) 229–32.

Block, B., Corbett, C. and Peay, J. *Ordered and Directed Acquittals in the Crown Court* (1993) Research Study No. 15, The Royal Commission on Criminal Justice. London: HMSO.

Bourcier, S. and Bruxelles, S. *Le Droit en procès* (1984) Paris: Presse Universitaire Française.

Brown, P. and Levinson, S. C. *Politeness: Some Universals in Language Usage* (1987) Studies in Interactional Linguistics 4. Cambridge: Cambridge University Press.

Carzo, D. and Jackson, B. S. (eds) *Semiotics, Law and Social Science* (1985) Rome: Gangemi.

Charrow, R. and Charrow, V. 79 *Columbia Law Review* (1979) 1306–74.

Danet, B. 32 *Semiotica* (1980) 187–219.

Davies, G., Lloyd-Bostock, S., McMurray, M. and Wilson, C. *Law and Criminal Justice: International Developments in Research and Practice* (1995) Berlin: de Gruyter.

Dershowitz, A. *Reasonable Doubt* (1996) New York: Simon and Schuster.

Dyson, B. *Liberty in Britain 1934–1994* (1994) London: Liberty.

Ewick, P. and Silbey, S. 29 *Law and Society Review* (1995) 197.

Findlay, M. and Duff, P. (eds) *The Jury under Attack* (1988) London and Sydney: Butterworth.

Galanter, M. 9 *Law and Society Review* (1974) 95.

Gold, V. 65 *North Carolina Law Review* (1987) 480.

Goodrich, P. *Legal Discourse: Studies in Linguistics, Rhetoric and Legal Analysis* (1987) London: Macmillan Press.

Hastie, R. Penrod, S. and Pennington, N. *Inside the Jury* (1983) Cambridge, MA: Harvard University Press.

Hollander, J. in Brook, P. and Gewirtz, P. (eds) *Law's Stories* (1996) New Haven and London; Yale University Press.

Jackson, B. S. *Making Sense in Law: Linguistic Psychological and Semiotic Perspectives* (1996) Liverpool: Deborah Charles Publications.

Jackson, J., Kilpatrick, R. and Harvey, C. *Called to Court* (1991) Belfast: SLS Legal Publications.
Jacquemet, M. *Credibility in Court* (1996) Studies in International Lingustics 14. Cambridge: Cambridge University Press.
Kauffman, S., *The Philanderer* (1953) London: Martin Secker and Warburg.
Kennedy, LJ *Criminal Law Review* (1996) 529–30.
La Buy, J *Manual on Jury Instructions in Federal Criminal Cases* (1965) St Paul, MN: West Publishing.
Lindley, D. *The Trials of Frances Howard* (1993) London: Routledge.
Lord Chancellor's Department *Your Role as Juror* (1996) London.
Moscovici, S. *Social Influence and Social Change* (1976) London: Academic Press.
Munday, R. *Criminal Law Review* (1996) 296–305.
——*Criminal Law Review* (1996) 530–2.
Munkman, J. *The Technique of Advocacy* (1991) London: Butterworths.
Ong, W. *Orality and Literacy* (1982) London: Methuen.
Raphael, A. *Grotesque Libels* (1993) London: Corgi Books.
Robertshaw, P. *Public Law* (1971) 169–88.
——47 *Australian Law Journal* (1973) 572–85.
——*Public Law* (1975) 113–36.
——50 *Australian Law Journal* (1976) 84–8.
——8 *Cambrian Law Review* (1977) 78–93.
——2 *Liverpool Law Review* (1980) 31–43.
——9 *International Journal of the Sociology of Law* (1981) 201–24.
——3 *Anglo-American Law Review* (1984) 357–79.
——*Semiotics* (1984) 527–53.
——8 *Oxford Literary Review* (1986) 198–207.
——50 *Modern Law Review* (1987) 971–81.
——*Rethinking Legal Need* (1991) Andover: Dartmouth.
——3 *International Journal for the Semiotics of Law* (1992) 215–19.
——*Criminal Law Review* (1992) 867–71.
——*Jury and Judge: The Crown Court in Action* (1995) Andover: Dartmouth.
Robertshaw, P., Cox, S. and Van Hoen, N. 20 *International Journal of the Sociology of Law* (1992) 271–81.
Robertshaw, P. and Curtin, C. 25 *Sociological Review* (1977) 289–309.
Robertshaw, P. and Thakker, R. 1 *Medical Law International* (1993) 33–56.
Royal Commission on Criminal Justice, *Report* (1993) Cm 2263. London: HMSO.
Sealy, L. and Cornish, W. ch. 4 in Farringdon, D. (ed.) *Psychology, Law and Legal Process* (1979) London: Macmillan.
Smith, J. *Misogynies* (1989) London: Faber.
Sobota, K. *Sachlichkeit, Rhetorisches Kunst der Juristen* (1990) Frankfurt am Main: Peter Lang.
Street, H. *Freedom, the Individual and the Law* 4th edn (1977) Harmondsworth: Pelican.
Stygall, G. *Trial Language: Differential Discourse Processing and Discursive Formation* (1994) Amsterdam: John Benjamins.
Viehweg, T. *Topics and Law* (1993) Frankfurt am Main: Peter Lang.
Wagenaar, W. A., Van Koppen, P. J. and Crombag, H. F. M. *Anchored Narratives: The Psychology of Criminal Evidence* (1993) Hemel Hempstead: Harvester Wheatsheaf.

Walter, B. *The Jury Summation as Speech Genre: An Ethnographic Study of What It Means to Those Who Use It* (1988) Amsterdam: John Benjamins.
Wilson, C. *Law and Criminal Justice: International Developments in Research and Practice* (1995) Berlin: de Gruyter.
Winter, R. 9 *Law and Society Review* (1970-71) 325.
Zander, M. *New Law Journal* (28 February 1997) 320.
Zander, M. and Henderson, P. *Crown Court Study* (1993) Research Study No. 19, The Royal Commission on Criminal Justice. London: HMSO.
Zwickey, A. 10 *Chicago Linguistics Society* (1974) 287–301.

Table of cases

English cases

(The prefix *R* v. is omitted)

Scottish cases

USA cases

Canadian cases 171–9

Index